# Finance, Institutions and Industrial Change: Spatial Perspectives

# Finance, Institutions and Industrial Change: Spatial Perspectives

Edited by E. W. Schamp, G. J. R. Linge
and C. M. Rogerson

Walter de Gruyter · Berlin · New York 1993

Eike W. Schamp: Professor of Economic Geography,
Johann Wolfgang Goethe University, Frankfurt am Main, Germany
Godfrey J. R. Linge: Professor of Human Geography, Research School of Pacific Studies, The Australian National University, Canberra, Australia
Chris M. Rogerson: Professor of Human Geography, University of the Witwatersrand, Johannesburg, South Africa

⊗ Printed on acid-free paper which falls within the guidelines
of the ANSI to ensure permance and durability.

*Library of Congress Cataloging-in-Publication Data*

Finance, institutions, and industrial change : spatial perspectives /
edited by E. W. Schamp, G. J. R. Linge & C. M. Rogerson.
XIX, 265 p. 23 × 15,5 cm.
Includes bibliographical references and index.
ISBN 3-11-012603-6
1. Finance. 2. Financial institutions. 3. International finance.
4. International economic relations. I. Schamp, Eike W.
II. Linge, G. J. R. III. Rogerson, C. M. (Christian Myles)
HG173.F488 1993
332.1 – dc20 93-31331
CIP

*Die Deutsche Bibliothek — Cataloging-in-Publication Data*

**Finance, institutions and industrial change** : spatial
perspectives / ed. by E. W. Schamp ... – Berlin ; New York : de
Gruyter, 1993
ISBN 3-11-012603-6
NE: Schamp, Eike W. [Hrsg.]


Printing: WB-Druck, Rieden. – Binding: D. Mikolai, Berlin. – Cover Design: Johannes Rother, Berlin. – Printed in Germany.

# Contents

# Figures

# Tables

# Contributors

György Barta, Ph.D., is Senior Economist, Regional Research Centre, Hungarian Academy of Sciences, Budapest, Hungary.

György Csáki, Ph.D., is Senior Research Fellow, Institute for World Economics, Hungarian Academy of Sciences, Budapest, Hungary.

Ayda Eraydin, Ph.D., is Associate Professor, Department of City and Regional Planning, Faculty of Architecture, Middle East Technical University, Ankara, Turkey.

Wolf Gaebe, Dipl.Volksw., Ph.D., is Professor of Economic Geography at the University of Stuttgart, Germany.

Outi Homanen, Licenciate in Economics, is Researcher in the Finnish Export Guarantee Board, Finland.

Richard Le Heron, B.A., M.A., Ph.D., is Associate Professor, Department of Geography, Massey University, Palmerston North, New Zealand.

G.J.R.Linge, B.Sc.(Econ.), Ph.D., is Professor, Department of Human Geography, Research School of Pacific Studies, The Australian National University; he was Chair of the IGU Commission on Industrial Change (1984-92) and is a Fellow of the Academy of the Social Sciences in Australia.

Roman Matykowski, Ph.D., is Associate Professor, Institute of Socio-Economic Geography and Spatial Planning, Adam Mickiewicz University, Poznań, Poland.

Erzsébet Poszmik, Ph.D., is Professor, Department of Microeconomics, Budapest University of Economics, Hungary.

Andy C. Pratt, B.Sc.(Hons.), Ph.D., is Lecturer, Department of Geography, London School of Economics and Political Sciences, United Kingdom.

C. M. Rogerson, B.Sc., M.Sc., Ph.D., is Reader in Human Geography and Associate Professor, Department of Geography and Environmental Studies, University of the Witwatersrand, Johannesburg, South Africa.

Eike W. Schamp, Dipl.Volksw., Ph.D., is Professor of Economic Geography at Johann Wolfgang Goethe University, Frankfurt-am-Main, Germany.

Mahindar Santokh Singh, B.A. (Hons.), M.A., Ph.D., is Professor, Department of Geography, School of Humanities, Universiti Sains Malaysia, Penang, Malaysia.

Tadeusz Stryjakiewicz, Ph.D., is Associate Professor, Institute of Socio-Economic Geography and Spatial Planning, Adam Mickiewicz University, Poznań, Poland.

# Acknowledgements

**The Editors** are indebted to many people who have assisted in the production of this book. Special appreciation is due to Jan Linge for her thoughtful editorial inputs throughout the project. In *Germany*: Cordula Neiberger and Heike Bertram gave invaluable word-processing assistance; and Gülnur Melan helped with translation. In *Australia*: Yvonne Byron, Merv Commons and Daniel Fritsch gave word processing advice; Ian Heyward skilfully prepared all the line drawings; and Margaret Burns and Mira Kwasik assisted with translation. In *South Africa*: Rolf Dauskardt, Rebecca Lammas, Harry Tate, Mrs S. Crankshaw, K.W.V. Garp, Douglas Green, and Helen Green made valuable inputs. C.M. Rogerson received financial support from the Richard Ward Endowment Fund and computer support by the Drummond Foundation.

**Outi Homanen** is grateful for the constructive remarks by Irma Adelman, Tariq Banuri, Reijo Helle, Erkki Pihkala and Robert Pringle: any misconceptions are the responsibility of the author. For financial support, she thanks the Union Bank of Finland, World Institute for Development Economic Research (WIDER), Helsinki School of Economics and Business Administration, and the Foundation for Economic Education (Finland).

**Richard Le Heron** is indebted to Mike Roche and Andy Pratt for helpful critical comments on an earlier draft, and to Anneke Visser for speedily word processing the manuscript. Support by the New Zealand Social Sciences Research Fund Committee and the Massey University Research Fund for research into the internationalization of New Zealand enterprises is gratefully acknowledged.

**G.J.R. Linge** warmly thanks Yvonne Byron and Christine Tabart for their library and other assistance.

**Andy C. Pratt** gratefully acknowledges support from Coventry Polytechnic for travel to the Eppenhain conference in 1989 where the paper on which his chapter is based was first presented. His research was partly supported by a grant from the Economic and Social Research Council (No. D00428327103).

Acknowledgement is made to Elsevier Science Publishers B.V., Academic Publishing Division, Amsterdam, The Netherlands, for permission to reproduce Tables 3.1 and 3.2 from Berg and Sachs (1988) in the *Journal of Development Economics*; and to Hillier Parker May & Rowden, London, for permission to reproduce Figure 7.1.

# Preface

Curiously, and with only a few exceptions, geographers have paid little attention to the sources of finance and the mechanisms and channels through which it gets into the hands of users. There is little appreciation that lenders (such as households) through their agents (such as the banks or building societies) can, and often do, fetter the spatial options of borrowers. Or again, texts purporting to explain global shifts in industrial activities usually pay scant regard to the role of currency exchange rates and the impacts that these have on short-term decision making and long-term corporate planning.

No one book can hope to adequately cover the vast and complex field that is so disingenuously summarized by the term 'financial markets', and which has now become symbolized by an image of young, hyperactive and grossly overpaid 'computer jockeys' using an arcane acronymic language of their own. This volume thus consists of eleven exploratory essays that may help towards a better understanding of some aspects of the interplay between the institutions of the financial system and the organization of industrial space.

Change and uncertainty have characterized financial markets during the last two decades. Deregulation, globalization and securitization have transformed the institutional arrangements and operating environment in the capitalist business world. Cross-border financial flows have not only become very much larger but also increasingly mobile. The uncertainty that all this has created is echoed in various ways through all the contributions to this volume, and forms one of the main themes linking them together. Related to this is the transient nature of many of the solutions adopted.

Chapter 1 by Linge and Schamp provides a broad overview of the topic covered by this book and shows why and how the financial world has increased in complexity, and how profound are its impacts on the geography of production. This is followed by an outline by Linge in Chapter 2 of the development of the global financial system since the Second World War. In particular he emphasizes the role of currency exchange rates — the so-called 'international management mechanism' — in influencing the location of economic activity. By drawing on examples from the motor vehicle industry, he illustrates how changes in the relative value of the yen reinforced decisions by Japanese companies to establish plants overseas which, in turn, stimulated counter-moves by North American and European producers. In fact much of the Japanese foreign direct investment (FDI) during the 1980s produced poor short-run returns, but it was essentially a hedge against possible trade barriers following the creation of regional economic blocs on both sides of the Atlantic. Even more uncertainty surrounds investment in, and loans to, developing countries. Most international lending to these economies is, as Homanen points out in Chapter 3, to the public sector or to the private sector with public sector guarantees. She argues that the assessment of sovereign risk (the ability of governments to back-up their guarantee of repayment) has concentrated on concrete measurements of the ability to match such undertakings while neglecting evidence about other, more abstract, elements that contribute to economic growth and stability. This reinforces a point made in Chapter 2 that one cause of the debt crisis precipitated by the default of Mexico in 1982 was the lack of bankers' expertise in appraising risks associated with nation states rather than with corporations.

A theme running through the book is the way the deregulation of financial markets, the development of new kinds of finance and loan packages, and the emergence of the necessary processing and communications technology provided new opportunities not only for reputable investment companies, banks and other financial agencies, but also for wheelers and dealers. A very visible aspect of this during the 1980s was the burgeoning of merger, acquisition and takeover activity. Alongside this was corporate raiding, much of which went hand in hand with the rapid rise and even faster fall of the junk-bond phenomenon. Before examining the case of a major New Zealand investment corporation which spread its wings and then had them clipped by the stock-market crash of October 1987, Le Heron in Chapter 4 examines the interface between the industrial and financial sectors in a political economy perspective. Although in any event he regards this approach as necessary to indicate the structural conditions affecting the form and extent of capital circulating into, within, and out of a country, it is particularly important in the case of New Zealand which turned during the 1980s from an essentially national orientation to an overwhelmingly international one.

Changes in the politico-economic environment as well as in institutional arrangements directly affect the existing system of financial intermediaries that form the interface between the world of finance and the world of investment for production. Although one of the most significant of these changes has been the globalization of the financial markets and the growth of cross-border capital movements, national regulations and operating procedures remain important. This is illustrated by the empirical country-specific evidence presented in Chapters 5, 6 and 7. Banks, long dominant in the provision of financial services in Germany, have been widening their roles in order to retain their clientele in the face of competition from other financial intermediaries which have been allowed to extend their range of activities. Yet it is only recently, as Gaebe notes in Chapter 5, that they have started to develop their networks overseas, lagging very much behind such countries as the UK, the US and Japan. Schamp in Chapter 6 reconnoitres the emergence of leasing as a new financial service, and asks whether this could be yet another factor weakening the close spatial ties that have long existed between banks and industry. In the UK, the finance industry has been playing an important role in providing the built environment for industry. Pratt presents evidence in Chapter 7 highlighting the fact that the industrial built environment has become both a commodity and a means of production and hence can thus enable or constrain the location and activity of firms. He, like Le Heron, argues the need for a political science approach as a way of incorporating new relationships into a theoretical understanding and explanation of the social and economic reproduction of localities.

There are several threads that link the final four chapters. Hungary, Poland and Turkey have all been forging trade and investment links with other players in the global economy, and trying to build or revamp institutional arrangements to enable these to work. Along with Malaysia, all three are vitally concerned to attract a substantial inflow of capital both to build and update productive capacity and also to provide infrastructure to enable it to function. Barta, Csáki and Poszmik argue in Chapter 8 that the particular 'pre-revolutionary' circumstances in each of the East European countries will leave their mark on the transition to a market economy and the shape it will eventually take. Even in Hungary, where a mixture of bureaucratic command and market coordination had emerged during the 1980s, the economy was still not being shaped by market forces, and hence the production and pricing structures were getting increasingly out of kilter with those in the outside world. To try to solve the trade deficit, the shortage of capital and the lack of technological know-how, efforts are being made to encourage Joint Ventures with firms from developed countries. Poland, discussed in Chapter 9 by Matykowski and Stryjakiewicz, is also encouraging Joint Ventures. Like Hungary it, too, is uncertain about the implications of selling-off state enterprises, and the long-run spatial consequences of attracting foreign capital. Ideally it would be desirable to use such inflows to rebuild backward or depressed regions, but in fact compromise is likely to be the reality because East European countries are not only competing with each other but also with other parts of the world. Moreover, events are showing that although it will take time to rebuild government, economic and physical structures, it will take even longer to change the attitudes and ambitions of people.

The importance of government policies in shifting Turkey from being a 'semi-closed' economy to a more integrated player on the world stage is outlined by Eraydin in Chapter 10. The changing character of international relations prompted fresh foreign trade linkages which, in turn, encouraged alterations to institutional arrangements and business practices. This is a neat illustration of the process by which greater outside involvement can induce structural change in a newly industrializing country even though Turkey retains many of its former characteristics, including the importance of small-scale firms making traditional products. In contrast, the group of countries examined by Singh in Chapter 11 — Thailand, Indonesia, Malaysia and the Philippines — are playing for higher stakes by seeking to play a role in the production of sophisticated high-tech goods. Much of the foreign direct investment they have been attracting is related to the production of exports, sometimes as an off-shore platform to enable Japanese companies to overcome trade restrictions imposed by the US and Europe. How ephemeral this kind of activity proves to be may well depend on the deftness with which the various governments manipulate the economic levers that they can control in a global environment where capital seems to be more in demand, more scarce and more volatile.

Reinforcing the main message that emerges from all these chapters — namely, the speed at which all these changes have taken place — are the circumstances under which the contributions to this book were prepared. They were to have been a selection of the papers delivered at the annual conference of the International Geographical Union's Commission on Industrial Change held at Eppenhain near Frankfurt-am-Main. That conference ended on the morning of Saturday, 9 September 1989. Late that night thousands of East Germans began streaming across the border from Hungary to Austria, against the wishes of their own government but with the full permission of the Hungarian authorities. It is doubtful whether anyone could have foreseen the developments that began that night and which initiated the transformation not only of the social and political landscape of Europe, but of the entire global political, economic and security balance. Suffice it to say that, in the light of these events, some chapters had to be completely rewritten and all the others extensively revised. In some instances, as is indicated in the contributions from Hungary and Poland, the changes are so profound that the outcomes remain far from clear: the best that these authors can do, therefore, is provide a reference point that will allow a better understanding of the events as they eventually unfold.

E.W. Schamp
Frankfurt-am-Main
Germany

G.J.R. Linge
Canberra
Australia

C.M. Rogerson
Johannesburg
South Africa

# 1 Finance, Institutions, and Industrial Change: Spatial Perspectives

G.J.R. Linge and E.W. Schamp

The last decade has seen massive changes to the international financial world. These have included the eruption of the world debt crisis dating from the first moratorium in 1982 when Mexico defaulted; the 'big bang' in October 1986 when the London Stock Exchange switched to electronic-based share trading, thus sounding the bell for a new age of global electronic financial markets; and the world-wide stock exchange crash a year later when the postwar upswing in the world economy came to halt.

Junk bonds (basically those not classified as investment grade), which were 'discovered' in 1983 in the US, led to an enormous takeover wave and previously unheard-of prices for acquisitions. About US$51,000 million (27 per cent out of the total raised in these kinds of bonds in the US between 1983 and 1989) were used to finance leveraged buy-outs. In 1988-89, however, the junk bond market broke down, company empires began to disintegrate, and brokers (who had burgeoned and become rich on these bonds) were bankrupted. The age of corporate raiders seemed to have ended. Junk bonds, it was said, symbolized the greedy 1980s: when their inventor, Drexel Burnham Lambert (a Wall Street investment bank), itself went bankrupt early in 1990 it spawned headlines about the end of an era.

During the 1980s Japan's finance capital was perceived as the largest in the world. That country's aggressive investment strategy — such as setting up overseas factories, acquiring businesses and buying securities — aroused fear in the US and Europe but hope in the Asia-Pacific region and some developing countries elsewhere that it would increasingly become a leading engine, a 'supercharged money machine', for sustained growth. By the early 1990s, however, it had lost some of its immediate vitality because of a downturn in the business cycle, falling land and asset values and sluggish domestic demand following the collapse of the 'bubble' economy. Adding to overall global uncertainty has been the demise of communism, the legacy of political and economic confusion in the countries and regions of Eastern Europe, and the dismemberment of the USSR with the declaration of a new Commonwealth of Independent States (CIS) in December 1991. Even this incomplete list is sufficient to explain the feelings of concern, crisis and insecurity that have led to the financial markets being described as the 'new international economic disorder'.

The turbulence in the financial world is having severe repercussions on the production system. Yet neither economic geographers nor regional economists have devoted much energy to teasing out the precise interrelationships between processes in the world of financial decision making and the spatial distribution of investments. So far, empirical research into the regional and interregional mobility of capital and the resulting regional and international division of labour has only analyzed the *use* of funds: Taylor and Thrift (1983: 359) rightly pointed out that the *sources* of funds were largely being ignored in explanations of regional development. Today, there is both growing recognition of how little is known about the relationships between finance capital and productive investments and their impacts on regional industrial change, and growing incredulity that human geographers have paid so little attention to matters of money and finance (Thrift, 1990: 1135).

A brief review of some basic paradigms will indicate the ways in which the relationship between finance and industrial change have traditionally been considered. The neo-classical theoretical view that capital is freely available and perfectly mobile (because markets are perfect) is under increasing attack. As Clark et al. (1986: 252) have suggested, 'perfect mobility of capital is connected with the assumption that capital will be allocated according to interest rates'. Consequently, the emerging tendency towards the inter-regional balancing of interest rates — hence equalizing costs of capital spatially — means that regional investment rates are becoming independent of regional savings ratios. Capital once invested will be fixed; that is, completely immobile (Chick and Dow, 1988). Capital mobility, then, can be seen as synonymous with locational choice, for instance of plants and firms.

In Marxist analysis a clear distinction is made between money and productive capital, but the interrelationship between them is not well understood at a specific place or over a specific period (Walker and Storper, 1981). It is basically hypothesized, however, that capital markets are institutions within a capitalist economy which are comparable to other markets. This means that they are governed by regulations and actions of the powerful but also that the limits of capital markets are clearly defined. Questions arise as to whether such limits can also be defined spatially and whether regional and national industrial change can be explained by discerning regional and national capital markets. Recent turbulence on the international financial markets indicates that changes in the financial system are becoming increasingly important for global and regional investments in manufacturing. In view of these events, it is arguable whether it is correct to suggest that a (totally) New International Financial System is emerging (Thrift, 1986a) and, if it is not, what the consequences might be for the spatial organization of industry.

## Institutions

Shifts in the relationship between finance capital and productive investments become clearly evident through changes in institutions. Following Dear (1988), three levels of analysis in the capital-investment relationship can be distinguished. First, at the structural level the principal mechanisms of capitalist economy can be discerned, including competition between enterprises and between territories striving for hegemony which, however, is constantly threatened by competition. Competition and hegemony form the major themes through the following discussion of the financial system and its institutional change. Second, the institutional level 'represents the phenomenal form of structure' (Dear, 1988: 63) which can be put in specific spatial and temporal forms. Third, there is the level at which the actors operate. These three analytical levels can be applied at spatial scales ranging from the local through the national to the international.

## Defining an 'institution'

Institutions are thus the crucial link between structural change in a capitalist world economy and actions of individual agents. However, because the term 'institution' can be enigmatic, it is helpful to distinguish between institutions *strictu senso* and organizations. A particular financial system can be regarded as an institution whereas the various financial intermediaries within it are acting as organizations. In general, the New Institutional Economics School (NIES) sees institutions as 'regularities in repetitive interactions among individuals' (North, 1986: 231). According to Bromley (1989: 41–2),

> institutions can be demarcated in two classes: (1) conventions; and (2) rules and entitlements . . . a convention is a regularity in human behavior that brings order and predictability to human relationships . . . An entitlement is a socially recognized and sanctioned set of expectations on the part of everyone in a society with regard to *de jure* or *de facto* legal relations that define the choice sets of individuals with respect to the choice sets of others.

The NIES considers institutions to be an important part of modern societies based on the division of labour. Increasing social and spatial division of labour implies a growing multiplicity of transactions and hence uncertainty in economic relations. Institutions may serve as an instrument of social control of transactions. Bromley (1989: 47) suggests that the four prerequisites needed to facilitate a working division of labour — order, predictability, stability, and reliability — are being established by institutions to facilitate economic actions; that is, they regulate markets. Given the general awareness of growing disorder in the modern world economy, the increasing interest in institutions is understandable. However, institutions may limit possible action choices the more they produce stability and predictability for a certain market, so that some of the actors may want to change them fundamentally. As institutions must be steadily reproduced through social action, the continuous tendency to alter them can result in contradictions leading to even more radical change. The current, quickly changing array of new financial instruments is indicative of the rapidly evolving nature of the financial system.

## Regulation theory

Regulation theory is a political economy approach to the theorization of capital restructuring (Aglietta, 1979; de Vroey, 1984; Boyer, 1986, 1990; Dunford, 1990; Tickell and Peck, 1992). Boyer (1988), among others, prefers the term *régulation* theory to emphasize that this concept goes far beyond the general meaning of regulation. This approach regards change as an historical process, tied to a particular epoch and nation, which occurs through crises.

Regulation theory developed as a means of understanding the evolution, reproduction and crisis of regimes of accumulation and, in particular Fordism. However, the theory is neither prescriptive nor deterministic: it is agnostic about the successor to Fordism (Tickell and Peck, 1992: 196).

Although it is generally accepted that a post-Fordist regime of accumulation is emerging, the nature of its successor is yet far from clear (Lipietz, 1985). Whether the leading capitalist economies are in a protracted period of crisis or whether the new regime is characterized by greater flexibility — of labour markets and processes, of consumption, and of production and its management — remains the subject of vigorous debate (Tickell and Peck, 1992: 196).

In this theory, social regulations and their institutions mark an historically explicit shaping of a regime of accumulation. Such institutional forms are the wage-labour nexus, type of competition, the mode of adhesion to the international regime, the form of state intervention and, not least, monetary and credit relationships (Boyer, 1988: 71–5). So far, however, empirical studies have mainly concentrated on the wage-labour nexus and neglected the monetary and credit relationship. There is thus a need to undertake a more detailed analysis of the role of the financial system. Because *régulation* theory considers the accumulation regime to be a national one whereas financial markets are becoming increasingly global, the question arises as to how far the national and global institutional forms are able to interact.

An historical explanation of global change cannot be confined to an examination of existing institutions. Over time, new actors appear which, because of their size and economic power, are able to search out fresh opportunities for action including the alteration of existing institutional arrangements. The emergence of multinational corporations and transnational banks, for example, changed the nature of global strategies by fomenting oligopolistic competition between a few dominant firms. Early studies analyzing the spatial repercussions of such competition revealed strategies of consultation and collusion to be part of their approach to conflict solving (Rees, 1978; Gwynne, 1979; Laulajainen, 1981). Such competition, however, can never be static: it can only create temporary 'solutions'.

Rivalry for the investments of these large oligopolistic firms is increasing as states try to improve the quality of locational factors not only through infrastructural and other expenditure but also by legal devices. The form of industrial competition is, therefore, shaped by regulations and institutions at the state level. Several scholars (such as Daly and Logan, 1986, 1989; Corbridge, 1988) have shown how this struggle for economic hegemony developed. As is illustrated in several chapters in this book, nation states revise regulations and institutional arrangements to improve their attractiveness, and hence modify the conditions under which enterprises develop their own strategies. As the rivalry between states is increasingly about enterprises that are internationalizing their activities, the emergence of the global corporation has provided a new parameter for their endeavours. The differentiation of enterprises and governments as actors is itself, of course, somewhat arbitrary because neither is an unambiguous or value-free term; it will, none the less, suffice for present purposes.

This may give some indication of the 'complex and highly differentiated web of interactions which bind together the capitalist world system' (Corbridge, 1989: 358), and point to some difficulties in the analysis and prognosis of specific historical processes. Because various groups of actors are interrelated in complex ways through direct interaction as well as more indirectly by determining conditions for the actions of others, it is not possible to anticipate historical processes of the capitalist world system but merely describe them *ex post*.

One way of tackling this is to segment events into different phases. Following the approach developed by Dear (1988), the evolution of actors and institutions during the last four decades are here considered at the global, national and regional scales. Given that accumulation regimes are national in character, the question arises as to whether the changing institutional arrangements in the financial sector signify the emergence of a new accumulation regime in a global system of enterprises and states. A fundamental change in institutions would be an indication of a new historical phase, as is suggested by many crisis theorists. However, the periodicity which lies behind many such theories has been upset because of an historically unique event — the bankruptcy of socialism and the turning of East European societies towards capitalism. Yet other impulses have arisen with previously semi-closed economies — like Turkey discussed by Eraydin in Chapter 10 —

fashioning new links with the world economy, and countries like India, the CIS and the People's Republic of China (PRC) moving towards making their currencies fully convertible. Such developments are bringing about an unprecedented and radical change to global financial institutions. Although its impact on the sectoral spatial organization of industry — not to say all economic activities — will be significant, the extent and direction of the wide-ranging ramifications are just beginning to unfold. The challenge of the 1990s is that, because it is the first decade since before the First World War in which a truly global market-place can exist for goods and services, structures have to be refashioned or even developed *ab initio* to integrate the mercantilist and former Marxist systems.

## The Global Financial System

Some essential features of the financial world which caused the contemporary 'disorder' of the global system and the high volatility of markets can now be addressed. Geographers have only recently begun to elaborate comprehensive descriptions and explanations of the international financial system (Edwards, 1985, 1988; Daly and Logan, 1986; Corbridge, 1988, 1989; Thrift and Leyshon, 1988). Three factors can be distinguished which have determined processes at the global scale during the last two decades. First, there was an enormous rise in international liquidity; second, new ways emerged in which liquidity was redistributed globally; and, third, finance capital became increasingly mobile. As a result international financial flows can be speedily driven by actual or expected changes in interest and currency exchange rates.

### The rise of international liquidity

There is no space here to review the extensive literature analyzing the increasing globalization of trade and production and the way it has given rise to a global financial system (some of the more recent examples being Leyshon and Thrift, 1992; O'Brien, 1992; and Swyngedouw, 1992). An important feature has been the gradual erosion of the absolute monetary and financial hegemony of the US nation and the US dollar. Among the many reasons were the rising trade deficit of the US in the wake of the Vietnam War (1965-73) and the growth of international liquidity. During the 1950s and 1960s there was an explosion in contractual savings involving insurance schemes, pension funds and unit trusts (a means of facilitating the collective purchase of shares and securities and spreading risk over a wider range of investments). In the UK and elsewhere, 'this greatly intensified the institutional control of funds [and heralded] a significant reduction of funds away from manufacturing and productive sectors of the economy towards non-productive, especially property and local authorities' (Taylor and Thrift, 1983: 377). After the breakdown in the early 1970s of the Bretton Woods Agreement, with its quasi fixed currency exchange rates (which in fact had to be altered with increasing frequency), and the transition to floating exchange rates, the emerging Euromoney market greatly expanded (cf. Linge in Chapter 2). Finally, the Western industrial nations caused increasing liquidity by adopting a Keynesian approach to master the crisis of the 1970s (Lipietz, 1985) which eventually, led to inflation and stagflation.

## Global redistribution of liquidity

The two oil price shocks from 1973 and 1979 led to massive capital transfers through the world economy, a redistribution process extensively described elsewhere particularly in relation to the indebtedness of developing countries. The debt problem itself was not new (World Bank, 1985) but its dimensions greatly increased as oil producing countries withdrew capital from oil consuming ones. Most of this, however, could not be invested directly but had to be spent as finance capital though the banking sector. International banks were thus forced to look for new forms of finance-capital investments. Furthermore, reduced demand in industrial nations lowered profit expectations and hence led to decreasing rates of investment.

Globally, the redistribution of capital led developed-country banks to seek new debtors and many found them in Third World countries. Indeed, a 'window of opportunity' seemed to present itself to some developing countries, though most in fact ended up with serious balance of payments problems that led to the debt crisis of 1982. This came about, on the one hand, because of external circumstances, like falling terms of trade for commodity exports, rising dollar values and interest rates, and the growing unwillingness of international commercial banks to continue voluntary lending. On the other, there were internal reasons, including the misguided use of credits and escalating debts. Eventually, governments were no longer able to pay interest, much less repay capital. Whereas Latin America experienced a net positive transfer of long-term debt until 1983 (because borrowing outpaced total debt repayments), during the 1984-89 period, in contrast, total net transfers amounted to minus US$153,000 million (equivalent to 15 per cent of the subcontinent's total exports). The threat of default led the international money market to halt most voluntary lending and the loans that did proceed went towards rolling over debt and capitalizing interest payments that were in arrears.

The debt crisis began to attract the attention of geographers when they perceived that it was influencing regional development processes in the world economy (Corbridge, 1988, 1989; Edwards, 1988). Increasingly, internal reasons were seen to be contributing to the debt crisis (World Bank, 1989), particularly as some states achieved high economic growth rates despite large debts whereas the majority got into crisis. It may be a characteristic of global capitalism that chances are distributed unevenly and, inevitably, there will be winners and losers. In any event, creditors were forced to search for new ways of assessing sovereign risk (cf. Homanen in Chapter 3).

A distinction should be made between public and private creditors. The debt crisis is nearly always exclusively discussed in connection with private bank creditors. Debtor countries are not all in crisis simultaneously so that the impact on creditor banks differs. There is, for instance, a close relationship between the spatial allocation of private bank credit and the geographical range of international trade (Fryer, 1988). Thus, US banks mainly operate in Latin America; British ones in Latin America and the 'old' British Commonwealth; German ones in Turkey and Eastern Europe; and Japanese ones in Third World countries and the US. The Bank of Boston (based in New England), for instance, has 32 branches in Argentina and 19 in Brazil; or again, ANZ-Grindlays has 56 branches in India (*The Economist*, 27 June 1992: 81). There are signs, however, that this situation is changing. Thus, Germany's largest commercial bank — the Deutsche Bank — now has a network of branches and subsidiaries in 17 countries of the Asia-Pacific region controlled from its Group headquarters in Singapore: with a 1992 profit of US$200 million, this has become the Bank's most profitable region outside Germany.

Furthermore, the present situation of bank creditors varies greatly according to the way national banking systems are organized. Thus, Molyneux (1989) distinguishes between the European Continental banking system which is dominated by general banks; the British system which is characterized by a strong separation between commercial and merchant banks; and the US hybrid form which has elements of both of these. Their ability to handle the debt crisis is further differentiated by national regulatory measures. For example, while German banks can obtain tax relief on depreciation for credit, US banks are unable to do so to anything like the same extent. Moreover, US banks are forced to call-in credits when interest payments become 90 days overdue.

The anti-inflationary policies of Western governments during the 1980s led to historically high interest rates and massive impacts on the world financial system (Edwards, 1988). On average, real interest rates in the 1980s were more than twice as high as in the 1960s and nearly six times higher than in 1974-79 (World Bank, 1990: 15). Rising interest rates and falling terms of trade increased the indebtedness of many countries. Thus, in Latin America, the additional annual burden of these high rates in relation to their 1963-80 average approached US$1,000 million (almost 1 per cent of GDP). Aggregate net financial transfers to developing nations (disbursement of long-term loans minus total debt service) swung from a net inflow of US$36,000 million in 1981 to a net outflow of US$30,000 million in 1989 (World Bank, 1991:18).

Global financial flows were thus completely reversed. Banks turned to new financial instruments in industrialized countries and to speculative markets such as futures or junk bonds (Browett and Leaver, 1989). Additionally, the technical and economic upturn in industrialized countries at the end of the 1980s, along with decreasing oil prices, opened up new investment opportunities. To this global redistribution of disposable capital must be added the flight of capital from many countries (despite government controls in some instances), the role of the Overseas Chinese network and, increasingly, the 'laundering' of drug money (Fryer, 1988). Adding to the complexity of the international financial scene is the problem that no one knows how much credit risk is floating — some might say gushing — around the world system and who ultimately bears it: as Thrift (1990: 1136) points out, 'the international financial system has become, in effect, a rogue state' which is almost beyond control.

## Increasing mobility of finance capital

The spatial distribution of foreign direct investment and the various strategies of multinational corporations have received considerable attention by geographers, although this is not the place to review the extensive literature which has in any case been summarized by Linge and Hamilton (1981:46–86), Thrift (1986a), Dicken (1992) and Vernon (1992). Investments of multinational corporations should not be equated with export of capital alone: they also export capitalist relations of production. This connotation of the internationalization of capital encompasses foreign plants of a multinational organization that are not necessarily linked to capital exports from its homeland. In fact, capital exports in this sense were no longer needed by global corporations in the 1980s because they could gain access to international financial markets as well as those of the host country. Decision power based on investments and origin of investment capital thus falls apart.

Geographers have not yet studied the emergence and operation of various kinds of banks in any depth. It is clear, none the less, that the relationship between the multinational corporation and the banking sector is changing (Cohen, 1981). When corporations were spreading globally, and again when petrodollars were being recycled, the emerging multinational banks gained in importance. For present purposes it is immaterial whether the multinational banks followed the multinational corporations, or whether it was they that propelled the globalization of capital by internationalizing themselves (Kindleberger, 1983).

Whereas small multinational corporations still need the banks to help raise outside investment funds, this no longer seems as true for the global enterprise. Many global corporations no longer depend on the banking sector for outside capital as they operate their own international finance companies in off-shore centres like Luxembourg or Amsterdam to fund their investments — wherever these may be — with Euromoney. In addition to operating their own finance affiliates, their emerging financial philosophy — well summarized by BASF Aktiengesellschaft (a leading German global chemical corporation) — is that each such group should 'be regarded as a network of risks and resources: it is the equity and earning power of the whole group which forms the backbone in case single group companies run into risks' (Paul, 1989). Whereas large corporations are increasingly farming out various functions and decentralizing decision power within the organization, this is not true of their control over finance. As the head office is better informed than an outside bank about the risks associated with various foreign investments, credits between companies belonging to the global corporation receive favourable interest rates; an outside bank, in contrast, has to add a premium to cover its risk. This philosophy is thereby justified both rationally by the lower interest rates available and strategically by the increased economic independence. Even so, global corporations still need the services of banks for, among other things, the global distribution of their share capital and the investment of finance capital when the corporation has high liquidity. Banks will thus be driven to innovate as the needs of their clientele change.

Even where it is illegal — as in the US and Japan — banks belonging to global corporations have endeavoured to become 'universal' ones: that is, they combine commercial banking (collecting deposits and making loans) and investment banking (issuing, underwriting, placing, and trading company securities). To some extent they now compete with major finance collecting institutions, such as insurance companies and pension funds. This, in turn, has led to innovations, one of the more important being securitization — an arrangement whereby a financial institution packages a portfolio of financial assets into negotiable marketable instruments and on-sells them. It is this process of issuing loan paper on securities markets rather than borrowing from banks which has contributed substantially to the growth of speculative transactions on financial markets. In effect, finance is raised in the form of marketable debt instead of through banks (Gibbs, 1991).

Such contemporary processes in the world economy have brought about what has been labelled a phase of 'disorder' (Thrift, 1986a; Browett and Leaver, 1989) which may give rise to a 'a new international financial system' during the 1990s (Thrift and Leyshon, 1988: 55). This notion of disorder stems from the emergence of new actors on world markets, the growing 'laxity of control' by governments (Edwards, 1988), and the resulting volatility and increasing uncertainty on financial markets. There can be scepticism about whether the developing-world's debt crisis has really been overcome during the last decade. Perhaps, insofar as it stemmed from a crisis in the global regulation of financial markets, the nature of the problem may have changed but many developing countries, especially in sub-Saharan Africa, are still running into increasing difficulties. As the Bank for International Settlements (1992: 226) observes:

> just when the old East-West dichotomy has lost its significance a divide is beginning to open up within the developing world, between countries making large strides forward and those left far behind. Perhaps they should no longer all be called by the same name . . . In more than one sense the extremes are moving further apart, on the one hand gradually reducing the areas of misery in the world but on the other making it even more urgent to enhance the specific strategies designed to help the worst-off cases.

Another dimension is that the latter part of the 1980s saw the focus of financial recycling shifting away from the developing world to exchanges between industrialized countries with large trade surpluses and others confronted by growing budget deficits (Leyshon and Thrift, 1992).

None the less, some see straws in the wind that a new, more orderly phase may be emerging during the 1990s. One of these is the introduction of new capital standards for commercial banks which came into full effect at the end of 1992. Under these 'Basle rules', negotiated under the auspices of the Bank for International Settlements, banks now have to back every commercial loan with capital equal to 8 per cent of the loan's value; half of that must be share capital or disclosed reserves ('core' capital). Another is the moderating role being played by the intervention — mainly by peer pressure — of the Group of Seven (G–7) industrial nations (US, Japan, Germany, UK, France, Canada and Italy). Yet another is the longer-term possibility that three currency blocs (based on the US dollar, the Japanese yen, and the European Currency Unit or Ecu) will emerge and give some stability to exchange rates.

There are, however, countervailing concerns about the adequacy and reliability of such developments. Faced with a period of recession and the tightening of credit in the early 1990s, bankers in some developed countries sought to have the capital standards relaxed even before they were fully implemented. The argument was that they would be able to lend more freely, feed credit-starved economies and stimulate growth.

In the US in the 1980s, when recession struck oil-producing states, regulators were persuaded to relax capital standards in Texas and elsewhere. This exacerbated the problems already facing the savings and loans associations (the so-called 'thrifts' that are elsewhere known as building societies) which until the 1980s had enjoyed a virtual monopoly in certain types of deposits and sorts of lending. When international and other kinds of funds increasingly became available, the thrifts lost their cartel advantage of being able to pay depositors less than the market price for deposits. To attract depositors they were forced to offer higher interest rates which they funded by investing in riskier ventures; this added to the existing problems arising from the mismatch of assets and liabilities produced by their policy of borrowing short and lending long at fixed low rates of interest. The Federal government's response to thrift insolvency — the relaxation of investment and capital standards — simply compounded a worsening situation. Thrift owners took even greater risks (while protecting their own funds); depositors (protected by federal insurance up to US$100,000) chose risky thrifts because they paid high rates of interest; and thrift owners gambled on new assets like junk bonds and interest-rate swaps. The total costs of the resulting bail-out by the Federal government are not yet known, as the mess is still being sorted out, but are likely to be over US$200,000 million. Most of this is being disbursed to thrift depositors who are presumably recycling it into the financial system. Contrary to popular belief, therefore, the loans and savings fiasco has neither imposed a huge burden nor pushed up interest rates: the real cost has been the diversion of scarce resources from more productive uses into offices, shopping malls and other property at places where it remains less than fully utilized.

The opening on 1 January 1993 of the European Single Market in financial services saw most of the necessary measures in place. Removal of restrictions on capital movements was agreed to in December 1989 and implemented (with some exceptions) in 1990; removal of restrictions on life and non-life insurance was agreed to in 1992 and will apply from July 1994; and a common position was reached on investment services in 1992 but with implementation being delayed until early 1996. In some cases, however, the EC Directives have yet to be enshrined in national legislation, or even issued (as in the case of bank deposit insurance schemes), and on some matters a few countries have lengthy derogations: for instance, foreign banks will not gain access to stock exchanges in Spain, Portugal and Greece until 1999.

Although institutions have been positioning themselves to grasp the opportunities offered by deregulation, many tensions remain to be resolved, such as the different forms in which relationships have traditionally operated between finance and industry in various member countries. These have been detailed by Leyshon and Thrift (1992) and need not be repeated here. There are also many concerns, exemplified by the suggestion that to safeguard cheap access to capital markets by small enterprises, the institutional separation of regional independent financial intermediaries from national/global ones should be maintained (McKillop and Hutchinson, 1990).

The events of 1992, when the Maastricht Treaty ran into political difficulties and the European Monetary System into economic ones, have raised questions about the effectiveness of attempts at better controlling global financial markets. Some even perceive the Maastricht Treaty to be a catalogue of vagaries, inconsistencies and flaws, and an inadequate basis on which to move towards a fully fledged European Monetary Union (EMU) with a single European currency and a Central European Bank by the end of the century. Little thought seems to have been given to the possibility that a common currency could lead towards a convergence of price levels: 'any tendency for claims to be made for an equalisation of wage levels in different EC member countries without regard to differences in productivity could have unwelcome unemployment implications in relatively low-income countries in the Community', especially Portugal, Greece, and Spain (Bank for International Settlements, 1992: 126–7).

The European exchange rate mechanism (ERM) which was established to provide stability may prove instead to be an engine of destruction with major currencies being devalued or suspended from the system. The Europeans made the mistake of putting a single currency — the German mark — at the centre of the system (thus repeating the error made in the 1940s when the US dollar was made the centre-piece of world currency arrangements). Other currencies in a fixed relationship with the mark thus have to pay interest rates higher than that in Germany to attract investors, making it more difficult for them to tackle the recession and reduce unemployment. In previous years countries were happy to borrow the German currency as it was regarded as sound, but reunification in 1990 put paid to this situation. The one-for-one parity of Ostmark to D-mark, without a strict fiscal policy, meant high interest rates and an inflow of US money (because of the low interest rates there). High net public expenditures of DM139,000 million in 1991 and an estimated net DM180,000 million transfer in 1992 (about 5.5 and 6.5 per cent, respectively, of West German GDP) created a tremendous demand for state borrowing, much of which was used for consumption purposes. Furthermore, capital exports grew to DM107,000 million in 1990 and DM92,000 million in 1991, including large bank credits to the CIS. This induced a massive increase in demand which outstripped supply; prices began to rise and the Bundesbank raised interest rates to their highest level for 30 years. This exposed the inflexibility of the ERM, which requires participants to keep their rates to within 2.25 per cent of that in Germany where options are fettered by its high rate of inflation. As one observer laconically commented, 'true market-building is a mighty intrusive exercise'.

### Technological change speeds the system

At a time when the nexus between flows of goods and flows of money is weakening, financial markets are mainly influenced by flows of information, whether this be factual, speculative or deliberately misleading. Advanced telecommunication and data-processing technology enables finance capital, which always looks for better interest rates and arbitrage profits, to be shifted rapidly round the world in response to fluctuations in exchange rates and stock and bond markets. As even seconds count, dealers have no time to check whether rumours about events that might have an impact on market trends have any substance. The resulting volatility has become a critical feature of the contemporary international financial system. Computerization requires standardization of commercial procedures and this, in turn, speeds up the pace at which transactions can be processed: the wheel spins ever faster.

Many of the software programs operating in the financial world seem to be based on the same logic; if traders start with similar attitudes towards the market, volatility will be increased. This was the case in 1987 when, after two years of modest monetary expansion, the US tightened credit: this caused a sharp rise in interest rates between February and early October. A gap between bond and equity portfolios then emerged that widened to more than 2 per cent — well above previous differentials. Along with the perception that speculation had already driven equity prices too high, this yield gap induced a massive shift in international portfolios from stocks to higher-yielding bonds. Computer software, programmed to trigger automatic responses to such situations on the basis of preconceived judgements and expectations among financial decision makers, was activated, causing the New York Stock Exchange to collapse on 19 October. The increasingly integrated global capital market instantly transmitted the New York price falls to stock exchanges around the world. Almost instantaneously, millions of dollars were slashed off the market values of companies in many countries including distant Australia, one of the worst hit, where market values of listed companies plummeted within a month by more than 40 per cent.

In another development, large investing institutions have become linked electronically so that they can trade between themselves even when stock exchanges are closed. In the two decades to 1990 the NASDAQ electronic market system run in the US by the National Association of Security Dealers grew from infancy to capture 40 per cent of the daily volume of American equity share trading.

About half of all international finance transactions are made through phones linked by satellite (Warf, 1989). Telecommunication services are increasingly based on a spreading fibre-optic network, an innovation inaugurated when London and New York were connected in 1988. Several projects are in hand, for example, to quintuple the number of submarine optical-fibre telephone circuits from Japan to the US and Asia to 290,000 by the mid-1990s. New services, such as electronic funds transfer, on-line price information and electronic mail services, are growing in importance, thus creating the 'electronic marketplace' (Langdale, 1985, 1987, 1989; Hepworth, 1989, 1990). Apart from banks, financial service firms, information brokers, and even global manufacturing corporations have their own telecommunication networks, as has been documented by Bakis (1987) in the case of International Business Machines (IBM).

The new technical infrastructure enabling the rapid circulation of information throughout global financial markets was made possible by deregulation in the telecommunication sector marked by breaking up American Telephone and Telegraph's monolithic Bell Telephone System in the US, privatizing British Telecom, and admitting private competition in the US, UK and Japan (Warf, 1989). Regulations and institutions form two sides of a coin: changes to regulations allow new techniques to be established which, in turn, may assist or require new regulations and institutions to emerge. Thus, the emergence of systems like NASDAQ raises the question of balancing the concern that trading be done on regulated exchanges to ensure investor protection and market surveillance with the desire not to stifle innovative markets.

## The National Financial System

The preceding summary of some of the processes influencing the global mobility of finance capital — the increasing international liquidity, the deregulation of financial markets and the new technological innovations that are breaking down information and regulation barriers — may give the impression that national space is no longer significant. O'Brien (1992) even sees the 'end-of-geography' flowing from the declining sovereignty of governments over financial markets. While there are certainly questions to be raised about the role of the nation state, there are several factors suggesting that it will continue to be an important influence on financial markets. Reportedly, for instance, some French politicians believe that much of the confusion in European money markets in the early 1990s was inspired by Anglo-Saxon financial institutions unwilling to see the creation of a European currency that could rival the US dollar.

First, despite the advent of Euromoney, much investment capital is sourced nationally. Some authors even point out that Euromarkets are not as independent of central banks as usually stated (Herr, 1987). The size and use of national income, which differ of course between countries, influence both the capacity to invest in and restructure domestic industry and also the amount and type of capital available for export. Second, the banking and financial systems differ between countries, and depend on different legal and institutional frameworks and social attitudes. Third, despite the much-touted 'euphoria' about the benefits of deregulation, national (and, in some cases, regional) governments still ultimately determine the degrees of freedom within which the financial intermediaries must operate. It thus seems premature to speak of a new paradigm emerging in which territorial development is entirely dependent on global finance capital. National governments, for example, use personal and company taxation arrangements to influence the ways in which savings are accumulated and expended.

## Household savings and pensions

After the Second World War most industrial nations experienced an unprecedented phase of prosperity with considerable growth in real income. In the Federal Republic of Germany (FRG), as a case in point, the purchasing power of net earnings quadrupled between 1949 and 1989. This rise in real income can be explained by the considerable improvements in productivity made during the Fordist phase of mass production, by the redistribution of profits in favour of wages achieved by the countervailing power of unions, and by the Keynesian policy of governments. Rising household earnings, especially in those countries like Japan and the FRG that accumulated large international trading surpluses, encouraged the development of a range of services to help people buy homes, educate children and anticipate old age. This was particularly so in the case of firms providing superannuation and life insurance, which became leading channels for collecting and accumulating the flow of savings arising from rising real wages and salaries, inflation and the benefits available from diverting otherwise taxable income in this direction. The share of household financial assets channelled into pension funds, insurance companies and other collective investment schemes rose markedly during the 1980s in most of the highly industrialized countries: in the US from 20.0 per cent in 1980 to 31.2 in 1990, in Japan from 15.6 to 26.4, in Germany from 22.6 to 35.1, in the UK from 41.5 to 58.6, in France from 10.6 to 36.3, and in Canada from 20.4 to 29.7 (Bank for International Settlements, 1992:

194). This created massive amounts of new investment capital: in 1990, pensions funds in Japan, the EC and North America aggregated US$4,200,000 million; by 2000 they are expected to be treble this amount (*The Economist*, 20 June 1991: 18). It was this greater institutionalization of savings that underpinned the expansion and sophistication of the securities market.

Such figures must, however, be treated with caution because the population structure of the developed world is ageing and thus each person in the workforce will have to support more elderly dependants. Unless productivity allows wage rises to keep pace, new contributions to savings will decline just at the time that the growing number of retired people will be drawing on the existing pool of savings. The impact on the financial system will vary between countries, depending on their demographic characteristics and the arrangements now in place to provide for future pensions. In Japan, 18 per cent of the population — a greater proportion than anywhere else — will be aged 65 or more by 2010: as companies there have not accumulated large pension funds, benefits for the aged will have to come out of profits or from increases in taxation. In Europe, where the problem will emerge a decade or more later, few countries have yet made adequate provision for the future. Indeed, the paucity of pension funds in Germany and Italy helps to explain why the stock markets there are relatively poorly developed, and why the major firms in those countries turn to London or New York to raise finance (*The Economist*, 20 June 1992: 17–19). Even in the UK, The Netherlands, Canada and the US, which do have well-established pension funds, capital will be scarce and more expensive, and financial markets may become more subdued and less imaginative. The implications of all this on the relative competitiveness of individual countries (and their groupings), and on the ability of industry to obtain affordable capital for innovation, are profound.

### New financial intermediaries

Since the Industrial Revolution 'the financial requirements of business organizations have progressively changed and this has necessitated constant evolution in the functioning of financial institutions' (Taylor and Thrift, 1983: 360). The system of financial intermediaries and services which has so far developed in industrialized countries is shown diagrammatically in Figure 1.1.

It is bound in time and space, and can be characterized as the 'institutional form' of the finance sector in a given country. In the FRG, for example, the banks lost much of their influence over private capital accumulation in favour of the insurance companies. Between 1982 and 1988, private household money capital held by the latter rose from DM28,000 million to DM40,000 million whereas that held by banks fell from DM66,000 to DM44,000 million (Händel and Patterson, 1990). In particular, life insurance companies are becoming the biggest collectors of private capital as this is the most important way people make provision for the future.

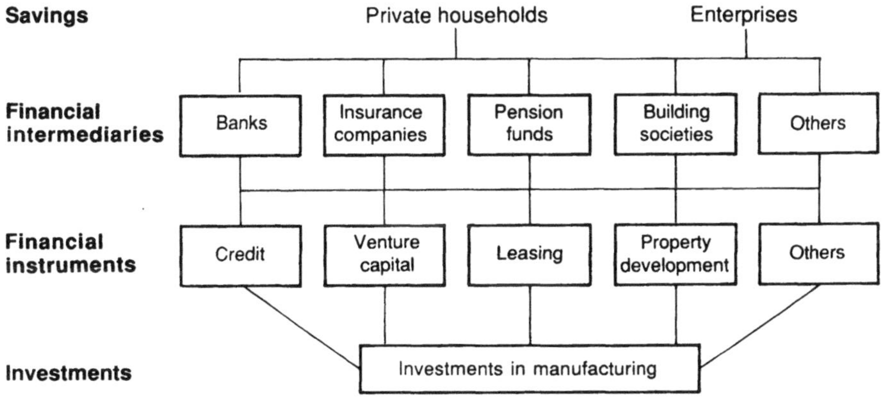


Figure 1.1: The system of private financial intermediaries in industrialized nations.

The public pension system in the FRG is based upon the so-called 'treaty among generations' in which retirement pensions are financed through payments by younger employees. Additional company pensions, in contrast, are accumulated within the firm and form reserves that can be used to finance investments. As the equity:capital ratio of enterprises is decreasing, reserves built up from pension payments are becoming increasingly important for investment purposes. This is quite different from anglophone countries where private household pensions have to be accumulated during the years of employment. As Pratt points out in Chapter 7, public-sector workers in Britain have been required since 1974 to invest in occupational pension funds which now form the biggest pool of private capital in that country. These new financial intermediaries are at the core of the New International Financial System (Thrift and Leyshon, 1988).

The prosperous industrial nations are soon likely to see a considerable increase in the number and value of mobilized private assets because many 'first generation' entrepreneurs of the 1950s will soon pass their companies to descendants, not all of whom may be willing or capable of managing these themselves. Personal assets' management companies are now emerging to look after the financial affairs of wealthy individuals.

Venture capital, which became a much vaunted product during the late 1970s and 1980s, illustrates how quickly markets can change. In the US where it played an important role in financing the formation of high-technology firms, it began as a small profitable niche business producing returns of over 20 per cent. The number of firms grew from 250 in 1980 to a peak of 650 in 1987 when the funds under management totalled US$29,000 million (*The Economist*, 7 December 1991: 96). Since then, when annual raisings were running at over US$4,000 million, circumstances have changed and new raisings have halved. On the one side, investors have become more wary as the returns on their high-risk outlays declined; on the other, favoured recipients like biotechnology and computer software projects, now require greater capitalization and longer lead times before producing results. Most studies of the regional distribution of this kind of investment relate to the US (Leinbach and Amrhein, 1987; Florida and Kenney, 1988), Canada (McNaughton and Green, 1989) and the UK (Martin, 1989; Gibbs, 1991) because these were where it became an important outlet for pension funds and insurance companies (Rothwell and Zegveld, 1985; Organisation for Economic Co-operation and Development, 1986; Thompson 1989). In Germany, by contrast, such sources have not been so important for supporting the formation of firms, in part because almost all the banks there administer venture capital funds and try to minimize this form of competition.

The main sources of finance for industrial change in developed countries are 'internal funds' (firms' retained earnings), bank loans, and equity capital. Conventional wisdom has long suggested that in Germany bank loans are the major source of investment capital for industrial companies, but this has now been challenged by Edwards and Fischer (1991). Their examination of data for the 1970-89 period showed that internal funds were by far the most important source of finance for German companies, providing 62 per cent of the total as against only 18 per cent through bank loans. They used comparable British data to show that banks there provided 24 per cent of the funds with, again, 62 per cent coming from internal funds (mainly retained profits), a finding that supports the earlier work of Thomas (1978). Netting out financial investments, British firms buy 20 per cent of their physical assets using bank finance but German firms only 11 per cent (*The Economist*, 7 December 1991: 89).

## State regulation

Financial institutions and systems grew up to mobilize capital to meet the demand for finance by industrialists and merchants. They have long been subject to legislative restrictions, ranging from the Jacksonian ethic in the US (Trescott, 1963) to the paralysing legal restrictions and centralization in France and the near free-enterprise environment in Scotland (Cameron, 1976). The financial systems operating today are thus a product of diverse political and economic histories in various parts of the world. In Africa and Asia, for example, the system remained largely undeveloped until countries gained independence. Thus, prior to the late 1940s, Nigeria was the only African country with indigenous commercial banks (incorporated in the territory and owned and operated by Africans), and there and elsewhere the system was orientated towards agricultural exports and the needs of the expatriate communities. In contrast, India when it became independent in 1947 had a well-developed, sophisticated indigenous banking structure that relied on an elaborate system of personal relations to finance local, mainly small-scale, activities (World Bank, 1989: 47). Different again was the situation in China where the foreign banks lost their dominance to locally owned ones in the 1930s and the whole system was taken over by the state after 1947.

The contemporary national banking systems in developed countries reflect the series of changes inaugurated after the Great Depression of the 1930s. In the US banks were prevented from holding equities in industrial and commercial companies, from investment banking, and from paying interest on 'on demand' deposits. 'Coupled with continuing restrictions on bank mergers and branching, these measures constrained the growth of commercial banks, which remained fragmented and were unable to meet the long-term financing requirements of American business' (World Bank, 1989: 46). These needs were met instead by the securities markets. Whereas countries like Canada, France and Italy also separated investment from commercial banking, Germany did not. Indeed it was the increased lending to industry by German banks during the 1920s, the failure of many companies in the 1930s, and the conversion then of debt into equity that has led to the continuing — and long-established (Böhme, 1978) — close relationship between banks and industrial enterprises which is discussed in Gaebe's chapter in this book. In Japan, investment and commercial banking were not separated until after the Second World War when the *zaibatsu* conglomerates were broken up and the development of the securities market encouraged. However, the system of corporate cross-holdings that re-emerged under the *keiretsu* business groupings (see Chapter 2) and the regulatory framework in which they have operated has maintained the close links between industry and the banking system (Goldsmith, 1983). As a consequence, the securities markets and institutional investors have played a relatively minor role in the financial system. This was also the case in Germany and other continental European countries where social security arrangements provided a safer way of accumulating savings. Important, too, were the tax and other incentives designed to encourage home ownership, with housing finance and contractual savings arrangements having fewer restrictions than bank deposits and credits.

After the Second World War, direct intervention by government in the financial systems of most developed countries increased. This took various forms and varied greatly between countries. Some large commercial banks were nationalized; specialized long-term credit institutions were encouraged; export credit banks were established; and post office and other public-sector banks were expanded. In Japan, the government-run postal-savings system — now the world's largest with accumulated deposits in 1992 totalling US$1,400,000 million — competes with commercial banks by offering higher interest rates (guaranteed for ten years) and charges no fee for withdrawing funds prematurely.

By the mid-1960s the high rates of inflation and the changing nature of the financial system were undermining many of the credit and banking controls then in use. There were also concerns that regulations could reduce efficiency, stultify innovation and divert business. It was the heavy-handed rules in the 1960s that caused New York to lose much of the Eurodollar market to London. Canada, UK and several Scandinavian and European countries undertook wide-ranging reforms which 'abolished the distinctions among different types of institution, relaxed both global and selective credit controls, removed branching restrictions, and liberalized interest rates on lending and wholesale deposits' (World Bank, 1989: 51). These deregulatory moves were temporarily halted between 1973 and 1979 due to the turmoil created by the 355 per cent increase in oil prices during the two years to January 1974. When they resumed, controls were eliminated or relaxed on credit, interest rates, foreign exchange and branching, and some of the restrictions on the activities of financial institutions and new financial instruments were removed. These steps were a recognition, in effect, that the growth of the Euromarkets, the development of new financial instruments, and the advent of electronic technology were all making it easier to find ways around restrictions.

Not only can regulation and deregulation induce or permit financial intermediaries to introduce innovations, but they can also have profound repercussions on the organization of industry and, more indirectly, also on locational choice. Thus, the US regulations prohibiting the use of internal firm pension funds for takeovers led to the invention of junk bonds as a way of financing large leveraged buy-outs in a deregulated market that favoured 'raiding' — a phenomenon discussed by Le Heron in Chapter 4.

The investment behaviour of pension funds since the early 1980s clearly illustrates the role of the state. When various countries relaxed their rules, these funds began to invest in risky sectors and in markets outside their national borders (Organisation for Economic Co-operation and Development, 1986): Swedish pension funds, for instance, pushed into the European property market. While deregulation enables financial activities to move from national into international markets, regulation by governments and collaboration between financial intermediaries can perpetuate market segmentation. This was illustrated in the 1980s by the formation of a so-called 'White Knight Fund' in The Netherlands by Amro Bank, the two largest Dutch insurance companies and the pension fund of Philips to counter hostile takeover attempts by foreign firms (Hirn, 1990). In the FRG, the power of the three largest banks, existing company law, and the worker co-management law are regarded as the main barriers to hostile takeovers. German insurance firms retain much of their economic power because state controls limit the entrance of foreign insurance companies. Given such examples, the significance of the interventionist role of the national state in global financial markets cannot be doubted.

More recently, the emphasis has turned to improving the monitoring and supervision of the financial system, a process that is even more important now that the players which make up the financial system are freer to engage in new forms of competition and offer more complex products, often derivatives of derivatives. A particular worry is that this may expose financial institutions to greater risk as they chase business, lower prices and emphasize short-term performance rather than long-term efficiency and stability. An example that well illustrates this is the French state-owned Crédit Lyonnais which doubled its assets in the four years to mid-1992 and spread across national borders to become Europe's largest banking network. However, its profits during the first half of 1992 fell to US$23 million, compared with US$309 million in the same period in 1991, largely because of an 85 per cent increase in provisions against bad loans, mainly to poorly performing Hollywood film-making studios, that had mounted to US$1,210 million.

## The Regional Financial System

In most developed countries, the current financial system evolved from humble local beginnings. Until the 1850s the needs of industry and commerce were mainly for short-term working capital rather than finance for fixed capital investment. Taylor and Thrift (1983) have traced the practical considerations and legal constraints that led in most countries to the centralization of the banking system. This process, however, was not without differences within and between countries. In the US, for example, the collapse of Southern banking after the Civil War (1861-65) led to a concentration of this activity in the northeast with New York being chosen as the central reserve city. National banks, denied the mortgage lending instrument, were restricted from operating in rural areas so that local banks there were given a virtual monopoly. They were thus able to charge high interest rates and the resulting large profits were channelled to the cities where they acted as deposits for the whole banking system. From the beginning of the nineteenth century in the UK, takeovers and mergers began to reduce the number of independent banks as these suffered from high overhead costs, an inability to supply the growing range of services being demanded, and the lack of representation in London which had clearly become the focus of all financial activities. By 1930, British banking had become dominated by the so-called 'Big Five'. From a regional point of view this was a double-edged sword: on the one side, the standardization of lending policies and procedure took away what has been called the 'local elasticity' of branch managers but, on the other, they could call upon their head offices to support much larger and more complex loans.

Chick and Dow (1988) maintain that financial factors, especially banking systems, have an important role in regional as well as national growth. Just as the banking system of a nation progresses through different stages of development, so too, they suggest, do the banking relationships in and between regions. This explains why various regional development theories can co-exist — be they neo-classical, Marxian, dependency or Keynesian in orientation — which differ as to the primacy of saving or of investment. The choice between them, Chick and Dow argue, depends on whether or not the relevant stage of banking development has been reached. They identify five such stages.

*Stage 1*: Banks collect regional savings and lend them to regional investors; growth is slow as investment must wait for new saving. Although the banks are small and their hinterlands limited, some savings will be attracted from other regions where investment opportunities are scarce.

*Stage 2*: Banks create credits on the basis of their deposits; a deposit multiplier comes into play and investments become independent of the regional yield of savings capital. The development of financial relationships between different regions leads to the emergence of a centre/periphery situation. As the peripheral economies are likely to be more volatile, the banks there need to retain a higher level of reserves, thus giving banks in the centre a competitive advantage. Head offices of banks and other financial institutions will congregate at the centre in which more information is available at less cost, leading also to a possible bias in favour of supporting firms and projects there.

*Stage 3*: Inter-bank lending begins and a coherent system emerges; bank expansion is more likely to reach the limits of the deposit multiplier and the multiplier process is more rapid. Even if banking in the periphery remains in the hands of branches of the centre banks, the value of credit in the periphery must still be sufficient to retain it there rather than being used to expand credit at the centre.

*Stage 4*: A central monetary authority accepts the function of lender of last resort so that banks can collectively expand credit without the risk of being caught short of reserves; various financial markets emerge in which speculation is possible so that credit no longer need be confined only to productive investments. The terms of regional credit reflects national monetary policy rather than local considerations.

*Stage 5*: Banks become 'liability managers' and meet the demand for loans by actively bidding for deposits through manipulating interest rates; they then use any reserves thus created to compete for lending opportunities, some of which may be speculative in character. Banks compete internationally to raise deposits, using instruments such as securitization, and begin to move outside the money markets regulated by central banks.

Although the Chick and Dow evolutionary model is a helpful way of bringing together the diverse approaches to regional issues, it does not take account of the ways in which governments can interfere with the development of the banking system. A prime example is the US which 'maintains the most detailed, fragmented, and complex system of legal controls on its financial system' (Holly, 1987: 633). To prevent the concentration of financial power, the Pepper-McFadden Act (*Banking Act*, 1927) stopped banks based in one state from having full branches in another. The states joined in: some limited branching to the central office county or its neighbours while others prohibited branching altogether. The result, as Holly (p. 633) points out, has been 'the creation and maintenance of a diverse and decentralised banking system' which supports 14,000 commercial banks and 30,000 chartered depository institutions. During the 1980s, however, various institutional devices were used to overcome these geographical restrictions, which in any case were being weakened by the growing use of credit cards and automatic bank teller machines, and by legal loopholes that allowed interstate quasi-banking operations. Massachusetts in 1982 and Connecticut in 1983 passed laws that authorized acquisitions of their own state's banks, provided the buyer was based in New England. In 1985 the Supreme Court ruled that states could legally make exceptions to the general federal prohibition against interstate banking. By then, 15 of the 21 states that had passed laws permitting out-of-state mergers had specifically excluded New York, thus allowing the rapid development of so-called 'super-regional' banks based away from that city. During the 1985-89 period about half the value of the 3,000 bank mergers in the US was accounted for by the 20-odd super-regionals, the assets of which grew during this period by about 50 per cent, compared with around 20 per cent for the six biggest New York-based banks.

In Japan, too, regional banking was strictly regulated until 1988 when moves were made to liberalize the nation's financial system. Previously these mutual savings and loans, or *sogo*, banks were only permitted to make loans to companies with fewer than 300 employees or capitalized at less than ¥400 million (US$3,280,000); moreover, loans to any one client could not exceed 20 per cent of the bank's capitalization or ¥800 million. Most of their business, therefore, was with nearby small firms. Under amended laws, they were allowed to change their status to *futsu* (ordinary) banks which gave them a freer hand but also exposed them to greater risk. Many of the 66 second-tier regional banks operating at the end of 1992 face deteriorating asset values and sharper competition as the deregulation process proceeds, and mergers seem likely to thin out their numbers. Japanese regional banks are also striving to compete with the larger 'city' counterparts by linking with foreign banks that can provide assistance and services to their clients establishing branches overseas.

It seems that, in reality, the extent to which regional financial systems remain viable largely depends on the particular historical, legal, social and other conditions applying in each country. In some situations loan and savings associations and cooperative banks have probably survived because, unlike the branches of centralized banks, they are better informed about local affairs and can be more flexible and hence responsive to the needs of local small and medium-scale enterprise. For instance in Germany, as Schamp points out in

Chapter 6, the local banking system, regarded as very stable, has maintained long-established close associations with local business and been very supportive of their efforts to restructure their activities. Hence, whereas the proportion of all bank assets in the FRG held by cooperative and loan and savings banks increased from 56 to 70 per cent between 1950 and 1987 that held by the major banks fell from 44 to 30 per cent (Bonus and Schmidt, 1990).

## Where to Now?

This chapter has been written in the context of the fundamental changes that are taking place in the structure and organization of the institutional arrangements conditioning the operation of the world economy.

Although the markets for labour, goods and finance have been internationalizing since the 1960s, it is only during the last decade that they reached truly global dimensions. For firms, the operating environment has become more uncertain and risky. Among the many sources are those stemming from fluctuations in interest and exchange rates. To existing uncertainties are being added a seemingly never-ending stream of additional ones, just as the new-found political awareness of the popular strength of concerns about the 'environment' (such as the depletion of the ozone layer) and health (like tobacco smoking) is leading to switches in policy and related legislation. The volatility of the international market-place is reinforcing moves by national and supra-national bodies to find ways and means of adding new checks and balances to the system to try to minimize wild aberrations, violent fluctuations and downright dishonesty. Ironically, this has created another kind of risk for firms. Much more effort now has to be expended to avoid unintentional non-compliance with the voluntary 'codes of conduct' devised by national and international industry groups and the even more complex (and often conflicting) regulations laid down by central banks (among them the Federal Reserve in the US, the Bank of England and the Bundesbank in Germany), corporations and securities agencies (such as the US Securities Commission), and agencies supervising many aspects of corporate operations. Some observers consider that uncertainty and instability will remain a fact of corporate life until the appearance of a lender of last resort able to set institutional conditions for financial intermediaries operating globally.

Another fundamental change is that the institutional order of the socialist world has broken down. Replacing socialist modes of production by those that have characterized capitalist societies marks a change of global rather than simply national importance. Hänkel (1990) applied the term 'underbanking' to describe the contemporary system in many developing countries but this is also true of the former socialist countries where decentralized regional banking and credit creation facilities are absent. Underbanking greatly hinders the development of regions and nations because, in the absence of such institutions or the ability to create credit independently, capital must be imported such as by direct investment. As Matykowski and Stryjakiewicz point out in Chapter 9, when investment decisions are made centrally and local capital markets do not exist, sectoral and spatial investment decisions can be swayed by ideological and political considerations rather than local needs. This situation is changing: too slowly for the reformers and too rapidly for the conservatives. None the less, there are signs that decentralized institutions are beginning to emerge. Thus, the argument that the socialist countries can be excluded from discussions about the 'new world economic order' because 'the case has to be convincingly made that they are an integral part of it' (Thrift, 1986a: 13) is becoming less tenable. (Joint ventures, which have become a particularly important mechanism helping to introduce capitalist ways of doing business into the former socialist countries of Eastern Europe, are discussed in Chapters 8 and 9.)

It is appropriate here to speculate only briefly about some of the possible spatial repercussions stemming from the changes occurring in the world financial system. Although it is possible to conceive of a unified global system, it will remain a fiercely competitive one, as between nations and regional groupings of nation states as well as between transnational enterprises engaged in productive and service activities. Japan and the FRG, which emerged as the largest commodity exporting nations during the 1970s and 1980s, have had a growing influence on the international distribution of short-term and long-term capital. The net assets held abroad by both these countries rose considerably during the 1986-91 period (from US$180,000 million to

US$383,000 million in the case of Japan, and from US$97,000 million to US$341,000 million by Germany), whereas the US saw its net foreign assets decline from +US$19,000 million to –US$362,000 million (Figure 1.2).

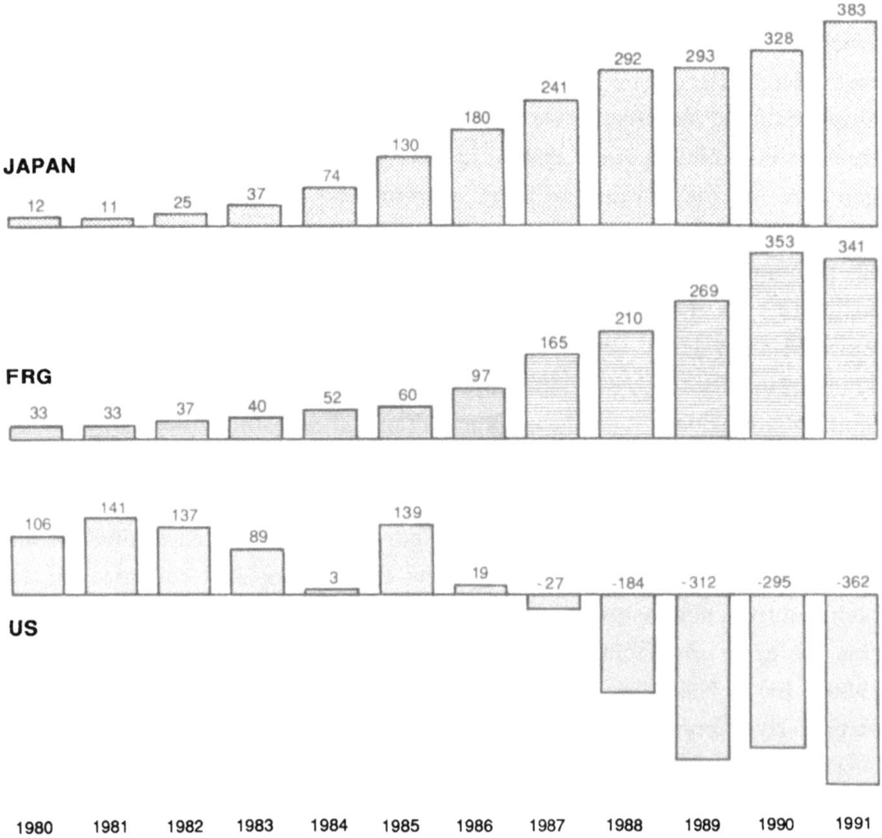


Figure 1.2: Value of net foreign assets of the US, Japan and Germany, 1980 to 1991 (US$000 m.). The German Democratic Republic excluded prior to 1991. *Source*: Deutsche Bundesbank, 1993.

This link between trade and investment seems to support the argument of some proponents of the *régulation* theory School. Lipietz (1989: 45), for instance, suggests that 'a loss of American industrial hegemony foreshadows an implicit loss of American financial hegemony'. Clearly, national regulation policies can greatly influence a country's position in the world production and trade systems. It is possible, therefore, to see advocacy of deregulation as an innovative way of trying to gain advantage on — or perhaps regain dominance of — global financial markets, while support for maintaining or even strengthening regulation could be regarded as an appropriate way for those states with some economic power to safeguard their own markets. Some even see the 'trade disputes' between Europe, Japan and the US that have rumbled on since the mid-1980s as part of a bigger 'war' being fought by anglophone countries to try to maintain the US dollar as the dominant global currency.

The emergence of an even newer 'new world economic order' — still centred on the internationalization of capital but incorporating the former socialist countries — makes it likely that the direction of capital flows will substantially change. During the 1980s both the FRG and Japan made substantial contributions to the capital needs of the rest of the world, especially those of the US. In 1989 German capital exports alone accounted for 64 per cent of the deficit in the US current balance of payments (Roche, 1990: 92). The integration of the former German Democratic Republic (GDR) with the FRG on 1 July 1990, together with the growing capital needs of the other East European countries, has meant that capital flows have been diverted away from traditional borrowers like the US. Net transfer payments by the German federal government amounted to more than half the total GNP of the eastern Länder during 1991. The former state-run enterprises there are generally not internationally competitive and sustained improvements in productivity and product quality will require massive investments over many years, as will the upgrading of transport, communications and related infrastructure. Much of this funding will have to come from outside the eastern Länder which, indeed, absorbed about one-sixth of all total private investment in the FRG in 1992.

Japan's direct overseas investment expanded for seven years before peaking at US$67,500 million in 1987 and then declined each year to US$41,500 million in 1991 (see Table 11.2); surveys suggest that this contraction will continue during 1992 and 1993. The greatest reduction has been to flows to the US and Europe, in contrast to those to Asian countries which overall have been growing. Japanese investors, mainly institutions like banks and insurance companies, are also retreating from foreign stock markets. Each year from 1980 (when official data were first collected) to 1991 they were net buyers, but in 1992 their sales, totalling US$36,300 million, exceeded purchases by US$3,000 million, much of it going to shore up otherwise dismal earnings statements. This has come about as the result of a mixture of both short and long-term and also internal and external influences which are discussed in Chapter 2. What is important to note here are some of the fundamental changes occurring to the agenda that underlay these capital flows and the likely consequences.

First, the leading investors, the Japanese car manufacturers, appear to have virtually completed their initial plans to establish plants in the US and Europe. Second, the US$80,000 million-worth of Japanese direct investment built up in the US by 1989 produced only poor returns before incurring a small loss in 1990 and a much larger one of US$1,300 million in 1991 (Bank for International Settlements, 1992: 92). This reinforces the view that much of this investment in so-called 'transplants' was aimed at defusing protectionist sentiment while at the same time securing a base in markets which might become even less open in the event of the collapse of the current lengthy 'Uruguay Round' of negotiations on the General Agreement of Tariffs and Trade (GATT). Third, only 198 overseas acquisition and merger deals were concluded by Japanese companies during 1992, a quarter fewer than the previous year, and the average size of these deals was also a quarter smaller at US$20 million. It appears that large-scale deals, like Matsushita Electric Industrial Co's US$6,100 million buyout of the US entertainment giant MCA Inc. in 1990, have become a thing of the past. Fourth, Japanese companies are facing a continuing deterioration of corporate profits and shrinking liquidity just at the time when the massive debts they incurred during the boom years of the 1980s are maturing. Similarly, Japan's financial institutions, real estate developers and other non-manufacturing concerns have little choice but to stop boosting overseas assets. Banks, for instance, have been trying to unload a mountain of non-performing real estate loans in Japan both to make up for substantial losses in their securities portfolios and also to raise capital-adequacy ratios that have fallen in the wake of slumping stock-market values.

Capital flows are increasingly becoming directed and controlled through a hierarchical system of financial centres (Cohen, 1981). Studies of places like New York (Sassen, 1989), London and Amsterdam (Ter Hart and Piersma, 1990), and Manchester (Gibbs and Gentle, 1990) all point to the existence of a multi-level city system of financial control and decision making (Shachar, 1990). Competition between them has intensified as a result of globalization and securitization. The ending of most exchange controls has broadened the search for the highest return for savings and the lowest cost for borrowing, while the replacement of traditional bank finance by tradeable debt has helped to loosen the bonds that tied investors and borrowers to place. Furthermore, as noted earlier, technological advances enable money and information to be shifted between places in seconds and, with the growth of systems like NASDAQ, in an almost disembodied way. All this suggests that financial centres should be disappearing as the services they provide become increasingly footloose: in reality, competition between them is growing.

The process of information gathering increases the pressure for clustering. According to *The Economist* (27 June 1992):

> Finance depends on information. The best way to gather it is to be near the centre of the business. Paradoxically, as information has become more complex and (thanks to computers) more widely available, the will-o'-the-wisp hunt for an information lead has become more pressing. That is a powerful impetus to market participants to gather close to one another and to their principal sources of information — the press, government, financial regulators and so on.

There are other practical centralizing forces — including the ability to maintain face-to-face contacts, to draw on a larger pool of skilled labour, and to lobby those in power — which outweigh the costs and disbenefits of crowding into one place.

However, it is not by chance that the three leading financial centres in terms of stock-market turnover, international bank-lending and foreign-exchange turnover — London, New York and Tokyo — are distributed round the world since this allows trading to pass round the clock from one to another. All three are likely to remain ahead of potential competitors, at least for the foreseeable future, despite the problems within their own national financial systems, like the collapse of the Japanese property market.

Intensifying rivalry between centres at the next level of the hierarchy, however, makes the outcome here less clear. This is particularly the case in Europe with most observers agreeing that 'the EC can only sustain a limited number of global centres' (Begg, 1992: 336). Competition among centres — in particular Frankfurt, Paris, Zurich, Amsterdam, Milan, Madrid — is growing as changes to procedures, facilities, taxation and legislation are implemented. Frankfurt and Paris, the two largest, have visions of supplanting London. This ambition of Germany's banks and securities houses to make their country an international financial centre is captured by the widely used title *Finanzplatz Deutschland.* The German government, for example, is supporting plans for the establishment of a holding company, the Deutsche Börse, which under Frankfurt's leadership would bring together the regional stock exchanges, the Deutsche Termin-Börse (futures exchange) and the country's settlement system. The fight to host the proposed European Central Bank is leading to a round of gamesmanship with some support in London being given to the claims of Amsterdam or Luxembourg in an effort to thwart the aspirations of Frankfurt, its main rival. This illustrates again that national aspirations and financial ambitions often run hand in glove.

Rivalry also exists in the Pacific Basin among Tokyo, Osaka, Hong Kong, Singapore and Sydney, with others like Seoul and Taipei emerging on the horizon. The main contenders, Singapore and Hong Kong, both have drawbacks, not the least of which is the government's propensity to control information in the former, and the uncertainty facing the latter when the PRC resumes sovereignty on 1 July 1997.

Most national capital markets are controlled by a handful of centres (Wheeler, 1986; Holly, 1987). Although rivalries exist — for example, between Toronto and Montreal in Canada, Tokyo and Osaka in Japan, and New York and Chicago in the US — financial power seems to be concentrating in a single centre standing head and shoulders above the others, as does Paris in France, Frankfurt in Germany, Milan in Italy and Zurich in Switzerland. Usually there are particular reasons for the continuing importance of other centres. Thus, Chicago has maintained its national and international dominance of futures and options business, and Osaka leads this kind of activity in Japan.

Regional capital markets can only exist where a traditional local banking system is well preserved or a new one created. Various studies stressed the importance of a local banking system for the well-being of small and medium-size enterprises and for economic growth in peripheral regions (e.g. Clark et al., 1986). Given the contemporary tendencies which have been demonstrated in the hypotheses outlined above there is, however, a danger that globalization of financial markets will intensify the segmentation of powerful multi-locational firms and weak small-scale enterprises. The new centralization of financial capital could, in the end, result in a growing external control of production as the possibilities of locally financing investments in small-scale industries are reduced.

Some geographers have interpreted the emergence of globalized banks more as a new form of world system control by emerging world cities (Friedmann, 1986) than as a new institutional form of globalizing financial markets. In this context, Shachar and Öberg (1990) have drawn attention to the dimension of economic and political power embedded in this process. This is exemplified by changes that have occurred in off-shore banking (Andreff, 1984). Since the US government permitted liberalized international financial activity in New York in 1981 and the Japanese government followed suit with Tokyo in 1986, some off-shore tax and regulatory havens such as Bahrein, Panama, Cayman Islands and the Bahamas have lost some of their prominence and changed their clientele. As 'old-world' wealth has dried up, it is being replaced by money from the newly rich of Latin America and Asia. A sign, perhaps, of the fundamental reorientation taking place is given by the incorporation in 1992 of a company in Bermuda by the PRC to raise US$80 million for a vehicle making operation in China.

The impact of changes in the financial system on the spatial organization of industry has been poorly addressed by geographers. Empirical research is needed which recognizes that the spatial organization of an economy is an historical process of contradictions, conflict and crisis. There are two critical premises for this work. One is the very significant role of political power in influencing and explaining capital mobility (and sometimes even its spatial inertia) — a theme that has run through this chapter. Corbridge (1989) was right to plead for a greater emphasis on the political economy approach which, indeed, Le Heron adopted as his theme in Chapter 4. The need for such an approach is underscored by the argument of Underhill (1991: 200), following Polanyi, that 'even in the case of internationalised financial markets, politics, through the medium of state decision-making, continues to determine the pattern of development'. His case studies of financial services in the Single European Market, of GATT negotiations on services and the determination of the 'Basle rules' on minimum capital adequacy ratios make it plain that both state decision making and historical events matter when it comes to explaining institutional change in financial markets. The other essential premise is that manufacturing activities will remain the leading generator of capital and hence its pattern of flows. Little credence can be given to the notion that free-floating financial capital, ever increasing by speculation, will shape the industrial production system. Undoubtedly, there will be disruptive episodes (such as the temporary reduction in liquidity in the early 1990s caused by the slump on Japanese property and financial markets), but there is no reason to doubt Cohen and Zysman's (1987) claim that 'manufacturing matters'. Indeed, this seems to remain the only viable base for the generation of surplus.

# 2 Financial Markets and Industrial Change

G. J. R. Linge

Geographers have not paid much attention to either the role of financial institutions or the impact of such influences as patterns of household savings and levels of national indebtedness on the organization of space. Moreover, they have paid only lip service to the importance of factors like interest and currency exchange rates, with which this chapter is principally concerned.

Yet, as was pointed out in Chapter 1, the last three decades have seen fundamental changes to the organization of financial markets and to the speed and intensity with which they operate. These changes, driven and underlain by innovation, technology and deregulation, are ubiquitous, with all levels of space sharing their consequences. During the 1980s and into the 1990s they have also become increasingly internationalized as a result of the growth of cross-border flows of goods, services and capital and the rise of multinational business and joint venture (JV) enterprise. In a real sense, too, they are becoming globalized as the Commonwealth of Independent States (CIS), the People's Republic of China (PRC) and the economies in eastern Europe open their doors to the external forces from the wider economic environment.

Capital and assets can now be moved around a world in which boundaries and barriers between national financial systems have been eroded and, in some instances, virtually demolished. No one has been able to measure the true size of the international capital market: data on some of its elements are fraught with problems of definition and double-counting as well as pierced with lacunae like the laundering of drug money. However, one partial indicator of the almost incomprehensibly large amounts involved is that the *daily* global trade in foreign exchange (and derivatives like futures, options and swaps) is estimated to be about US$900,000 million; another is that during 1991 net cross-border portfolio flows (largely funds being invested abroad by institutions such as pension funds and insurance companies) amounted to perhaps US$102,200 million; and yet a third is that the global stock of foreign direct investment (FDI) is thought to stand at about US$1,700,000 million. A perspective is given to such figures by recalling that the annual value of trade between the US and Japan amounted to only US$148,000 million in 1992.

The actual amounts involved are only one part of the story. Perhaps even more significant is the short-run volatility of the system and the great speed at which some of the longer-run trends have been emerging. By 1991, for instance, the stock of 'international' bank lending (that is, cross-border lending plus domestic lending denominated in foreign currency) had reached US$7,600,000 million whereas in 1980 it amounted to only US$324,000 million (*The Economist*, 19 September 1992: S9). To keep abreast of changes of such magnitude, producers must now monitor stock levels, labour costs and commodity prices every few days, and scan stock-exchange prices, currency exchange fluctuations and interest rate relationships every few hours, rather than more leisurely every few weeks or even months.

In effect, the international financial markets are now largely setting the pace and the agenda, leaving national governments to cope with the aftermath, whether this manifests itself like the savings and loan fiasco in the US, the boom and bust of the bubble economy in Japan, or the dole queues in Australia. The complexity of the task facing governments in manipulating a range of monetary and fiscal levers to achieve long-run national objectives is exacerbated by the speculative nature of much of the cross-border financial activity. The capital standards and voluntary codes of conduct set by central banks still leave plenty of scope for manoeuvre. Moreover, attempts to influence movements in exchange rates consistent with national economic and social policy objectives by central bank intervention (such as by buying and selling reserves) seldom have much effect unless backed up by monetary policy related, for instance, to interest rates. In short, as Browett and Leaver (1989: 32) have noted,

> whilst some geographers have recognised the significance of the spatial impacts of the growth in the internationalisation of production . . . as much, if not more, attention needs to be devoted to shifts from public to private economic power and from order to disorder in international financial markets.

That challenge is taken up here by first summarizing the main phases through which the global financial system has evolved since the Second World War, and then indicating — with special emphasis on the role of exchange rates — some of the ways in which the location of industrial and other activities has been affected. This is then later illustrated by an outline of circumstances in the motor vehicle industry which has become Japan's leading exporter.

## The Global Financial System

The present shape of the global financial system began to emerge in the late 1950s and early 1960s with the establishment of the Eurodollar loan and bond market (Mistry, 1987). The Eurodollar concept was originally that of a US dollar held outside the US — initially in London — when the administration there imposed a 15 per cent tax on interest paid to non-resident owners of US securities (Swedberg, 1987: 324). Governments (especially the former USSR) and institutions (including multinational enterprises) also wanted to hold and freely invest in dollar balances in jurisdictions where these could not be seized, frozen or otherwise controlled (Tew, 1977; Barclays Bank Ltd, 1979). The Eurodollar market began as an inter-bank lending system with the main operators being the European and US commercial banks, although it soon developed into a securities market as well. Deposits rose from less than US$20,000 million in 1963 to US$200,000 million in 1972 and possibly, though nobody knows for certain, to as much as US$800,000 million in 1979 (Swedberg, 1987: 324).

Prior to the development of Euromarkets the movement of funds mostly took place within national money markets. As Flight and Lee-Swan (1988: 50) point out, monitoring was relatively simple: 'flows could be restrained when necessary through exchange controls or other financial regulations in accordance with the monetary controls of a country that sought to maintain exchange rates at specific target levels'. The Euromarkets, as they expanded into a very large global banking system, operated independently of national governments and central banks and thus became the first truly supranational form of money (Wachtel, 1986). Moreover, 'this money escapes the ken, much less the control, of any governmental authorities' (George, 1988: 36). These flows of funds, which reflected free market assessments of countries and their currencies, made it more difficult for governments to control exchange rates.

The expansion of world trade, the build-up of very mobile Euromarket funds, the debilitating impact of the Vietnam War (1965-73) on the US economy and its subsequent decline from world pre-eminence, and the growth of the private demand for gold were all factors leading to the demise in 1971 of the Bretton Woods Agreement of July 1944 (Swoboda, 1986). This had fixed the price of the US dollar to gold, with other currencies being defined in terms of the US dollar at fixed rates within a ±1 per cent range. Two turbulent years followed, but by 1973 it had become clear that the fixed exchange-rate system had broken down, and the major currencies were allowed to float. This triggered various responses: even in 1986, the currencies of 94 countries were pegged to another, 13 had 'limited flexibility', 26 were 'more flexible', while only 17 were independently floating. 'Pegged relationships often reflected historical trading ties, and the reluctance to abandon fixed exchange rates usually implied some domestic political necessity, or the fear of the consequences of freeing up the system' (Daly and Logan, 1989: 78). As a case in point, the European Monetary System (EMS), introduced in 1979 as a compromise between fixed and floating exchange rates, required the governments involved to keep currencies within narrow exchange-rate bands and thus promote trade and investment within the European Community (EC).

The collapse of the par value system had special implications for developing countries (Kafka, 1978). The International Monetary Fund (IMF) had frequently acquiesced to their adopting various floating rate arrangements when problems arose: now they had to live with the floating rates of developed economies. In effect, the developing countries gained no additional freedom yet became subject to greater uncertainties. In turn, this led the majority of them to maintain a fixed peg against a single intervention currency — most commonly the US dollar, the French franc or the pound sterling (Crockett and Nsouli, 1977).

### Oil 'shock' and mounting debt

The quadrupling of oil prices in 1973 led to increased global inflationary pressures and a rise in interest rates. Oil funds boosted Euromarket deposits and enabled commercial banks — supported by Western governments — to undertake the global recycling of funds, mainly to developing countries whose credit on international markets was largely untested. By the end of the 1970s more than a thousand commercial banks had taken over from governments and international organizations as the largest group of creditors to the highly indebted economies, holding 69 per cent of their debt as against 27 per cent in 1974. Over half the loans to developing countries during the mid-1970s were provided by US banks, but their share declined to about one-third when the European and Japanese banks moved in to take advantage of the quick profits available (Moffitt, 1983: 104; Swedberg, 1987: 331). Overall, the debt of non-oil developing countries to foreign banks rose from about US$50,000 million in 1974 to US$254,000 million in 1981.

All this resulted in an environment of risk and uncertainty, exacerbated by a recession in industrialized economies. Syndicated commercial bank loans became the main vehicle for transferring financial resources: syndicated Euromarket lending, alone, to developing countries rose from US$4,000 million in 1972 to a peak of US$45,000 million in 1981. Superficially, the commercial banks appeared to be doing a good job of recycling surpluses because the realities and risks of what was happening were being swept under the carpet. The emphasis was on increasing the volume of lending rather than on assessing the risk, so that some loans were even made to developing countries at negative real rates of interest. One reason was that bankers had been trained to appraise corporate risks but had had little experience of assessing those of nation states, especially those in the developing world where appropriate financial data were often inaccurate or incomplete.

### The debt crisis in the 1980s

Inflation in the US reached record levels towards the end of the 1970s, thus leading to a tighter monetary policy, a rise in interest rates, and a slow-down in the growth of world trade (International Monetary Fund, 1986: 100). Mexico's announcement in 1982 that it would be unable to meet its full debt-servicing obligations was soon echoed by other Latin American countries. The recklessness of the 1970s was thus exposed, and the dimensions of the debt crisis facing the global financial system revealed. The IMF responded with a plan to encourage further lending and debt rescheduling to give defaulting countries time to reduce their expenditures and repair their economies. In the event, the countries that had encountered debt-servicing difficulties remained very vulnerable to unfavourable global circumstances. The weak performance of many of the more heavily indebted Latin American and African countries led to US initiatives in October 1985 that sought to encourage debtor countries to pursue effective growth-orientated programmes. In the event, the reform process could not be sustained, and large sums continued to be dissipated on 'white elephant' projects that contributed little to economic growth or to generating foreign exchange to service borrowings. From 1985 through 1987 interest and principal repayments by Latin American countries exceeded capital inflows by US$42,000 million; during 1988 alone, the debt of the 49 countries in arrears increased by US$11,000 million to US$52,000 million.

The recession of 1982 hurt world trade in general but particularly that of developing countries. Many, encouraged by favourable terms of trade and the ready availability of foreign loans to finance the resulting current account deficits during the 1970s, had allowed their effective exchange rates to appreciate. This, in turn, led to growing reliance on imports instead of on domestically made substitutes and this, along with controlled interest rates in some instances, precipitated a flight of private capital. Those countries which had been pursuing more outward-looking strategies were better placed to cope with the impact of the recession by such steps as lowering exchange rates. In this way, several of the newly industrializing countries (NICs) in Southeast Asia became more competitive during the mid-1980s (Figure 2.1) and were able to boost the volume of their exports, particularly to the US and Japan (Maitland, 1989).

Further compounding the uncertainties of the 1980s were the swings in the price of oil (which doubled from 1979 through 1981 before again drifting down) and a prolonged decline in commodity prices, both of which made it harder for commodity-producing countries to manage demand and exchange rates. Oil price increases and the surge in the value of oil exports put upward pressure on the producers' exchange rates and thereby harmed non-oil exports and encouraged imports. This condition, which became known as the 'Dutch disease', affected high-income countries such as The Netherlands and the UK as well as low-income ones like Nigeria and Egypt (World Bank, 1989: 9).

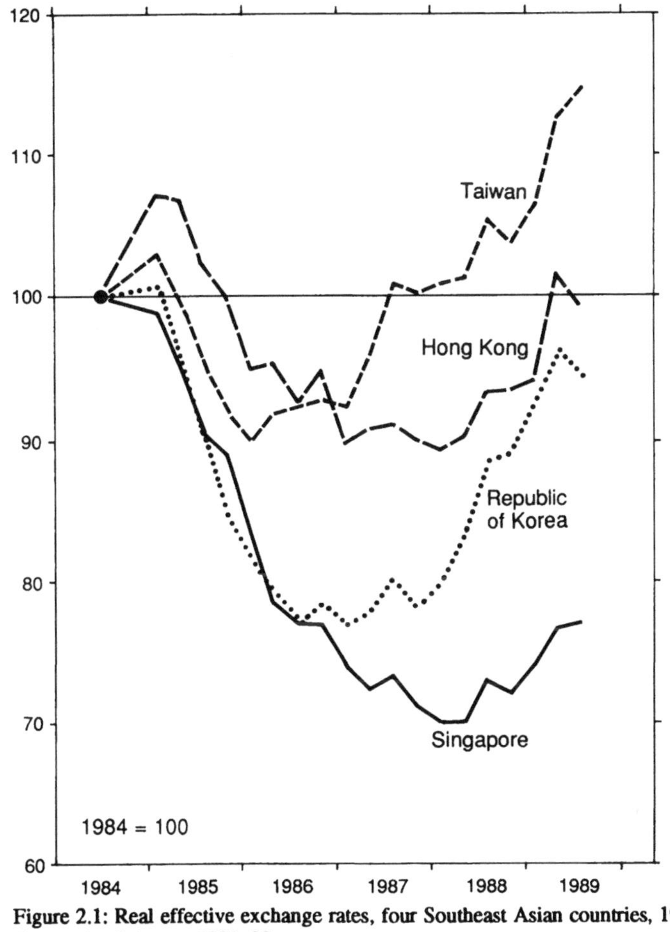


Figure 2.1: Real effective exchange rates, four Southeast Asian countries, 1984 to 1989. *Source*: *The Economist*, 5 August 1989: 88.

The lack of freedom of some developing economies to manage their exchange rates have had unfortunate repercussions. The 14 African countries in the colonial legacy known as the 'French Zone' still remain linked to France by 'a monetary umbilical cord'. Since 1948 the Communauté Financière Africaine (CFA) has had a fixed rate against the French franc, with the Banque de France acting as lender of last resort to the two regional African banks in Dakar and Yaounde. Many of these countries have rising balance of payments deficits caused by drought, low prices for export commodities (like oil, coffee and sugar), and the cost of servicing external debt. Thus, the poor prices for

Senegal's main exports, phosphates and ground-nuts, means that its attempts to become an export-driven economy are being frustrated, while its indebtedness to the Banque de France is growing, reaching perhaps US$300 million in 1990 (Medlock, 1989; Wiznitzer, 1990). Devaluation would enable this and other countries in the group to cut the dollar value of their exports and raise CFA prices on the domestic market. In fact, however, the CFA rate has been rising against the US dollar because the rigid link to the French franc in turn ties it to the EMS and hence to the strengthening German mark. As *The Economist* (30 March 1991: 41) reflected: 'French businessmen no longer lobby for special privileges in African ex-colonies now almost worthless as producers or customers'.

**The G–7 moves**

By the mid-1980s the industrialized countries were also facing problems relating to the structure of payment imbalances. Their recovery from the 1982 recession had been fuelled by an expansionary agenda in the US. This and a world-wide anti-inflationary monetary policy led to high real interest rates (especially in the US), an appreciating dollar, and a boom in US consumer expenditure and imports (World Bank, 1989: 8). By the end of 1983 a rising US trade deficit signalled that the dollar was fully valued — even over-valued, but it was not until 1985 that international financial institutions moved to reduce its value against the Japanese yen and other leading currencies. In September that year the Group of Seven (G–7) leading industrial countries (US, Japan, Federal Republic of Germany [FRG], UK, France, Canada and Italy) attempted, in the so-called New York Plaza Agreement, to arrange both a dollar depreciation that would cut the US trade deficit and also a yen appreciation and other measures that would reduce Japan's current account merchandise trade surplus. This had soared from US$2,125 million in 1980 to US$55,986 million in 1985. The inter-bank exchange rate against the US$ rose from ¥216.00 in September 1985 to ¥160.10 in December 1986 and peaked at ¥122.00 in December 1987, a revaluation of 77 per cent (Figure 2.2).

By 1987 the financial markets were losing confidence in the depreciating dollar. The G–7 Louvre Accord, signed in February, tried to prevent a chaotic slide in its value by agreeing to concerted central bank intervention. This failed to convince the financial markets, resulting in uncertainty and turbulence (including higher interest rates), and contributing to the stock-market crash of 19 October 1987.

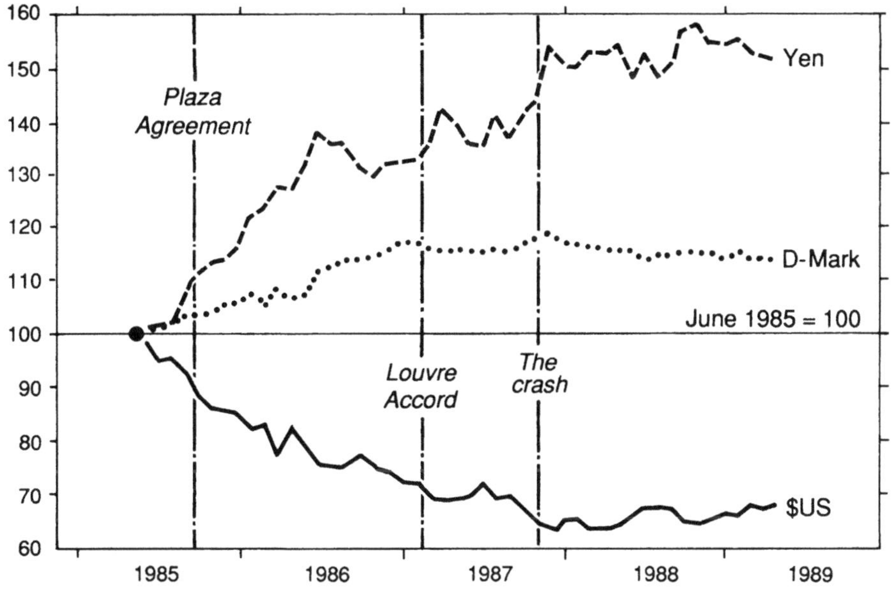


Figure 2.2: The changing relationships between the Japanese yen, the West German mark and the US dollar, June 1985 to April 1989. *Source*: *Financial Times*, 25 May 1989: Sii.

Ironically, the support given by Japan to the Louvre Accord precipitated yet another hastily arranged G–7 meeting in Paris in April 1990. The loosening of Japan's monetary policy to help prop up the dollar and stimulate domestic demand led to a surge in its money supply. The resulting explosion in equity and land prices reduced yields which, in turn, encouraged investors to seek higher returns overseas. The yen weakened because the net outflow of long-term capital (in the form of bonds, equities and FDI) exceeded Japan's current account surplus. Yet, even though the yen had declined since the end of 1988 by 21 per cent against the dollar and 25 per cent against the D-mark (Figure 2.3), the Paris G–7 meeting decided to take no action. In effect, Japan was left to solve its problems through domestic policy initiatives, such as increased interest rates.

Behind this decision was the view that the yen had been over-valued against the dollar in purchasing-power parity terms (see later), and thus some downward adjustment was due. It was also thought that G–7 intervention might simply continue to patch over or delay much-needed domestic reforms. Critics argued, for example, that the Louvre Accord had allowed the US to continue its profligate borrowing and defer the harsh measures needed to reduce its current account deficit. Wall Street, it was suggested, would have been less reckless in promoting highly leveraged transactions if Japan had not acted like a lender of last resort to Washington by purchasing about a third of the US Government bonds and Treasury notes on offer.

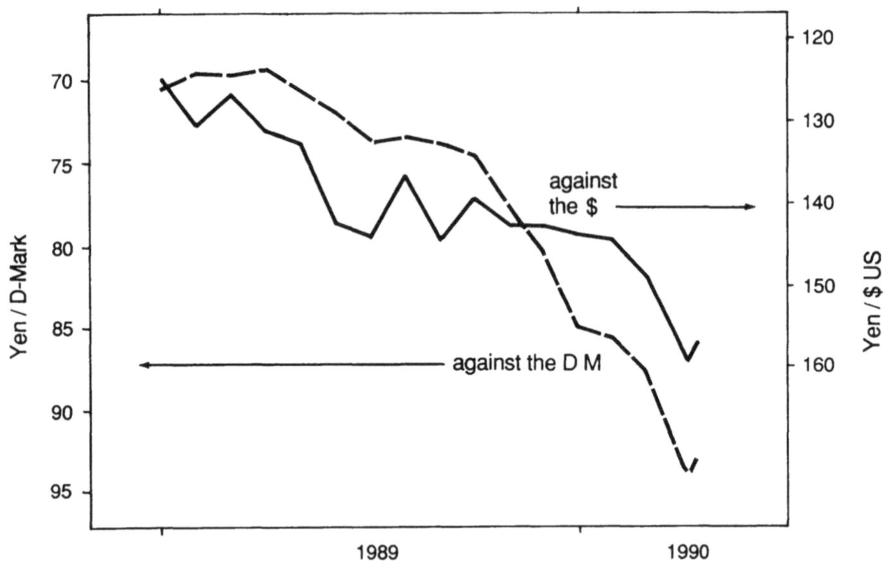


Figure 2.3: The decline of the Japanese yen against the US dollar and the West German mark (note inverted scales), January 1989 to April 1990. *Source*: *The Economist*, 14 April 1990: 75.

However, it was recognized that a reduction in the value of the yen against the dollar could not in itself solve the US deficit with Japan: action was also needed to reduce the gap between US gross saving (13 per cent of GNP) and gross investment (15 per cent of GNP). Thus, so-called 'structural impediments initiative' (SII) talks were arranged between Japan and the US early in 1990, during which both sides sought trade concessions and exchanged prescriptions for changes to each other's economic and social policies. These appear to have been something of a side-show for the benefit of the respective domestic audiences: 'at the risk of overstating the issue', suggested Sasaki (1990), 'it could be said that the main objective of the SII talks was to contain the growth inside the U.S. of the so-called revisionist theory, which emphasizes alleged differences between Japan and the U.S.'.

The US argued that 'unfair' trade practices which block its exports of goods like satellites, superconductors and wood products were the main reason why Japan had maintained a trade surplus with the US of over US$40,000 million for five successive years to 1989. Then, after falling slightly for two years the surplus rebounded to an estimated US$44,000 in 1992, thus rekindling trade as an issue between the two countries.

More important than actual exchange rates in terms of explaining this continuing trade imbalance are rates expressed in real terms. As Figure 2.4 indicates, following the collapse of the Bretton Woods regime in the early 1970s the yen continued to rise — with some pauses — by an average of 5 per cent annually against the US dollar. This graph also shows that since the early 1980s, apart from a brief period in mid-decade, the yen remained considerably over-valued in relation to its purchasing-power parity (the exchange rate at which a basket of tradeable goods and services in Japan equals the same price in the US). Despite the soaring yen after the G–7 intervention in 1985, Japanese exports remained competitive because, as discussed later, production costs were quickly slashed. Some estimates suggest that in the early 1990s the yen remained over-valued against the US dollar by more than 50 per cent (Burstein, 1990).

It may appear, then, that the Plaza Agreement failed to achieve its goals. Two points can be noted. On the one hand, the US share of Japan's trade surplus dropped from 86 per cent in 1985 to 49 per cent in 1991; on the other, 66 per cent of the US trade deficit by 1991 was with Japan as against 40 per cent in 1985 (Honda, 1992). Thus, the bilateral trade imbalance endured largely because, even though the total trade deficit of the US decreased, simultaneously Japan's total trade surplus grew. The Plaza Accord could not have anticipated the ability of Japanese producers to remain competitive by reducing costs so much and so quickly, nor was historical evidence available to suggest that changes in domestic demand are likely to have a much bigger influence than currency movements. Moreover, it could not have been foreseen that about three-quarters of the chronic imbalance would stem from the trade in various high-tech products, the demand for which outstripped US production capacity, and more importantly from vehicles and vehicle components. Whereas it was thought that Japanese 'transplant' factories (discussed later) would buy components locally, they have in fact shipped many of them in from their network of suppliers in Japan.

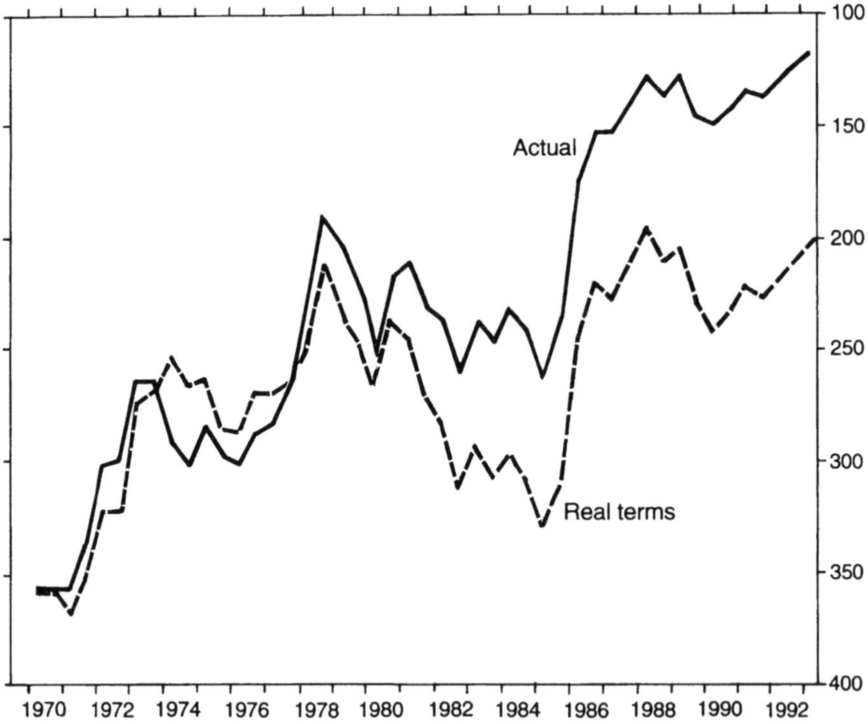


Figure 2.4: The long-term rise of the yen against the US dollar in actual and real terms, 1970 to 1992. Real terms calculated by adjusting for difference in producer prices since 1970, US and Japan. *Source*: *The Economist*, 27 February 1993: 86.

The level of exchange rates even in real terms is, of course, not the only measure of competitiveness. Price has to be weighed against attributes like quality, reliability, longevity, delivery times and after-sale service arrangements (Dunnett, 1989). Indeed, it was uncertainty about the availability of spare parts that undermined efforts by the USSR and some East European countries to build up an export trade in favourably priced passenger cars and farm tractors during the late 1970s and early 1980s.

## Exchange Rates and Investment Flows

During the regime of fixed exchange rates some currencies were, or became, under or over-valued. Several countries benefited by having under-valued currencies: at least part of the explanation for the RoK's rapid growth after the 1960s was the way the exchange rate was manipulated to reduce the price of exports and raise the cost of imports. In contrast, others suffered the consequences of over-valuation. The rapid expansion of the overseas-owned *maquiladores* ('in-bond' plants) along the Mexican-US border after 1966 came about mainly because of wage differentials (in the late 1970s foreign-owned companies were paying their US workers US$3.10 per hour as against US$1.23 to those in Mexico), but then the 'increasing value of the peso, spurred by domestic inflation and a failure to devalue fast enough, eroded this differential, and heightened the desirability of other locations further south, in Central America and the Caribbean' (Harris, 1987: 79). Not only did Mexico lose industry and export income but the remaining production was biased towards domestic markets. Moreover, cheaper imports and overseas borrowing encouraged investors to rely on imported materials and equipment rather than on domestic substitutes.

### Foreign direct investment

Until the mid-1950s, US business was reluctant to invest overseas because of the many economic, political and military uncertainties, but by 1967 the stock of direct US investment abroad was worth six times more than the US$9,900-million stock of FDI in the US. This imbalance continued through the early 1970s, with US investment in European manufacturing being quadruple that in the reverse direction. The variety of 'push' and 'pull' imperatives involved have been discussed elsewhere (Linge and Hamilton, 1981: 68-9; McConnell, 1983), but one of the most important was the way the exchange rate system operated.

Under the Bretton Woods Agreement, as noted earlier, each nation undertook to keep its currency within ±1 per cent of par value by central banks selling or purchasing their own currencies on foreign exchange markets. By running persistent and large capital-account deficits in its balance of international payments, the US effectively forced foreign central banks to buy excess dollars with their own currencies in order to decrease the supply of dollars in circulation. This provided American investors with the francs, marks and other European currencies necessary to buy assets in France, the FRG, and elsewhere. Hence, as the price for international stability, foreign central banks were put in the awkward position of financing the takeovers of their own country's industry (Bluestone and Harrison, 1982: 113).

The stock of US FDI thus continued to rise, from US$56,600 million in 1967 (54 per cent of the total for all developed market economies) to US$101,300 million in 1973 and US$137,300 million in 1976, 79 per cent of which was in developed countries. A study of 180 large US-based multinationals showed that from 1951 to 1975 they established 13,800 foreign affiliates, of which 6,890 were engaged in manufacturing. Of the 4,690 in developed countries, 35 per cent were newly formed and the rest resulted from acquisitions. Over 70 per cent of US FDI was accounted for by 250 to 300 firms (United Nations Department of Economic and Social Affairs, 1973: 7; Curham et al., 1977; United Nations Economic and Social Council, 1978: 236).

European business responded to this 'invasion' by the formation of defensive amalgamations leading to the so-called 'merger boom' at the end of the 1960s. In the UK, for example, more than 5,000 British companies were involved in corporate mergers in 1967 and 1968 (Tugendhat, 1971: 87). Most were between firms operating in the same country: of the 1,861 mergers occurring in the six EC countries from early 1961 to mid-1969 only 257 — mostly small ones — were across borders.

Following the 1971-73 currency realignments and the depreciation of the US dollar, flows of FDI to the US (mainly from Western Europe, Canada and Japan) rose from US$13,300 million in 1970 to over US$50,000 million in 1979 (McConnell, 1983: 338). In contrast, the US corporations' share of the total FDI flows of the 13 OECD countries that keep such records halved from an average of 61 per cent during 1961-67 to 30 per cent during 1974-78 (Bluestone and Harrison, 1982: 142).

During the 1980s the flow of investment funds to the US increased substantially, and by the end of 1988 had reached US$328,900 million —

mainly from the UK (31 per cent), Japan (16 per cent), The Netherlands (15 per cent) and Canada (8 per cent). Of crucial importance is that most of this was portfolio investment in stocks, bonds and Treasury Bills which mainly reflected both the low value of the dollar and the over-valuation of currencies like the yen. Other reasons included the

> competitive strengths of foreign groups; the magnetism of the huge US market; corporate restructuring responding to, and in turn accelerating, global integration; efforts to skirt trade barriers and get closer to the markets; and a growing foreign understanding of US business practices, particularly on the part of newcomers such as the Japanese (Riddell, 1989).

Even though the rate of US FDI slowed, none the less, it rose from US$215,000 million at the end of 1980 to US$327,000 million at the end of 1988. These flows carried with them very considerable implications for

> the diffusion of technology, the extent of technological and organizational interdependence among companies and countries, the patterns of commodity trade, the competitive advantage of industrial corporations and countries, and the dynamics of political and social change. Equally important [they] . . . influence[d] industrial location patterns, regional growth dynamics, domestic business and employment conditions, and related public policy issues (McConnell, 1983: 338).

## Exchange Rates and the Motor Vehicle Industry

Events in the motor vehicle manufacturing industry can be used to illustrate in more detail how shifting exchange rates can influence the spatial organization of manufacturing. Exchange rate regimes, of course, reflect real and perceived strengths and weaknesses of economies, and are not in themselves the sole consideration underlying long-term investment strategies. However, as this example shows, the dramatic realignment of the Japanese yen and US dollar in 1985 precipitated a series of events in the vehicle industry that are continuing to have profound impacts on the operation of the global economy (Linge, 1991).

During the 1950s the Japanese Ministry of International Trade and Industry (MITI) designated the embryo vehicle industry as a strategic sector, a move reinforced by high tariffs on small cars. Production of cars increased from 20,000 in 1955 to 165,000 in 1960. During this latter year the government set in motion an 'income doubling plan', one aim of which was to encourage exports. After some teething problems, Japanese small cars gained acceptance overseas and helped that country achieve a trade surplus on current account from 1965 through 1972. This challenge by Japanese producers led to reactions abroad, including strengthening protectionism and, in particular, to currency realignments following the floating of the US dollar in August 1971. The quadrupling of oil prices in 1973-74 turned Japan's trade balance back into deficit from 1973 to 1975, and brought even more pressure on manufacturers to cut costs. At the same time, the car makers were able to take advantage of a swing in consumer preference to smaller fuel-efficient cars, especially in the US where local makers were slow to discard the long-held 'small car, small profit' slogan. By 1976 motor vehicles had become the leading export, with the number of cars and trucks sent overseas reaching, respectively, 3,947,000 and 1,954,000 in 1980: by then, cars built in Japan had captured 21 per cent of the US market.

The success of this drive to export cars, colour television sets, steel and other products caused further trade friction between Japan and the US, Canada and Europe. One Japanese response was to accept 'voluntary' restrictions, such as limiting annual car exports to the US to 1,670,000. Another was for manufacturers to open manufacturing facilities overseas — beginning, in the case of cars, with those of Honda of America in November 1982 at Marysville, Ohio. As will be shown later, this strategy of 'transplant' production which helped to reduce trade tensions in the 1980s has become an even greater and more intractable problem for the 1990s.

The *endaka* (strong yen) that followed the Plaza Agreement in 1985 had profound impacts on the motor vehicle and other industries. Recognizing that costs would have to be more than halved to enable them to stay internationally competitive, Japanese firms redoubled their ongoing attempts to squeeze every waste and inefficiency from the production system: thus, even more emphasis was placed on the 'just-in-time' approach in which only as much is made as is actually required (Cusumano, 1985; Sayer, 1986; Gertler, 1988; Schoenberger, 1989; Linge, 1991).

Japanese car makers speedily moved to maintain their export markets: as the yen rose, they started to ship higher-value vehicles to the US, thus pushing into yet another segment of the market. They also advanced plans to set up further 'transplant' operations in North America and, increasingly, in Western Europe to reduce their vulnerability to exchange rate fluctuations and the threat of trade barriers. Reinforcing this strategy was an anxiety to position themselves prior to the establishment of the North American Free Trade Area (NAFTA) and European Single Market at the beginning of 1993. By 1990 eight of the eleven Japanese motor vehicle manufacturers had full-scale production lines in operation or under construction in the US, Canada, UK, Germany, Spain and Portugal representing a total investment of about US$10,500 million. The eight plants in the US and three in Canada can produce nearly three million units a year but in the early 1990s had captured about a quarter of the domestic market while operating at less than full capacity. To increase flexibility even further, R & D facilities were in some cases associated with these transplants so that production could be tailored to local markets or to 'niche' markets elsewhere. Cars built in these transplants are now being shipped to Japan: in September 1992, for example, Toyota started sending such 'retro imports' there from its facility in Kentucky, aiming initially at an annual target of 45,000 units.

In Europe, Japanese car makers have so far concentrated most of their transplant activity in the UK, leading France's Peugeot to describe Britain as a 'Japanese aircraft carrier floating off Europe poised to attack'. The three car plants (built by Nissan at Sunderland and opened in 1986; Honda, Swindon, 1992; and Toyota, Burnaston, 1992) will have a combined capacity of 500,000 units when fully operational. About 70 per cent of the output will be shipped to continental Europe where annual sales in the early 1990s totalled about 13,500,000 vehicles. Under a monitoring system set up in 1991 by Japan and the EC, the two sides negotiate adjustments in Japanese vehicle exports to the EC after reaching agreement on demand forecasts. This system is intended to limit Japanese exports during a transition period from 1993 through 1999, allowing European car makers to regain competitiveness. Under this accord, Japanese car exports to the EC were limited to 1,185,000 units in 1992. The Japanese argue that this leaves them free to export their UK-made vehicles to the remainder of the EC, a claim hotly disputed by France and Italy, both of which have their own tight restrictions on the import of cars built in Japan. These EC restraints, along with increases in the price of imported vehicles caused by the rising value of the yen and the poor profit results from their operations in Japan, have stimulated more transplant proposals. Mitsubishi Motors Corp. plans to start joint production with Volvo and the Dutch government in The Netherlands starting in 1995, while Isuzu Motors Ltd, Suzuki Motor Corp. and Daihatsu Motor Co. have similar projects in the pipeline. At the end of 1992, after the failure of its negotiations with the Ford Motor Co. to establish a JV in Germany, the Mazda Motor Corp. remained the only major Japanese car maker not to have announced a specific plan to build vehicles in Europe. Together with political persuasion, the high yen is forcing these EC transplant operations to consider sourcing a greater proportion of the components locally instead of shipping them from Japan.

During the latter part of the 1980s the small-volume car makers in Western Europe were also affected by exchange fluctuations and their consequences. Previously companies like Jaguar, Saab, Porsche and Volvo were reporting record profits because, as Done and Garnett (1989) note,

> They were making windfall gains from an over-valued US dollar; their sales in the US market soared as European up-market cars became the status symbols of American luxury car buyers. And the promised introduction of flexible manufacturing systems, of computer aided design, manufacturing and engineering, appeared to offer much lower break-even points for profitable car making.

Although flexible techniques helped the 'niche' car makers, it assisted the volume producers even more: as the speed at which model changes were introduced quickened, the big producers could spread the costs of design and retooling over a larger volume in a shorter time. Common to all the European car markers in 1989 was

> the blow struck by the plunge in the value of the US dollar in the years from 1985 to 1988. The recent strengthening of the dollar is not helping yet, as hedging arrangements lock in the lower dollar rates until 1990-91. In 1989, Jaguar is at the worst point in the currency cycle. The Europeans raised prices sharply in the US to recover diminishing profits, alienating their customers. Demand weakened and sales volumes began to drop alarmingly. They have been forced to discount and offer incentives to "move metal". Jaguar has not

been able to raise prices in the US since October 1987, and for the 1990 model year it is actually cutting prices (Done and Garnett, 1989).

These problems, the subsequent turn-down in consumer demand, and the manoeuvring in preparation for the advent of the European Single Market resulted in a chain reaction of closures, mergers and takeovers with consequent impacts on local economies. Sweden's A.B. Volvo, for instance, has announced plans to close its passenger car plants at Uddevalla — opened only in 1989 to provide employment for displaced shipbuilding workers (Nilsson, 1991) — and Kalmar, and concentrating production at its plant in Göteborg. Some industry observers believe that this restructuring is in preparation for a merger with the French state-owned Renault in which Volvo has a capital partnership.

In Japan, in contrast, the rapidly appreciating yen (along with the gradual removal of virtually all tariff and non-tariff barriers on vehicles imported into Japan) also meant that the prices of foreign-built cars — mainly executive and luxury models — declined so that their sales were boosted from 50,000 units in 1985 to 220,000 units in 1990 (two-thirds of which were from the FRG). Since then annual sales have fallen off to about 190,000 units largely because of the recession in Japan. The main importers — Volkswagen Audi Nippon KK, BMW Japan Corp. and Mercedes-Benz Japan Corp. — have attempted to consolidate their position by establishing dealer networks and vehicle preparation and maintenance training centres. Some industry observers believe that foreign car imports into Japan may rise to 400,000 units, or 10 per cent of the market, by 1995. In part this is due to the tenacity of European car exporters but it is largely the result of the relaxation of the myriad obstacles placed in their way by a Japanese government anxious to avoid a 'Fortress Europe' backlash against Japanese cars and other exports in the European Single Market of the 1990s.

## Exchange Rates and Global Uncertainty

As hinted earlier, events during the 1980s were creating a store of fundamental economic problems which are now beginning to emerge and being compounded by further, more recent dilemmas. It is not difficult to diagnose most of the basic maladies affecting the global economic system but a prognosis of the possible course of events is made much harder because many fundamental issues remain unresolved. Whatever happens, however, the role of exchange rates as both indicating and influencing relative international strengths and weaknesses will remain centrally important.

## Confrontation or cooperation?

After the First World War the UK was unable to sustain its role as the manager of the gold standard: after more than a decade of international politics and intrigue, it suspended gold convertibility in September 1931. The US then became the world's strongest economy so that the Bretton Woods system of fixed exchange rates was based on the dollar but tied to gold. Following the collapse of this arrangement in the early 1970s, the capitalist world changed in two basic ways. First, economic superiority became spread between North America, Japan (and the other Asia-Pacific countries within its sphere of influence), and a German-led more integrated Europe. Second, as has been documented in Chapter 1, massive amounts of relatively footloose capital became available to institutions that could move it around the world almost instantaneously in seemingly endless games of 'passing the parcel', with each player trying to avoid being left with the bundle of financial problems. Everyone, however, is operating in an uncertain environment.

One of the main uncertainties is the future of the Uruguay Round of trade negotiations which began under the auspices of the General Agreement on Tariffs and Trade (GATT) in September 1986 and were scheduled for completion in 1990. Although moving towards the resolution of many of the issues involved, the participants have become bogged down over, principally, trade in agricultural produce, a sensitive topic on which politicians on both sides of the Atlantic are hostage to strong farm lobby groups.

In parallel to these discussions about freeing up world trade, groups of countries have been entering into regional trade associations of one kind or another. The eight organizations that existed in 1960 to promote regional economic cooperation, involving 38 member states, had grown by 1990 to 19 organizations involving 113 states (Ding, 1990). The ratification of no fewer than 16 regional trade arrangements during 1992 has been ascribed in part to the continuing reluctance of the rich countries to commit themselves to a new GATT Agreement. While some of these agreements stem from new links between East European and Western countries, others represent an increasingly important manifestation of the autonomous liberalization occurring in Latin America and Asia. Although opinions differ (*The Economist*, 31 October 1992: 73), such regional agreements need not necessarily undermine the multilateral system — indeed several have been based on GATT principles, but they do indicate that developing countries are no longer prepared to dance attendance on the industrialized nations and what has been criticised as their 'General Agreement to Talk and Talk'.

**Towards a tri-polar world**

There has been a trend from loose forms of cooperation to closer ones like NAFTA (yet to be ratified by the respective governments) and the European Single Market. In turn, this has sparked the emergence of the notion of a tri-polar world trading and, possibly, financial system, an idea that gained momentum with the launching in November 1989 of an Asia-Pacific Economic Cooperation (APEC) forum to promote trade and development around the Pacific Rim. The founding members — Australia, Canada, Japan, New Zealand, the RoK, the US, and the countries belonging to the Association of South-East Asian Nations (see Chapter 11) — were joined in 1991 by the PRC, Taiwan and Hong Kong, and opened a permanent secretariat in Singapore late in 1992.

However, this symmetrical organization of the world economy, with three blocs of cooperating countries led by the US, Germany and Japan, no longer seems so neat or certain. There is space for only a brief review of some of the main reasons.

The US has been struggling under the weight of its military expenditure and, more especially, its growing international indebtedness and reliance on foreign capital. The annual budget deficit is running at about US$300,000 million and is likely to continue to rise as projected debt-reduction plans will barely keep pace with the escalating costs of programs (such as social security) that are already in place and fiercely defended by the electorate. Yet, unless action is taken to reduce the deficit, interest rates will remain high and continue to dampen growth. Despite the problems of the early 1990s, there are positive signs suggesting that in some fundamentals the US economy has strengthened. In particular, the manufacturing sector through the 1980s has become much leaner, more productive and better able to compete on world markets, not only because of the lower dollar but also in terms of quality and product innovation. In the longer-run this will help to reduce the trade deficit with Japan — an issue that has become a fixation on both sides of the Pacific. That problem, however, stems from the fact that the US (and Europe) invest more than they save whereas Japan saves more than it invests.

During the early 1990s the outlook for Europe has changed, with growing concerns in some countries about the political and economic consequences flowing from the provisions of the Maastricht Treaty and the Single European Market. In particular, Germany's expected role as the engine of a more unified Europe is now in question as the result of the greatly underestimated costs of transforming the eastern German economy, the problem of absorbing (or limiting) the annual inflow of 500,000 refugees, and an increasingly uncompetitive industrial sector. The promise to raise wage levels in the Eastern Länder to those in the rest of Germany by 1994 is absorbing about US$60,000 million a year in social benefits, unemployment pay and wage subsidies, while another US$30,000 million is being spent on upgrading infrastructure. German public-sector borrowing, running at about 8 per cent of GDP, is well above the 3 per cent upper limit regarded (by Germany itself) for responsible European monetary union. To curb this, the level of subsidies paid to German industries (about US$60,000 million a year) will have to be slashed and, despite constitutional prohibitions, state-owned businesses privatized. Overnight, it seems, Germany is having to face up to a massive reorganization of its economy and many of the traditional habits that have underpinned it. The pain of all this is being transmitted throughout Europe — via the exchange rate mechanism, discussed in Chapter 1 — because of the maintenance of high German interest rates necessitated by the mounting public-sector debt and the fear of inflation.

Japan, too, is facing fundamental changes of a kind not previously experienced. More than other developed economies, it showed great ability to cope with economic perturbations like the 'oil shocks' and price rises of the 1970s and the high yen of the 1980s, but the recession of the early 1990s is seen to be different. The immediate cause is the bursting of the so-called bubble economy manifested by the sharp decline in land and asset prices. Thus, the Nikkei 225 index of share prices, which quadrupled during the 1980s, more than halved from its peak on 19 December 1989 to the end of 1992. Similarly, land prices which had doubled during the 1980s began to decline in 1990. At the end of 1992, about half the total outstanding loans of the country's eight listed housing-finance companies were thought to be non-performing, in turn creating problems for banks (their main shareholders), agricultural finance cooperatives and other exposed financial institutions. Personal spending and capital investment, the two main forces driving domestic demand, became sluggish.

The short-term obvious result has been recession but, additionally, it has raised serious questions about the appropriateness and viability of many of the bases on which Japan's postwar prosperity has been founded. Among these are the roles of economic planners (like MITI) and of institutions and mechanisms like the *keiretsu* with their corporate cross-holdings; the banks and other financial players and the regulatory environment in which they operate; and the traditional close relationship between business and labour. Adding to these concerns are others relating to 'quality of life', ranging from the length of working hours, to the rigidity of the education system, the role of women and the neglect of infrastructure. Some flavour of this is given by Fallows (1989: 42) who argues that Japan, which

> has the largest overseas investments in the world also has by far the highest consumer prices, the highest proportion of unpaved roads among developed countries, the lowest per capita endowment of parks, sporting areas and other public facilities and, across the board, the least materially bountiful life. Some of Japan's under-consumption reflects an unavoidable lag in putting its recent wealth to work but most is caused by the economy's continuing bias towards corporate profit and foreign investment rather than individual consumer welfare.

Although in difficulty, the Japanese financial system is unlikely to collapse. The probability is, however, that the costs of bailing out housing finance and other institutions (such as by lowering their interest liabilities) will make loans during the 1990s generally more expensive and less freely available. A particular immediate problem is the refinancing of maturing corporate debt which was borrowed for as little as 1 per cent interest in the boom years of the 1980s but now costs four or five times as much. A good deal depends, too, on how the recession in the short-term, and the ageing of the population in the longer-term, impact on the level of household savings that have played such a critical role in Japanese postwar expansion. The trade surplus, which amounted to US$133,000 million in 1992 is expected to grow (and hence stimulate the domestic economy) but much depends on the trade policies adopted by the incoming US Administration and any pressure the G–7 Group may place on Japan to manipulate the value of the yen. An even stronger yen would raise the price of Japanese exports, choke demand and help reduce the trade surplus. This, however, would adversely affect the profits of exporting firms, like the vehicle makers which ship out about 40 per cent of their output, just at the time when domestic demand has slumped. Arguably, however, reduced export earnings would trim the demand for imports so that the net impact on the trade surplus would be lessened. Although a higher yen would reduce the costs of imported consumer goods and manufacturers' inputs (every ¥1 rise against the US$ reduces annual fuel bills by ¥11,000 million), much of this saving may be used to prop up declining profits rather than to reduce prices to the consumer.

Although the global economy will continue to be dominated by, and very much depend on, the outcome of the problems facing the US, Germany and Japan, circumstances elsewhere are of potential importance even if currently surrounded by uncertainty. For instance, the extent to which the 15-member APEC group will become globally influential remains unclear. Several of the Asian members (especially Malaysia) are apprehensive about formalizing this forum, fearing that it could become dominated by the US and Japan. For this reason, along with a desire to avoid yet another potential source of friction with the US, Japan is reluctant to play a leadership role, especially as there is some doubt about the likely success of any moves towards free trade, given the diverse nature of the economies involved. None the less, there are already signs that, once the credit squeeze is eased, Japanese FDI will increasingly be directed towards developing Asian countries rather than, as in the 1980s, to Western Europe and North America. One reason is that Asian investments return higher profits more quickly than those elsewhere; another is that it makes sense for Japanese firms to supply the rapidly expanding consumer markets using labour that is relatively cheap compared with that in Japan; and yet another is that Japanese business already has a well-developed or, as in the case of the PRC a rapidly growing, presence in these countries. It remains uncertain at this stage to what extent corporate Japan will be prepared to invest in other areas like the Russian Far East (Linge, 1992) and Eastern Europe.

The events of the early 1990s — the slow-down of economic activity in the leading industrialized nations; the gradual if uncertain integration of Eastern Europe, the CIS and the PRC into global structures; the rapid development of East and Southeast Asian nations; and even the reinvigoration of some Latin-American countries — are fundamentally reshaping the global economy. For example, the costs of German reunification and the deflation of the bubble economy in Japan are casting doubts on the ability of these countries to play their expected dominant role as the power-houses of the world.

More generally, the role of the state, too, seems to be changing. On the one side, governments of all political persuasions are relinquishing the ownership of a variety of activities and deregulating the milieu and structures in which they operate. On the other side, the extent of political corruption (as in Japan and Italy), the evidence of financial mismanagement (as in the loans and savings affair in the US and the collapse of state banks in Australia), and the emergence of new sources of power (such as the drug cartels) are all re-emphasizing the need for new approaches to economic management. Undoubtedly, the events of the early 1990s will rekindle the debate about the actual and appropriate role of exchange rates — the so-called international management mechanism — and whether they should be fixed or allowed to float. As this chapter has indicated, the outcome will have a considerable bearing on the way activities become organized in space. Hopefully, geographers will begin to recognize this and therefore not simply leave the debate to others.

# 3 Sovereign Risk Analysis: A Qualitative Approach

Ó. Homanen

This chapter focuses on sovereign risk, namely risks associated with long-term loans to governmental and parastatal bodies in developing countries. The discussion derives from Sachs' (1984: 11) argument that:

> Pure borrowing models should differentiate between the private and public sectors and take seriously the empirical facts that most international lending to developing countries is to the public sector, or to the private sector with public sector guarantees. In these circumstances, debt-servicing capacity depends not only on national wealth but on the public sector's ability to tax that wealth.

The intention here is to describe contemporary sovereign risk analysis, and to illustrate that analysts in this field could gain substantially by incorporating the results of scientific research on economics and politics into their assessment procedures. The sovereign risk analysis practised today, as with more theoretical studies, characteristically lacks an understanding of causalities. Practising analysts are not using scholarly inter-country studies on the determinants of economic growth in a meaningful way. Furthermore, such studies are not directly applicable to sovereign risk problems: in particular, a clear framework of the debtor's payment ability and willingness is largely absent.

Various linkages between institutional or qualitative factors of the polity and its economic performance, as well as theories of governmental behaviour, are introduced in this chapter. The risks considered here are primarily derived from the qualitative and institutional features of the domestic economy, based on the first of Calverly's (1985: 114) three sections of key political risk aspects:

(a) interactions between political developments and economic policy;

(b) radical political changes;

(c) interactions between political developments, foreign confidence and capital inflows (and outflows).

Although the issues in the latter two sections have significance to sovereign creditworthiness, they fall outside the scope of this chapter. Furthermore, the hazards connected with 'country' or 'political' risks in the case of private sector buyers, namely the effects of national economy decisions on investments and purchases of private enterprises, merit a separate study; non-publicly guaranteed private external debt has been omitted from this analysis.

## Sovereign Risk Defined

Sovereign risk as defined here is limited to loans made to, or guaranteed by, sovereign governments. These are repayable in a currency other than that of the debtor and, like other forms of international lending, the sovereign credits appear in the balance of payments of both debtor and creditor countries. Their uniqueness lies in the fact that a sovereign government has the ultimate responsibility for repayment (Heffernan, 1986: xiv). Basically, the sovereign risks concerned may be divided into the debtor's ability to pay and willingness to pay. The latter depends on the foreign exchange accumulating capability of the economy and on the public sector's ability to 'tax' the wealth of the nation, whereas the former is dependent on rational calculations of the cost of defaulting and internal political considerations (Sachs, 1984: 11; Krugman, 1988: 4). According to this definition, only one of the four aspects mentioned, namely the quantity of foreign earnings, can be estimated on the basis of current economic figures; the other three must be weighed against the nature of the leadership and politics in the debtor country.

Frequently, the terms 'political risk' and 'country risk' are used synonymously when financial transactions in developing countries are discussed. There is a tendency to associate the former term particularly with investment projects that might be affected by decisions of the host government. A more detailed definition, however, breaks country risk into 'credit risk', 'transfer risk', and 'political risk'. Credit risk relates to the borrower's lack of local currency; transfer risk to the debtor country's restriction on currency transfer and other factors affecting the debtor's ability to pay; and political risk which, although of a less direct economic nature, may have potentially severe consequences. The 'government taxing capability' risk (referred to above) can be considered a fourth category which draws the concept of country risk closer to the definition of sovereign risk.

In this discussion, the terms sovereign and country risk are used in parallel although some differences in their meaning have been identified: political risk is strictly reserved for those relating to the political structures of the country.

## Existing Methods of Sovereign Risk Analysis

The sovereign risk analysis methods used by practical analysts are mostly directed toward the concrete aspect of payment ability and the foreign exchange earning capability of the debtor country. The importance of calculating future debt-servicing obligations is also identified. More abstract aspects, including debt-servicing willingness, rational calculations of the cost of default, internal political considerations and the public sector's ability to tax the wealth of the nation are not usually specifically addressed. These aspects are thought to be adequately covered through consideration of the country's debt-service history and present political developments. Rational calculations of the cost of default should be analyzed partly on the basis of international sovereign credit market information: often, however, the nature of the market is not completely understood and the issue is underemphasized.

### Creditor's risk analysis routines

The three most important sources of sovereign credit to developing countries are commercial banks, international agencies and official Export Credit Agencies (ECAs). In theory, sovereign credit markets are composed of supply and demand: the expected return on foreign 'risky' lending to developing countries should be higher than the interest rate on 'safe' domestic investment. In practice, the sovereign credit market does not adhere to this model. Instead, each major creditor group finances particular activities (trade, project or balance of payments funding) with different interest margins. Moreover, the lending is often in the form of 'concerted' credits (a package composed from each of the three groups). Nowadays profit maximization is not the primary motivation for lending; rather, creditors have to give underpriced new loans to debtors to protect their existing claims. As limited enforceability of loan contracts is the major characteristic of sovereign lending, the lender has limited possibilities to withdraw its funds from debtor countries.

The country risk assessment routines of ECAs warrant particular attention as most long-term trade financing to developing countries is guaranteed against the political risks identified by such agencies. The risk assessment procedure of the commercial banks is similar to that of the ECAs although the banks are biased toward short-term financing in high-risk countries. ECAs (40 in 1989) operating in various countries, and regulated by the OECD and Berne Union agreements, promote national exports through the direct provision of export credit and guarantees on privately financed transactions. They function in the political risk field as non-profit organizations. Export credit insurance, however, is neither a form of development aid for the buyer country nor a subsidy for the exporter. In theory the guarantees are provided on a commercial basis.

With the emergence of the debt crisis era after 1982, the ECAs have had to accept their role among 'responsible' creditors. The continuous succession of debt reduction programmes are negotiated in the Paris Club — the rescheduling forum of official creditors — which provides agencies with firsthand information on future rescheduling applicants and countries in economic difficulties as well as knowledge about the International Monetary Fund (IMF) and the World Bank opinions and future credits. Generally, the ECAs and international commercial banks have adopted an 'IMF-tied' stance towards countries in debt-servicing difficulties. A Paris Club rescheduling requires in most cases a previous understanding with the IMF and a positive attitude from the London Club — which is the analogous rescheduling forum of the private banks — and commercial creditors (World Bank, 1985: 27).

The country risk analysis process can be divided into three phases: risk identification, risk assessment (estimating the probabilities of risks), and risk control. In the ECAs, risk identification is based on existing quantitative financial material, such as balance of payments figures; debt and other macroeconomic data; and information illustrating the qualitative or structural features of the country such as population and natural endowments. Nonquantifiable information on politics, ownership structure and labour markets is also gathered. The material is acquired in cooperation with other agencies, private consultants, the IMF/World Bank reports and other sources. Normally the procedure includes constructing spread-sheets of the most important financial and structural variables and a written report which analyzes political developments. The choice of, and importance attached to, the various indicators vary between the agencies. There are also great differences in preparing numerical material: some agencies use sophisticated statistical and econometric techniques as the basis for risk assessment processes while others accept forecasts provided by other institutions such as the IMF. Risk control methods, ranging from contract clauses to lending restrictions and political pressure, are employed according to the risks perceived.

Practising analysts tend to overvalue the importance of economic or financial figures and, at most, these reflect underlying economic fundamentals which are affected by various internal and external developments. In general, causalities behind financial figures are insufficiently considered.

**Scholarly publications**

Until recently, the literature on sovereign credit analysis following a statistical approach only evaluated the forecasting ability of financial indicators (such as amount of debt-service costs per export revenue, and available foreign exchange reserves). However, such methods were found to be incapable of forecasting country risk/payment default in a longer time span and their short-term forecasting ability was questionable (Heffernan, 1986).

Some recent studies dealing with the problem of sovereign creditworthiness have adopted a new approach that draws on the economic growth studies of the political economic tradition, and on political science research. Their common feature is the use of quantifiable structural data as the explanatory factor of economic or even debt-service performance. The structural factors include political instability and polarization, income inequality, education and the labour structure. A straightforward form of cultural determinism is not considered under 'qualitative' factors, primarily because of the volatility of general opinion around the issue. Indeed, studies using the 'qualitative' approach tend to be based on the concept that cultural differences are evident in the development of institutional structures in each country.

Berg and Sachs (1988) provide a good example of the use of non-traditional financial indicators in explaining debt-service performance. These authors share the criticism introduced earlier in this chapter, and emphasize that previous statistical cross-country studies have concentrated on the symptoms of crisis (such as debt-service ratios) rather than the causal reasons (Berg and Sachs, 1988: 272). They attempted to explain debtor country performances through a statistical analysis of structural characteristics of 35 market borrowers. Four explanatory factors were used, namely the trade regime, income inequality, the share of agriculture in GNP and the level of per capita income. The model performs well in separating rescheduling and non-rescheduling countries (Tables 3.1 and 3.2).

Table 3.1: Countries in order of decreasing predicted probability of rescheduling[a]

| Country | Rescheduling | Country | Rescheduling |
|---|---|---|---|
| Peru | Yes | Tunisia | No |
| Brazil | Yes | Kenya | No |
| Mexico | Yes | Indonesia | No |
| Argentina | Yes | Sri Lanka | No |
| Chile | Yes | Malaysia | No |
| Costa Rica | Yes | South Korea | No |
| Ivory Coast | Yes | Thailand | No |
| Uruguay | Yes | Taiwan | No |
| Yugoslavia | Yes | India | No |
| Turkey | Yes | Hong Kong | No |
| Philippines | Yes | Singapore | No |
| Colombia | No | Israel | No |

[a] Calculated from probit estimation on the sample of 24 commercial borrowers for which all data are available.

*Source:* Berg and Sachs, 1988: 290.

Table 3.2: Basic independent variables used by Berg and Sachs

| Name | Rescheduler[a] | Income distribution[b] | | | Trade regime[c] | Ag/GNP[d] | GNP/capita[e] |
|---|---|---|---|---|---|---|---|
| | | Lowest quintile | Highest quintile | Ratio quintile | | | |
| ***Latin America*** | | | | | | | |
| Argentina | Yes | 4.4 | 50.3 | 11.4 | 1 | 9.7 | 2,560 |
| Brazil | Yes | 2.0 | 66.6 | 33.3 | 3 | 13.1 | 2,220 |
| Chile | Yes | 4.5 | 51.3 | 11.4 | 3 | 7.6 | 2,560 |
| Colombia | No | 2.8 | 59.4 | 21.2 | 2 | 28.6 | 1,380 |
| Costa Rica | Yes | 3.3 | 54.8 | 16.6 | 2 | 20.3 | 1,430 |
| Ecuador | Yes | 1.8 | 72.0 | 40.0 | na | 15.1 | 1,180 |
| Mexico | Yes | 4.2 | 63.2 | 15.1 | 2 | 9.5 | 2,250 |
| Panama | Yes | 2.0 | 61.8 | 30.9 | na | 11.8 | 1,910 |
| Peru | Yes | 1.9 | 61.0 | 32.1 | 1 | 9.9 | 1,170 |
| Trinidad/Tobago | No | 4.2 | 50.0 | 11.9 | na | 3.0 | 5,670 |
| Uruguay | Yes | 4.4 | 47.5 | 10.8 | 3 | 10.2 | 2,820 |
| Venezuela | Yes | 3.0 | 54.0 | 18.0 | na | 5.9 | 4,220 |
| ***Average*** | ***83%*** | ***3.2*** | ***57.7*** | ***21.1*** | ***2.1*** | ***12.1*** | ***2,259*** |
| ***East Asia*** | | | | | | | |
| China | No | 7.0 | 39.0 | 5.6 | na | 32.5 | 300 |
| Hong Kong | No | 6.0 | 49.0 | 8.2 | 4 | 1.3 | 5,100 |
| Indonesia | No | 6.6 | 49.4 | 7.5 | 2 | 28.7 | 530 |
| South Korea | No | 6.5 | 45.2 | 7.0 | 4 | 20.3 | 1,700 |
| Malaysia | No | 3.5 | 56.0 | 16.0 | 3 | 26.4 | 1,840 |
| Philippines | Yes | 3.9 | 53.0 | 13.6 | 2 | 25.9 | 790 |
| Singapore | No | 6.5 | 49.2 | 7.6 | 4 | 1.7 | 5,240 |
| Taiwan | No | 8.8 | 37.2 | 4.2 | 4 | 18.1 | 2,528 |
| Thailand | No | 5.6 | 49.8 | 8.9 | 3 | 27.7 | 770 |
| ***Average*** | ***11%*** | ***6.0*** | ***47.5*** | ***8.7*** | ***3.3*** | ***20.3*** | ***2,089*** |
| ***Other*** | | | | | | | |
| Egypt | No | 4.6 | 48.4 | 10.5 | na | 24.5 | 650 |
| Hungary | No | 10.0 | 34.0 | 3.4 | na | 18.1 | 2,100 |
| India | No | 4.7 | 53.1 | 11.3 | 1 | 40.6 | 260 |
| Israel | No | 8.0 | 39.0 | 4.9 | 3 | 5.3 | 5,160 |
| Ivory Coast | Yes | 2.4 | 61.4 | 25.6 | 2 | 26.1 | 1,200 |
| Kenya | No | 2.6 | 60.4 | 23.2 | 2 | 35.1 | 420 |
| Mauritius | No | 4.0 | 60.5 | 15.1 | na | 18.2 | 1,270 |
| Morocco | Yes | 4.0 | 49.0 | 12.3 | na | 18.2 | 860 |
| Portugal | No | 5.2 | 49.1 | 9.4 | na | 13.6 | 2,520 |
| Spain | No | 6.0 | 45.5 | 7.6 | na | 8.2 | 5,640 |
| Sri Lanka | No | 6.9 | 44.9 | 6.5 | 2 | 28.6 | 300 |
| Tunisia | No | 6.0 | 42.0 | 7.0 | 3 | 18.3 | 1,420 |
| Turkey | Yes | 2.9 | 60.6 | 20.9 | 3 | 23.8 | 1,540 |
| Yugoslavia | Yes | 6.6 | 41.4 | 6.3 | 2 | 13.2 | 2,790 |
| ***Average*** | ***29%*** | ***5.3*** | ***49.2*** | ***11.7*** | ***2.3*** | ***20.8*** | ***1,866*** |
| ***Overall average*** | ***43%*** | ***4.8*** | ***51.7*** | ***14.1*** | ***2.5*** | ***17.7*** | ***2,123*** |

[a] Rescheduler: the dependent variable for the probit regressions.

[b] Income distribution data: estimates of the country-wide size distribution of income by households.

[c] Trade regime: effective rate of protection, direct trade controls, export incentives and exchange rate overvaluation. The countries are classified 1 (inward orientated) through 4 (outward orientated).

[d] Agriculture/GNP: the share of agriculture in GNP, averaged over the period 1970 to 1981.

[e] GNP/capita: in thousands of 1981 US$.

*Source:* Berg and Sachs, 1988: 280–1.

It is clear, however, that the factor variables are far too few and simplified to give a comprehensive picture of causalities. Although the authors work from a political and sociological background, they lack a comprehensive theory of country or state characteristics and behaviour. Despite reference to the work of various experts, their method of choosing variables is random, although statistically proven (the authors tested six other explanatory factors). The 'human' factor, largely absent from the study, could be indicated by education which correlates with economic performance (Kuznets, 1988; Oshima, 1988) or measures of domestic confidence, probably shown by the inflation figure.

Berg and Sachs (1988) emphasize that the agricultural production share in GNP is important to agricultural stability but the stability of an export-orientated agricultural sector is questionable. Not only is export agriculture at the mercy of climatic conditions, but it is also exposed to the volatilities of international commodity markets. In terms of the importance of the trade regime, a correlation between it and economic performance will always exist because of regional similarities and inter-regional dissimilarities in these factors due to historically evolved structural features in each region. These authors also find that GNP explains the development level of an economy which, in turn, correlates directly with debt-servicing capability. Countries with higher GNPs are likely to face higher debt repudiation costs, thus inducing compliance. High income inequality is utilized as a negative explanatory factor because it 'undermines the political stability and political effectiveness needed for successful macroeconomic management' (Berg and Sachs, 1988: 284) by pressuring for redistributive policies in favour of economic élites and enhancing their power to resist taxation. Furthermore, labour militancy and the government's dependency on the army increase. The authors note that the economic success of Japan, South Korea and Taiwan is partly due to the extremely low inequality of income distribution allowing governments to focus on issues of growth rather than redistribution. The importance of income equality is stressed by Kuznets (1988: 15–17) who follows Adelman in saying that a radical asset redistribution is more likely to precede than follow rapid growth.

Although the Berg and Sachs article may be criticized for lacking a theory of state behaviour, it represents a move towards rectifying the missing concept in sovereign risk analysis and provides interesting insights into the relevance of structural factor to debt-service performance. The concept of introducing more ratios or indicators on to the country spread-sheet, even if of improved quality, is unappealing without a theoretical framework outlining their status and importance among the 'identified' country risk factors.

### Scope for Concepts and Theories

According to the sovereign risk analysis philosophy suggested in this chapter, the quantitative foreign exchange earning capacity of a nation is seen merely as a partial explanation of the future debt-servicing behaviour. The starting point of the philosophy is the fourfold division of payment ability and willingness:

(a) the foreign exchange earning capacity;

(b) the taxing ability of the public sector regarding national wealth;

(c) rational calculations of the cost of default;

(d) internal political considerations.

As indicated already, rational calculations of the cost of default are partly derived from the nature of international credit markets, the discussion of which is beyond the scope of this chapter. Analysis based on foreign-exchange earning capacity is adequately covered by practical sovereign risk methodology and is excluded. Although the three other aspects mentioned will not be comprehensively analyzed, some ideas suggesting a better understanding of them are introduced. The point of departure is 'Keynesian', referring to the role of the developing nation state as an active participant in the economics of the country. The state must intervene in the country's foreign debt position to keep credits flowing and maximize benefits or minimize losses — although this does not necessarily mean that the country must attempt to meet its debt as, in certain instances, it may be in its interest to repudiate and reschedule them. The state must control its own borrowing behaviour, and in many countries the state has guaranteed a major share of private-sector debt obligations.

## Threshold theory

By concentrating on the interplay between domestic structural factors and economic performance, the concept of threshold theory based on a Keynesian assumption of a 'stabilizing' government is being employed (Liviatan, 1984; Heffernan, 1986; Krugman, 1988). The 'threshold' emerges as each debtor has a limited amount of income that can be used for foreign debt purposes:

A country, like a firm, has an expected stream of earnings, but not all of this stream is potentially available to service debt. Instead, some fraction of national income represents the maximum resource transfer that the country can be induced to make . . . The maximum level of resource transfer is determined ultimately by the country's willingness to pay, which in turn reflects both rational calculations of the cost of default and internal political considerations (Krugman, 1988: 4).

Willingness to pay depends on the political structure and economic situation of the country. The case of moratoria or non-payment is always a result of a mixture of unforeseen events, and conscious economic and/or political decisions. Needless to say, it is impossible to calculate the exact level of debt-service threshold for the next year and certainly not for a decade ahead. The nearest approximation is to calculate the amount of available foreign exchange and reduce the probable amount of 'surplus for domestic political purposes' estimated on the basis of previous years.

Contrary to the traditional approach which normally departs from 'how much money is needed for debt servicing', the threshold approach begins by assessing 'how much is needed for domestic political purposes'. Although a government can influence the amount of available resources in the short-run by providing incentives such as exchange rates and tariffs, or in the longer-run by investment decisions, that aspect is not considered here where central interest is how to analyze the decision-making environment of the government, government utilities, and decision-making constraints. Simplifying, it can be assumed that the time of interest is year t + 1 and that the probability of major natural or exogenous political disasters (such as war) is zero. The maximum quantity for debt service is given by A – B, where A is the amount of available foreign exchange and B is the 'domestic political surplus' (Figure 3.1). On one hand, B is affected, by the power of the government to decide about issues such as a budget deficit without risking a *coup d'état* (government fragility) and, on the other, by the realistic scope of governmental decision making and implementation constrained by poor legislation and administration (government capability) (Clapham, 1987: 79).

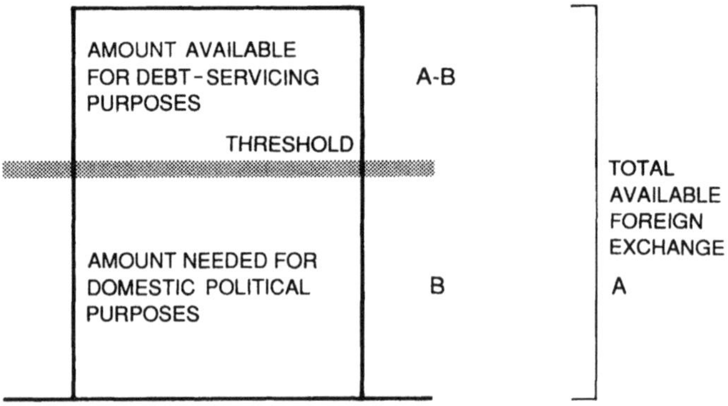


Figure 3.1: The threshold theory.

The threshold approach highlights the significance of differential rates of flexibility and the adjustment ability of different countries with dissimilar political systems. What remains to be considered are the 'systems' within which different factors influence the threshold level, government strengths and the scope of action. Even if each country is unique and worthy of separate analysis, a systematic theoretical approach can be pursued by using cross-country data on structural factors and economic development.

## Government as a Decision Maker

Sovereigns, or states, are not themselves decision makers. Decisions are made by various rulers, ranging from democratically elected governments to tyrants or military juntas. Rulers (the term government is here used synonymously), as any other decision makers, have preferred utility functions and constraints for their actions. The concept of *homo economicus* or that of a permanent 'social welfare' utility function, however, is not well suited to describe the government of a developing country (nor, indeed, of any country). Killick (1983: 361) borrows from the modern theory of the firm:

We have to view governments as "satisficers" — as pursuing solutions that are "good enough", as being satisfied with any one of a range of possible outcomes, as placing a premium on risk-avoidance and flexibility — a point well conveyed by the cliché that politics is the art of the possible.

The 'principle of bounded rationality' may be included in the image of the state. This principle (Simon, 1957) refers to the restricted capacity of the human mind in problem solving. Similarly, Rawls' (1971) 'principle of postponement' suggests: 'other things being equal, rational plans try to keep our hands free until we have clear view of relevant facts' (Killick, 1983: 358, 360). Typically, the government of a developing country has very little information about the future, and the 'governmental' utility function tends to fluctuate according to the interplay of power group balances; the objectives of a policy 'will only be revealed *ex post*, rather than being available *ex ante* for use in the preparation of medium term plans' (Killick, 1983: 359). It appears that a government more often formulates its policies to hold office than to pursue any preconceived, socially benevolent policies.

It must be asked about what constraints on decision making are faced by governments (apart from those formed by natural endowments and geopolitics). Internal constraints exist. A government is not a unit, but usually comprises a political regime, a bureaucratic élite and a military establishment. These may have differing interests, sometimes illustrated by the reluctance of bureaucracy to carry out political decisions. This condition constitutes a weakness of government capability or capacity. In some cases the political élite may be popular among the masses and face no major opposition on the political field, but at the same time be vulnerable to the threats of its own military. This lack of organic unity is incorporated by the concept of 'governmental fragility', which further includes the absence of legitimacy (Clapham, 1987: 76-8).

A second category of constraints emerges from oppositional forces within a country. The state is 'a prize in political competition' contested by the present ruling groups and opposition forces. The polity of a developing country is characteristically top-heavy, usually with a weaker administrative apparatus than in an industrial state. The rulers of developing countries are more motivated to stay in power than their counterparts in industrialized countries as the paucity of legislation and a controlling apparatus permit greater status than in the organized First World. In certain instances, however, the opposite may be true. A chaotic political situation may attract rapacious wheelers and dealers who use the opportunity to take the money and run. The extent of flexibility and manoeuvrability available to a government depends on the degree of political instability in the country, which may be explicit or underlying. Often political instability is triggered by economic instability.

Political instability results from the country-specific mix of society, attitudes and institutions. Rapkin and Avery (1986: 104) maintain that no relationship necessarily exists between the level of economic and political instability across countries: 'this assertion implies that domestic political factors must play an important mediating role: they may either dampen or magnify (or not affect at all) the destabilizing external (and internal) influences'.

Important factors determining the level of political instability are connected with sharing the burden of economic instability between different interest groups and the tradition of domestic conflict likely to result in violence or other extra-legal actions. Thus the developing-country government often has to spend more resources on avoidance and resolution of conflicts than is the case in industrialized countries. Furthermore, government violence is more pronounced in the developing world.

Threshold theory indicates that debtor country governments — as well as sovereign risk analysts — have to take internal political realities into consideration when calculating the amounts available for servicing the external debt. Describing the government as a decision maker suggests, however, that we cannot expect it to behave rationally and that analysis of domestic political linkages is required.

## Relevant Existing Approaches

The question arises as to how the behavioural concept of government decision making can be used in analyzing a country. At least, three types of approaches exist, namely the Public Choice School, the Concept of Polarized Society, and the Theory of Conflict and Governance. The first is characterized by the concept of the state as a political market-place with a passive role, and by the use of economic methods; the second sees the state as reflecting the interests of the group in power (Marxism falls into this category); and the third interprets the state in the role of conflict management and mostly applies the tools of political scientists (Frey, 1984; Amadeo and Banuri, 1988a).

### Theories of exchange society

Public choice theory is a method of explaining the behaviour of any country's government. This approach interprets the fluctuating utility function of a government by the interaction of the economic power groups, which attempt to maximize their own interests. The basic focus of the school is on politics as a field of exchange of benefits. Analysis proceeds on the assumption that political actors behave like *homo economicus*, for the benefit of themselves and not altruistically for the whole society. Groups pursue extra 'rents' for themselves or for their constituencies. The equivalent of 'rent' in the present case is the oversized payments sought by proprietors of certain monopoly goods or rights (oversized from the point of view of an effective macro-economic management of the economy). As Buchanan (1986: 22) notes:

> Even without the normative implications, however, the public choice perspective on politics directly draws attention to an approach to reform that does not emerge from the power perspective (of traditional political science) . . . attention is more or less necessarily drawn to the interaction process itself rather than to some transcendental evaluation of the outcomes themselves. How does one "improve" a market? One does so by facilitating the exchange process, by reorganizing the rules of trade, contract, or agreement. One does not "improve" or "reform" a market-like exchange process by an arbitrary rearrangement of final outcomes.

This approach comes closest to an idealistic democracy with a neutral, unbiased administrative body. Clearly, a typical developing-country state cannot be directly analyzed with this theoretical framework.

### The concept of polarized society

Alesina and Tabellini (1988) provide an exemplary theoretical study on polarization in relation to sovereign risk, using the state as an arena of political competition in which the party in power is not obliged to bargain with its opposition. The study links the seemingly irrational openness of the capital market in Latin America with political polarization and instability. Their model is of a Latin American economy consisting of two polar parties, the workers and the capitalists, and they empirically illustrate the tendency of each type of government to increase its constituency's share of the GNP (Table 3.3). The model suggests that there is no state in the world in which it would pay either of the parties to minimize capital flight, as there are certain costs associated with totally restricted capital markets. Naturally, a greater number of measures for reducing capital market openness are likely to occur under a labour government:

Under the plausible assumption that the flight of workers' capital is much smaller than that of the capitalists, we find that capital flight should be particularly high when right-wing regimes are expected to collapse (Alesina and Tabellini, 1988: 111).

The same phenomenon of polarization and political instability explains the over-accumulation of external debt. The current government does not fully internalize the costs of debt servicing as it is probable that 'others' will be in power when the payments come due. The 'other' government then only has the choice of repudiating or decreasing the endowment paid to its own constituency. A workers' government, however, is more likely to choose to repudiate than a capitalist government because of the possibility that creditors would seize private assets abroad to sanction repudiation.

Alesina and Tabellini recognize that they have only considered the polarization between the owners of physical capital and the owners of human capital. They note that their approach could be applied to trade-offs between other social groups, between 'tradeable' and 'non-tradeable' groups or industry and agriculture, which are more significant to understanding Latin America than Marxist conflict analysis. It appears that the concept of polarized society is particularly applicable in considering volatile economies like those of the Latin American countries: there, however, the more significant division of polar parties is between the tradeable and non-tradeable groups rather than between workers and capitalists.

## Table 3.3: Political regimes and capital controls, 1967 to 1986 [a]

| Country | Period | Political regime | Level of capital restrictions |
|---|---|---|---|
| Argentina | 1967-72 | right-wing | 0.67 |
| | 1973-75 | Peronist | 2 |
| | 1976-83 | military dictatorship | 1.25 |
| | 1984-86 | centre-left | 1 |
| Brazil | 1967-78 | right-wing | 1.67 |
| | 1979-84 | centre-right | 2 |
| | 1985-86 | centre-left | 2 |
| Chile | 1967-70 | centre-left | 2 |
| | 1970-73 | radical-left | 2 |
| | 1974-86 | military dictatorship | 1.54 |
| Mexico | 1967-86 | centre-left | 0.34 |
| Peru | 1967-68 | centre-right | 0.5 |
| | 1969-76 | 'left' military | 1.75 |
| | 1977-79 | 'right' military | 1.67 |
| | 1980-84 | transition to democracy | 1 |
| | 1985-86 | centre-left | 2 |
| Philippines | 1967-72 | right-wing democratic | 0.5 |
| | 1973-85 | right-wing dictatorship | 1 |
| | 1986 | centre-left democratic | 1 |
| Venezuela | 1967-69 | centre-left | 0 |
| | 1969-73 | centre-right | 0.2 |
| | 1974-78 | centre-left | 0.6 |
| | 1979-83 | centre-right | 0.8 |
| | 1984-86 | centre-left | 1.67 |
| Uruguay | 1967-72 | centre-left | 0.83 |
| | 1973-76 | 'right' military | 2 |
| | 1977-81 | 'centre' military | 1.2 |
| | 1982-84 | transition to democracy | 0 |
| | 1985-86 | centre-left | 0 |

[a] Each IMF report 1967-87 contains a summary table of exchange arrangements and exchange restrictions in all countries of the world. For each year, the countries in this table are assigned 0, 1 or 2 points, depending on whether they have no capital restrictions (0 points), either 'separate exchange rates for some or all capital transactions' or 'restrictions on payments for capital transactions' (1 point), or both (2 points). To calculate the restrictiveness of a political regime with respect to capital transactions, these points are summed over and divided by the number of years the regime is in power. Thus, a higher value may be interpreted as characterizing a more restrictive regime. If a regime ends early in a year, this year is counted for the following regime. When uncertain about the attribution of a transition year to two regimes, this year is assigned to both regimes with weights ½, ½.

*Source:* Alesina and Tabellini, 1988: 19–20.

**The theory of conflict and governance**

This theory is postulated by Amadeo and Banuri who (1988a: 4) see policy-making by the state 'as the constrained decisions of one actor among many actors operating in a situation of conflict and tension, rather than autonomous actions of an independent and omnipotent actor'. The state acts as a manager of social conflict. It is in the interest of the rulers to pursue stability in an environment of institutional constraints, an adaptation of the Keynesian ideal state. This is called a 'pragmatic state', in contrast to Myrdalian concepts of hard and soft states which seek, respectively, to repress or postpone social conflict (Amadeo and Banuri, 1988a,b). (It should be noted that Myrdal constructed his categorization of state types before the emergence of the *dirigiste* ones, which would perhaps have warranted a third category.) The 'hard' or 'soft' policy alternatives, namely repression or postponement of conflicts, are likely to be costly and ineffective in the long run. Both of these methods can, however, be used for winning time to create the institutions required by the type of crisis faced. This is relevant because, according to Weir and Skocpol (reported by Amadeo and Banuri, 1988a: 5), 'the structural features of the state affect the ability of the government to innovate, institutionalize, and implement different types of economic strategies'. There is no pre-ordained adjustment programme that is likely to be entirely suitable for an economy. Rather, adjustment measures must always take account of historically formed structures and institutions.

An analysis of conflict and governance situations starts by identifying power groups with controversial interests, and assessment of the mechanisms through which such groups can influence social decision making. Comparing the potential influence mechanisms with the existing institutional reality will reveal the scope of action available for the government and, at the same time, the potentially necessary institutional changes. Amadeo and Banuri (1988a,b) raise the issue of conflict between the interests of labour and capital on one hand (a Marxian conflict), and between those of capital and industry on the other (a Keynesian conflict). As in the theory of public choice, each of these groups tries to maximize its influence using either indirect or direct measures. In their analysis, based on the experience of Latin American and Asian countries, Amadeo and Banuri (1988a: 24) find that:

> The existence of well-organized labour groups will, by creating wage-resistance in the economy, erode the effectiveness of "market-type" economic policies . . . Second, the existence of financial openness will reduce the effectiveness and increase the costs of interventionist and regulatory policies.

In Latin America the strength of labour unions and the openness of the financial markets leave governments much less freedom of action than is the case in Southeast Asia (where there is some labour union strength and closed capital markets) or in East Asia (where there are weak labour unions and less capital market openness), although of course there are considerable differences between these countries. As Amadeo and Banuri (1988a: 31) note, the analysis of a 'pragmatic state' or as a manager of conflicts is:

> relevant mainly for major conflicts in the country, which impact upon the nature of the society as a whole: such as conflicts between labour and capital, between finance and industry; or even conflicts between various ethnic groups in culturally heterogeneous societies . . . Where a conflict of major proportions can be neither suppressed, nor postponed or managed, the result is a breakdown of the civil order, such as in Lebanon, or in some African states.

The 'manager' state is also an idealized concept but closer to the real political functions of government in many nations. Even if the government in a developing country has not acquired its power by free elections, it often plans to stay in power for a lengthy period. The government has to act as a manager between different interest groups in order not to fall into the fragility trap — avoiding a *coup d'état*.

## Conclusion

The need to analyze the causal aspects of sovereign risk points towards the conscious use of political science methodology. Assessment of the utilities of different power groups, the restrictions faced by government decision making and governance, as well as the structure of power and property relations in the society, need to be included. The approaches introduced above may prove useful in constructing a final framework of analysis. The developing country state is at its best 'a conflict manager' but in the circumstances of accelerating political instability it is likely that the characteristics of a competitive and polarized state will be increasingly evident. This chapter suggests that there is a need for further attention to political literature for constructing a theoretical framework and testing it by a range of country studies. The methodology for these would probably be based on recent case study methods and it is likely that regional similarities will emerge.

# 4 Corporate Raiders: The Case of Brierley Investments Ltd, New Zealand

**R. Le Heron**

Corporate raiders polarized the business and wider community in some advanced industrial nations in the 1980s over their much publicized role in forcing changes in the ownership and use of corporate capital *(Business Week,* 24 November 1986, 74–93). Depending on perspective, corporate raiding is either rigorously opposed or enthusiastically applauded. At one extreme, advocates view such activity as the quintessence of competition and efficient resource allocation while, at the other, alarm springs from concern over asset-stripping and job loss. For all the media coverage and dramatization of raiders like Kohlberg Kravis Roberts and Drexel Burnham Lambert, and associated phenomena, and activities such as leveraged buy-outs and junk bonds, mezzanine financing, mega-mergers and industrial destabilization, the business literature remains principally anecdotal or simply suggestive of strategies for the corporate victim or predator (Jennings and Mazzeo, 1986; Adler and Sneath, 1987; Bruck, 1989; Magowan, 1989; Reinmann, 1989). Few attempts have been made to ascertain the structural and historical significance of the corporate raider as a phenomenon (Coffee et al., 1988; Leland, 1989).

This chapter uses a broad political economy framework to probe the structural dynamics of, and developments in, capitalism that are implicated with corporate raiders and their activities. It is suggested that to make sense of the corporate raider and raiding, considerable effort should go into theorizing the conditions conducive to their development as well as to conceptualizing the specific histories of various raiders and raiding. Two sections of discussion are presented. The first contains a short digest of recent theory and method relevant to the domain of corporate raiding — the interface between the industrial and financial sectors. This covers basic relationships and interactions likely to yield outcomes such as mergers, acquisitions, takeovers and raiding. The second section details the behaviour and growth of a major investment company in New Zealand, Brierley Investments Ltd (BIL). It also considers New Zealand's industrial and financial restructuring against the backdrop of developments in the world economy, discusses the competitive responses of enterprises in New Zealand's structural setting and focuses on the growth trajectory and wider restructuring impacts of BIL. This company and the New Zealand scene are especially suited for investigation because it is the most conspicuous of corporate investors in New Zealand (including being the No. 1 Listed Public Company in 1986 and 1987) and because, with growth, the corporation effectively outgrew the New Zealand economy. The chapter concludes that a fuller understanding of the changing nature and geography of corporate raiders and industrial restructuring requires a framework that blends structural and enterprise analysis, takes a long-run view of industrial change and enterprise evolution and emphasizes the changing mix of structural forces and variety of enterprise behaviour.

## Framework

It is increasingly acknowledged by industrial geographers that developments in the world of business can be better understood if they are examined from a political economy perspective. In the mid-1980s, Taylor and Thrift (1986) offered a useful consolidation of approach, distinguishing four separable but related dimensions to any study of industrial change. These are structural context, industry environments, corporate environments and urban/regional contexts. The approach therefore stresses:

(a) theorization of capital's history to obtain informed knowledge of the latest maturation of capitalist production relations;

(b) conceptualization of structural processes germane to each explanatory focus or outcome, thereby enabling the identification of relevant relationships and constraints on interactions;

(c) investigation of industry and corporate environments in order to discuss concrete developments;

(d) examination of urban-regional settings to gain some measure of wider impacts of change.

While there is probably broad agreement about the basic ingredients of the political economy approach for corporate study, individual researchers have tended to specialize in particular dimensions, with most gravitating to the industry and corporate levels. Importantly, however, the assumed interconnections amongst the dimensions are being explored. Moreover, progress in each dimension is increasingly being fed into current research practice on other dimensions. Perhaps most critically, the steady momentum of theoretical research on higher-order structural processes continues to generate significant insights for those interested in corporate and industrial questions.

## Underlying Relationships: Internationalization and Regulation of Capital

Work by industrial geographers in the late 1980s has extended the theoretical frontier. Debate has centred on two main literatures: the 'industrialization of capital' school (Gibson and Horvath, 1983; Andreff, 1984; Daly, 1984; Massey, 1984; Bryan, 1987) and the 'internal restructuring or regulationalist' school (Jenkins, 1984; Lipietz, 1986; Jessop, 1988, 1989). The former literature probes the basic idea that the 'natural space' of capital is the world and that greater cognizance must be given to capital's circulation through three circuits, those of production, trade, and finance. The latter literature emphasizes the regulation of capital by the nation state and highlights the importance of establishing the institutional setting through and in which capital, in various forms, circulates. Synthesis of the two literatures (Fagan, 1988, 1990; Fagan and Le Heron, 1990; Le Heron, 1990a) offers potential for reinterpreting enterprise behaviour and industrial change — both of which are central to decoding the 'corporate raider'.

The synthesis rests on several premises about capitalist dynamics. Capital circulation is always potentially global in scale, moving through the three circuits of production, trade (realization), and finance (reproduction). Nation states play a major role in determining the opportunities for capital, with state policy impacting in two ways. First, at the level of total capital, state action alters the possibilities for capital circulation in each circuit and at different geographical scales (especially inside or outside a nation). For any nation state, at any time, regulatory policy differentiates capital into four fractions on the basis of the combinations of capital circulation. Bryan (1987) terms these the global fraction (featuring global circulation for realization and reproduction, with production being national); the national fraction (involving national circulation in all three circuits); the market-constrained fraction (a special case of global capital where reproduction as well as production is confined to the nation); and the investment-constrained fraction (a special case of national capital, with realization being international in scope, but reproduction and production being national). It is most important to appreciate that a range of institutional environments might equate with state policy that 'opens up' or 'closes down' the global circulation of capital through the different circuits. The point is vigorously argued by the regulationalists who, while identifying the importance of the external link, have tended to concentrate on the internal implications for accumulation of state policy. Second, at the level of individual capital, state policy impacts differentially on individual capitals, reflecting the inevitable variety of circumstances. The theoretical conclusion is that, regardless of state action, some capitals will be advantaged and others disadvantaged. This follows from the fact that any change in state policy may involve a reinsertion of territorially resident capital in the global circuits or a reinforcement of existing advantages or disadvantages facing resident capital.

An important conclusion is that structural conditions favouring accumulation and reproduction of capital in total have altered historically, necessitating responses by individual capitals. The changing conditions stem from the shifting importance of a particular circuit or circuits at different times. A tentative sequence has been proposed. Early capitalist expansion centred on trade. A period of crisis ensued during which the finance circuit played a critical role in disciplining the restructuring of production and trade. This was followed by the ascendancy of the production circuit and more latterly by the reassertion of the finance circuit. Late in this century, greater integration amongst the three circuits, at both the levels of total and individual capital, appears to be a tendency. This means that systematic forces seem to be encouraging flexible circulation of capital into and out of different circuits.

This statement puts a premium on examining the interplay between the international circulation of capital and the national regulation of capital. Contemporary analyses of corporations and industrial change adopting the political economy model are thus compelled to address global, national and local developments relating to production, trade and finance, as well as recent changes in state regulatory policy bearing on the insertion of the national territory into global circuits of capital and the recomposition of individual capitals within different structural contexts. Such analysis could incorporate a comparative component, cross-referencing national developments to more general developments in world capitalism. This chapter now examines more closely the production/finance relationship.

## Domains of Interactions

The industry/finance relationship has received little theoretical attention. Taylor and Thrift (1983) asserted that different relationships affecting the sources of funds exist for the periods of monopoly and global capitalism, and that the extent of separation or integration of industry and finance varies between nations. Its significance, however, is undeniable. Thompson (1977: 247) theorizes that banking and other commercial capital, through lending and borrowing practices, 'can determine "where" accumulation might take place (in terms of under which organisational form and entity)' and in what type of production. Further, attention is drawn to the different 'calls' on surplus value made by entities in each circuit. Moran (1981) warned that relations between the industrial and financial sectors are highly political, necessitating empirical investigation of specifics. The basic idea has not been explored further by incorporating recent developments in the international financial sector, such as new instruments used to raise capital; the way these are placed; the size and nature of the market in which they circulate; the rise of merchant banks and other commission-based intermediaries; extension of futures markets; and so on. Drucker (1986: 768) perceptively noted that 'capital movements rather than trade have become the driving force of the world economy'. The few geographers examining the interrelations between finance and industry or finance and property (Taylor and Thrift, 1983; Daly, 1984; Daly and Logan, 1986; McGee, 1986; Huxley and Berry, 1988; Rimmer, 1988; Pratt, Chapter 7 in this volume) have done so without explicit reference either to the internationalization or the regulatory dimensions already mentioned.

The industry/finance relation can be viewed in two ways. From the standpoint of industrial capital (spanning food and fibre, manufacturing, energy, and construction) relations with the finance sector are needed to meet cash-flow requirements (arising from labour costs, short and long-term loan obligations, and raw materials), expansion of facilities, and addition or replacement of equipment. The accent is thus on expanding the productive base. This may necessitate contact with various money markets and institutions. Conversely, from the standpoint of finance capital, involvement in other sites of production is governed by assessment of the productive assets as a commodity in their own right. It is the latter perspective which forms the basis of corporate investment strategy that involves repeated takeovers and the name 'raider'.

The two standpoints are theoretical positions and must be seen as such. Therefore, in any nation, a tendency towards or away from one pole may be discernible and individual corporations may adjust and change their growth strategy. Industries cannot be viewed only in technological terms but need to be seen from the potentially contradictory perspectives of production and finance, which can lead to diverging assessments of industry opportunities for growth, based either on production expansion or efficiency, or on financial returns from asset and share sales, revaluation and appreciation. Likewise, corporations should be seen as agencies with an internal structure that is far more complex than generally assumed. In particular, a distinction must be made between ownership and capital structure, organization and asset structure, and shareholder objectives and management of debt. The second entity in each pair reflects the addition of a financial component, internalized into corporate structure and strategy (Easterwood et al., 1989; Leland, 1989). Again this component is largely missing in the work of business historians (Chandler, 1962; Channon, 1973; Scott, 1986).

## Industry and Corporate Environments

At least two intermediate level concepts of industrial structure and organizational change (both drawn from the industrial economics literature) provide a bridge between the structural conditions and individual companies. They are useful after structural analysis (at a higher level of abstraction) has clarified the structural dimensions making up the field of possibilities open to capital. Such possibilities of course may not be perceived, or understood, or even attained by individual capitals. Indeed, corporations are likely instead to focus on more accessible and understandable parameters. Industrial structure, the immediate competitive external environment and linkage network of a firm, forms one of the main constraints on the ability of individual companies to respond and adapt to changing conditions. This arises because industrial structure shapes profitability, the nature of competition, and the type and extent of inter-firm and intra-firm transactions. According to Hay and Morris (1979), there are three elements of industrial structure: scale of production (in relation to industry size, measured by the proportion of industry output provided by a plant of minimum economic size); concentration of industry activity in the largest firms (influenced by the number of firms in an industry and the relative sizes of the market shares of companies); and product differentiation.

By contrast, organizational change constitutes a major mechanism for altering the production base, market positioning or financial viability of a company. Britton and Perry (1987) identify three types of organizational change: administration, organizational structure, and ownership, and link these to three common restructuring tactics: mergers and acquisitions, divestments, and closures. Mergers refer to all types of requisition of assets or stock of part or all of another firm that results in operational control of some or all the other firm (Narver, 1964: 2). A horizontal merger designates a merger of firms whose products are viewed by buyers as virtually identical. Such mergers may involve geographical diversification. The key distinction of a vertical merger is a functional relationship between the acquired and acquiring firms. Though the term conglomerate merger is often used to classify the residual of merger activity, Reid (1976: 87–8) proposes a distinction between a circular merger (involving diversification through product extension into broadly related activities, aimed at achieving a set of corporate objectives) and a conglomerate merger, which should be reserved for a combination of completely unrelated products and/or services (see also Channon, 1973).

Coyne and Wright (1986) argue that the term divestment covers a spectrum of rearrangements which hinge on the nature of ownership severance, the relative frequency with which such behaviour takes place and the post-divestment ownership form of the part of the company released. Their interpretation thus relates divestment to organizational growth and adaptation and avoids isolated treatment of such phenomena as mergers, acquisitions and closures.

Several studies (Mandel, 1975; Reid, 1976; Utton, 1981; O'Connor, 1984; Maycock, 1986; Marshall, 1987) indicate that merger activity at the national level is bunched with rising stock markets, regulatory change and economic upheaval, a periodicity that appears to precede global depressions. The association broadly matches Harvey's (1982) third phase in the accumulation cycle. Reid's (1976: 16) analysis for the US, covering the years 1948 to 1971, showed a relative distribution of horizontal (19.4 per cent), vertical (11.9 per cent), circular (47.2 per cent) and conglomerate (21.4 per cent) mergers. Moreover, merger activity was confined to comparatively few merger-active companies (Reid, 1976: 70), with the leading 25 of the big 200 companies accounting for 59 per cent of the total assets acquired by the 200 largest manufacturing companies. More recent evidence for the US (Reinmann, 1989: 18) reveals that the 'Q ratio, or the market value of corporate assets as a proportion of current replacement cost, had declined to about 50 per cent by 1981', providing scope for a fresh round of corporate consolidation. Moreover, certain taxation provisions assisted the rise of leveraged buy-outs. Leland (1989) argues that the tax deductibility in favour of new debt holders, resulting from greater debt servicing with a higher debt/equity ratio from a takeover, had a major bearing on the surge in leveraged buy-outs. Indeed, Easterwood et al. (1989) show that between 1978 and 1985, the 50 or so large successful buy-outs in the US averaged US$560 million. Accompanying the buy-outs were substantial changes in stakeholders, away from pre-buyout public stockholders, bondholders and employees to private buy-out teams.

## Corporate Raiders and Raiding

The foregoing discussion suggests that waves of merger activity might be explored in terms of fundamental shifts in the form and mix of the three circuits of capital in different nation states. In such a context particular 'types' of corporate entities, identified on the strength of patterns of business behaviour, may play an especially significant role in shaping the direction and detail of industrial change.

The definition of the term 'corporate raider' presents several problems. First, mergers, acquisitions and takeovers, whether 'friendly' or 'less than friendly', result in concentrations of capital, whose form, history, geography and significance cannot be adequately discussed without reference to underlying structural conditions. The business literature contains several typologies of such outcomes but little systematic discussion of the wider forces permitting and encouraging the outcomes. Second, government policy will always be implicated in any explanation of conditions stimulating or suppressing merger and related activity, having either a direct or indirect part, whether through tax codes (affecting depreciation options, interest deductibility, treatment of debt); rules governing financial markets (affecting different stakeholders); lending requirements and restrictions; foreign exchange regulations; and so on. Third, corporate raiding forms a subset of acquisition and takeover activity, insofar as it demarcates intentions behind takeovers that diverge from a production-orientated motivation. While billion-dollar raiding reaches the limelight, much parallel activity of modest scale undoubtedly goes unreported. Fourth, evidence from several countries clearly indicates that only a few companies sustain an aggressive acquisition/takeover posture for extended periods, thereby inviting the label 'raider'. Although Coffee et al. (1988) suggest special qualities are needed by the management of such enterprises to ensure success from the strategy, the interdependence of corporate behaviour patterns, the regulatory environment and developments in the financial sector cannot be overlooked. Fifth, the theorization and literature review suggest that the notion of a 'pure' form is quite inappropriate. Instead, corporations engaging in raiding should be interpreted as changing entities with shifting bundles of external and internal relationships. Only empirical analyses of specific organizations and industries in different contexts can clarify concrete cases.

## Brierley Investments Ltd

The remainder of the chapter reports on the evolution and impact of BIL in New Zealand. The empirical analysis establishes links between the structural context and company strategy and growth but does not explore in depth the industrial milieu entered or left by BIL. The discussion begins with a brief introduction to the change in regulatory order and new windows of opportunity afforded by the reinsertion of New Zealand into the world economy: it is confined to the 1980s, the period when BIL growth strategies changed several times.

## New Zealand Economy, State Intervention and Growth Limits

New Zealand's participation in the post-war long boom of the world economy was carefully managed by the state, initially through border protection for manufacturing and extensive state expenditure on infrastructure and welfare, and then in the 1960s and 1970s through industrial assistance to foster exports (Franklin, 1978; Britton and Le Heron, 1987). The insulated New Zealand economy formed a distinctive arena for accumulation, in which national (mainly industrial and farmer) capital was advantaged relative to global capital and market-constrained capital operating behind protective barriers.

### New Zealand corporate profile 1980

Corporate growth in New Zealand from 1945 to 1980 was primarily a feature of company growth within the manufacturing and primary processing sectors. Several waves of mergers occurred (Le Heron, 1977) reflecting business responses to tightening commercial conditions. A few steadily growing companies, almost entirely of domestic origin, emerged as New Zealand's main corporations. Through advantages endowed by regulation, early positioning, industry conditions and management, these firms were able to and chose to take advantage of the growth possibilities of the post-war economy. The most important, both in terms of market capitalization and employment, were essentially 'commodity corporations', dependent on the industrial processing of land-based commodities and 'manufacturing corporations' springing from the protected manufacturing base (Jesson, 1987). Further, the pattern of industrial concentration and centralization dramatically changed. Whereas most industries had only modest levels of industrial concentration, the extent of concentration in the largest three enterprises had risen appreciably. Those enterprises that had grown had done so partly by horizontal and vertical integration, but also by diversification. Evidence on the extent of diversification of New Zealand's largest corporations during the late 1970s (Le Heron, 1980) suggests that this growth route should not be overstated because the majority of new investments and acquisitions were in related activities. By the 1980s, growing concentration and centralization (Ellis, 1976; Le Heron et al., 1989) may have given the New Zealand economy two very different groups of companies, with the tendency of key corporations to both concentrate and centralize activities not being mirrored in small and medium-size enterprises. Hamilton's (1986) aggregate analysis of the degree to which manufacturing enterprises were diversified in 1981 showed quite low levels of diversification in comparison to the UK (Utton, 1977).

The growing level of concentration in the economy did not go unnoticed by corporate leaders. Hugh Fletcher, the Managing Director of Fletcher Challenge Ltd (FCL), New Zealand's largest listed company, spoke in 1981 of the absence of projects in New Zealand of sufficient scale to generate adequate levels of corporate profitability (Fletcher, 1982).

## Components of re-regulation in New Zealand

Starting in the mid-1970s, but especially from the mid-1980s, New Zealand saw a progressive re-regulation and opening of the economy (Bollard and Easton, 1985). This direction in government regulatory policy reversed a long history of increasing intervention in the economic sphere and was largely in response to the failure of interventionism to solve New Zealand's balance of payments problems (Ayto and Bollard, 1987; Roberts, 1987; New Zealand Planning Council, 1988). The principles underpinning the changed role of the state were sufficiently general to span all sectors of the economy. Manufacturing was systematically targeted by the Industries Development Commission between 1975 and 1984 with a review of 20 industries. Several industry development plans set in motion substantial enterprise restructuring.

In 1984 the newly elected Labour Government introduced a comprehensive re-regulation policy (usually, but incorrectly, referred to as deregulation) which included the accelerated opening of the economy, further reductions in manufacturing protection and new regulations for New Zealand's financial sector (Carew, 1986; Harper, 1986). Previous controls on interest rates, deposit-taking activity and the direction and level of lending by financial institutions (e.g. compulsory ratios) were removed. Likewise, exchange controls limiting capital movements were eliminated. These included restrictions on private-sector borrowing overseas (such as the fixed term of at least 12 months and at an interest rate no greater than two percentage points above the London or Singapore interbank rate); access to the New Zealand capital market by overseas-owned companies operating in New Zealand; prohibitions on New Zealand financial institutions from borrowing overseas; and prohibitions on New Zealand residents from purchasing foreign exchange for investment purposes. Further, there were regulations governing entry into banking, foreign exchange dealing and the short-term official money market (Carew, 1986; Savage, 1986, 1988). Patterns of financial re-regulation in New Zealand closely followed those adopted in the UK, Australia and other nations (Cooke, 1986; Hall, 1987). Accordingly, the 1980s saw a fundamental change in the structural conditions facing business, from an essentially national orientation at the beginning of the decade to an overwhelmingly international orientation by its end.

## BIL: Conglomerate Structure and Strategy

BIL was formed in 1961 as an investment company to

> take over or acquire substantial holdings in certain public companies in Australia and New Zealand with a view to ultimate participation in management and the reorganisation and improvement of their finances. This will apply particularly to "dead" companies which have considerable assets but low earning capacity, due to poor management [and to undertake] investment in companies and industries where it is believed that rationalisation and mergers are inevitable in the normal course of events (Brierley Investments Ltd, 1981: 6–7).

Acting as a 'corporate catalyst' BIL grew steadily, reaching the leading 10 companies by market capitalization in 1981. Significantly, the annual reports for 1980 and 1981 forecast the structural development of the New Zealand economy. It noted three aspects. First, BIL recognized that the 'present phase has, perhaps, another three years to run. Thereafter, the character of the market, at least in New Zealand, will have permanently changed through the large number of mergers and absorptions and as a consequence our own role will also have to change'. Second, the 'restructuring' of the New Zealand economy was foreseen with some 50 to 60 much larger and more specialized companies, each firmly established in a relatively dominant position in one or more commercial and industrial sectors. Third, the pattern of recent major mergers (especially that of New Zealand South British and Fletcher Challenge Ltd) was seen as a trend-setter for a 'think big' philosophy which was 'certain to pervade the market for some time ahead' (Brierley Investments Ltd, 1981: 9). BIL had argued a year before that if

> a company such as our own aspires to continue to perform a role as catalyst for "Industry Rationalisation" (a trend which we are convinced will intensify in the future) it is imperative that we have the resources to support a worthwhile level of investment in significant companies and industries. The alternative is to concentrate solely on the smaller end of the market where there are some useful opportunities but which do not offer the same scope for long term advancement (Brierley Investments Ltd, 1980: 8).

In 1988 BIL was number two in the market capitalization stakes behind FCL, having slipped from the first rank in 1987. BIL's 1980s growth involved several dimensions: an industry rationalization strategy in New Zealand; internationalization involving Australia at first but extending to the US and UK, an equity-centred strategy made possible by the massive expansion of the New Zealand and Australian stock markets in the mid-1980s (Cooke, 1986: 4); and a period of divestment occasioned by the share-market collapse at the end of 1987.

## Growth from industry rationalization

BIL's New Zealand growth during the 1980s is summarized in Table 4.1 which itemizes the industries that BIL entered and the form of the business restructuring. Investment of one type, such as share purchases, was often submerged by later developments, such as full takeover of board membership, that extended or reduced the initial investment.

Table 4.1: Profile of major BIL New Zealand investments, 1980 to 1988

| Year | Industry [a, b] |
|---|---|
| 1980 | Meat (H); Gas (H); Textiles (H); Printing (H); Engineering (H); Mining (A) |
| 1981 | Brewing (A) |
| 1982 | Pharmaceuticals (S); Engineering (H); Metals (H); Gas (H); Printing (H); Wines (H); Retailing (H); Property (H) |
| 1983 | Wine (H); Printing (H) |
| 1984 | Wine (H); Retailing (H); Food (A); Motor vehicle distribution (A); Radio (H); Food (S); Textiles (H) |
| 1985 | Timber (S) |
| 1986 | Gas (H); Medical (H); Radio (H); Electrical (H); Printing (H); Liquor distribution (H); Textile (V); Horticulture (A); Insurance (S); Brewing (A); Pulp/timber (A); Newspaper (A) |
| 1987 | Rubber (A); Insurance (S); Textiles (S); Engineering (S); Entertainment (A); Food (S); Liquor (A) |
| 1988 | Metals (D); Petroleum (D); Electronics (D); Newspaper (D) |

[a] A loose industry classification is used because the annual reports only provide information on the activity areas of companies in which BIL invested. Moreover, some investments were in companies with fairly diversified operations. Following Reid (1976) these can be viewed as comprehensive investments satisfying several objectives.

[b] H (Horizontal); V (Vertical); S (Share purchases); A (Acquisitions); D (Divestments – includes sales of subsidiaries and major shareholdings). Since BIL has not changed its ownership status, all investments involving ownership have been acquisitions and not mergers.

*Source:* Brierley Investments Ltd, *Annual Reports*, 1980-88.

The 1980-84 period featured substantial consolidation by the company in industrial sectors already within its orbit. Horizontal acquisitions far outweighed other investments in New Zealand. Strikingly, the enterprises taken over by BIL were mostly in industries with very low concentrations in the leading three firms (e.g. printing and packaging, textiles) and where no obvious technological barriers were evident (e.g. wine).

The sheer size of BIL as a New Zealand corporation can be gauged from Table 4.2 which details its employment by industry group. With a total workforce of over 22,000, the company is one of the largest industrial employers in New Zealand. Britton and Perry (1987: 156) estimated that the Auckland employment of BIL and its subsidiaries was at least 4,400 in 1986.

Table 4.2: New Zealand employment by BIL sector

| Activity sector [a] | 1985 | 1988 |
|---|---|---|
| Building and construction | 6,458 | 4,331 |
| Energy | 290 | 640 |
| Food and beverage | 5,065 | 5,837 |
| Manufacturing and assembly | 1,457 | 4,006 |
| Printing, publishing and media | 4,884 | 3,152 |
| Wholesale and retail | 2,277 | 3,905 |
| Shipping | 1,183 | — |
| Other (property) | 15 | 786 |
| Total New Zealand | 21,629 | 22,657 |

[a] Based on 1988 BIL classification of subsidiary companies. The breakdown in Brierley Investments Ltd (1985b: 2–11) is more detailed. Some difficulties arose in reconciling the two classifications. A major company represented in printing and packaging in 1985 was reassigned to wholesale and retail in 1988; and companies associated with several activity sectors changed completely.

*Source:* Brierley Investments Ltd, 1985a, b, 1988.

## Dimensions of internationalization

Even before the 1980s, BIL was a trans-Tasman corporation by virtue of the parallel growth of its Australian subsidiary, Industrial Equity Ltd (IEL). Discussion of the New Zealand scene must therefore take account of this enduring relationship. Throughout the 1980s the company maintained its expansionary strategy in New Zealand but also accomplished comparable (though fluctuating) growth rates in other countries. Table 4.3 summarizes BIL performance on sales, assets and profit sources; this is based on BIL consolidated accounts, so that the Australian figures probably estimate the contribution of IEL, while those for the US summarize Industrial Equity Pacific Ltd (IEP).

The ratios for assets and sales are surprisingly stable suggesting perhaps a carefully balanced management of total company growth. Moreover, there is little evidence to suggest any attempts to integrate production with either subsidiaries or companies in which BIL has an interest. Profit attribution by sphere of operation shows a sharp fall off from New Zealand post-1985. Available figures for 1986 to 1988 record a decline in the New Zealand share from 61 to 38 per cent.

Table 4.3: Aspects of BIL internationalization (NZ$ m.)

| | 1983 | 1984 | 1985 | 1986 | 1987 | 1988 |
|---|---|---|---|---|---|---|
| ***Sales*** [a] | | | | | | |
| New Zealand | n.a. | n.a. | 993 | 1,900 | 3,310 | 3,260 |
| Australia | n.a. | n.a. | 933 | 921 | 1,338 | 1,484 |
| UK | n.a. | n.a. | } 552 | 511 { | 1,935 | 2,338 |
| US | n.a. | n.a. | | | 5,710 | 31 |
| New Zealand percentage | — | — | 40 | 57 | 46 | 45 |
| ***Assets*** [b] | | | | | | |
| New Zealand | 302 | 636 | 1,102 | 2,210 | 4,532 | — |
| Australia | 400 | 874 | 1,121 | 1,790 | 3,932 | — |
| UK | 5 | 15 | 104 | 891 | 1,998 | — |
| US | 13 | 41 | 472 | 754 | 1,365 | — |
| New Zealand percentage | 41 | 40 | 39 | 39 | 38 | — |
| ***Profits*** [c] | | | | | | |
| New Zealand | n.a. | n.a. | n.a. | 111 | 153 | 114 |
| Australia | n.a. | n.a. | n.a. | 61 | 152 | 47 |
| UK | n.a. | n.a. | n.a. | } 8 | 37 { | 58 |
| US | n.a. | n.a. | n.a. | | | 45 |
| New Zealand percentage | — | — | — | 64 | 63 | 47 |

[a] Sales from goods and services.
[b] Total corporate assets.
[c] Profits from all sources.
*Source:* Brierley Investments Ltd, *Annual Reports*, 1983-88.

## Growth from investments

The change in corporate growth strategy advertized in 1980 and 1981 is identifiable (providing the forewarned lag of three years is remembered) in Table 4.4 which presents the value of total corporate assets spread over investments and fixed assets. After 1984, investments (mostly in shares) account for a much higher percentage of total assets. Two further indicators corroborate this trend. Table 4.5 shows the apportionment of investments in listed New Zealand, Australian and other foreign companies. BIL investment in the New Zealand share market was relatively conservative, concentrating on mainstream land-based production and manufacturing. Le Heron (1990b) calculates that up to half the value of BIL share investments was held in a set of 30 land-based companies, mostly established. To some extent the investment figures in Table 4.5 may be misleading as they are not inflation adjusted and may contain substantial share-value appreciation. A less ambiguous measure is profits attributable to trading and investment activity. The two years shown in Table 4.6 reveal the strong absolute importance of trading profits to total profits.

Table 4.4: Asset spread of BIL group (NZ$ m.)

| | 1980 | 1981 | 1982 | 1983 | 1984 | 1985 | 1986 | 1987 | 1988 |
|---|---|---|---|---|---|---|---|---|---|
| Investments | 90 | 176 | 192 | 232 | 573 | 1,080 | 2,195 | 6,361 | 5,457 |
| Fixed assets | 85 | 83 | 178 | 210 | 411 | 562 | 1,171 | 1,947 | 2,657 |

*Source:* Brierley Investments Ltd, *Annual Reports*, 1980-88.

Table 4.5: Value of New Zealand and overseas shares of BIL group (NZ$ m.)

| | 1980 | 1981 | 1982 | 1983 | 1984 | 1985 | 1986 | 1987 | 1988 |
|---|---|---|---|---|---|---|---|---|---|
| New Zealand listed | 15 | 32 | 48 | 55 | 142 | 294 | 246 | 1,005 | 819 |
| Australian and other foreign listed | 48 | 100 | 105 | 138 | 334 | 596 | 1,477 | 4,594 | 3,421 |

*Source:* Brierley Investments Ltd, *Annual Reports*, 1980-88.

## Divestment for growth

The aftermath of the October 1987 share-market collapse, combined with a recession in New Zealand, saw BIL enter a phase of divestment (Table 4.1). Brierley Investments Ltd (1988: 10–11) carefully qualified the strategy shift:

The market has mistakenly interpreted this "back to basics" approach as being a new strategy based on disposals. The reality is that in the easier funding conditions that previously existed we tended to retain the majority of the assets we acquired . . . The key to ownership is the continuing enhancement of value. [The] Group [will] always have a core level of trading entities and operating earnings although the companies which make up these businesses will change from time to time.

Table 4.6: Before-tax trading and investment profits, BIL group (NZ$ m.)

| | 1986 | 1987 | 1988 |
|---|---|---|---|
| Trading activities | 168 | 408 | 433 |
| Building and construction | 42 | 45 | 32 |
| Energy | 17 | 40 | 6 |
| Food and beverages | 71 | 138 | 110 |
| Manufacture and assembly | 4 | (3) | 34 |
| Printing, publishing and media | 8 | 16 | 26 |
| Wholesaling and retailing | 27 | 171 | 161 |
| Investment activities | 257 | 577 | 624 |
| Trading/Profit ratio | 47 | 70 | 69 |

*Source:* compiled and calculated from Brierley Investments Ltd, *Annual Reports*, 1986-88.

The move reflected a review of BIL's position after the stockmarket collapse. The company had drawn several conclusions. Investment companies were no longer regarded as the 'flavour of the month' and this was judged to impact on the availability of equity and in turn, debt, such that BIL would have to look to more efficient utilization of existing resources. Behind this assessment were problems connected with recent acquisitions whose assets included speculative shares; an exposure to the New Zealand property market, both directly and through trading subsidiaries as well as joint venture investment in property and one-off losses associated with two greenfield projects; the failed Auckland newspaper *The Sun*; and the loss-making airline Ansett New Zealand Ltd.

## Conclusion

By using a political economy framework this chapter has revealed the importance of delineating the structural conditions affecting the form and degree of circulation of capital into, within, and out of a nation. An interest in industrial restructuring presupposed examination of the interrelations between the industrial and finance sectors. Corporate raiding was discussed as an activity or outcome involving the initiation, financing and completion of takeovers aimed at immediate or longer-run realization of profit from asset and share sales and asset and share appreciation, rather than from increased revenue from expanded production or productivity through application of different management regimes. The theoretical hallmark of raiding is therefore the pursuit of profit from the commodity value *per se* of an industrial operation and not the income stream from the operation's production base. In reality the theoretical division is hard to uphold. Corporate growth strategy changes in response to internal and external pressures and opportunities, so that the term 'corporate raider' must be employed advisedly. Though 'raider' may imply universality of investment strategy, the exigencies of context will almost certainly ensure a limit to the extent and duration of raiding.

This study of BIL has illustrated the theoretical assertions. BIL, an avowed corporate investor transformed itself from a minor investment company into a very large (by New Zealand standards) global corporation with a financial presence in Europe, Asia and North America. If the thrust of early growth was industry rationalization with an accent on profit from asset rearrangement, the trajectory followed during the internationalization phase seemed to suggest a slow erosion of this strategy, both in spirit and in operational behaviour. Unobtrusively, but steadily, BIL amassed one of New Zealand's largest industrial combinations, forming a new constellation of financial power from takeover and interlinkage. The reported shift to a divestment strategy revealed a longer-term investment horizon than might normally be attributed to raiding companies, a development which, on the surface, runs counter to a raiding philosophy. How far the conglomerate trend reflected an inability to liquidate, or a desire to retain until opportune disposal was possible, was not probed. What is obvious, however, is that a relational kaleidoscopic lens is needed to keep up with changes in the company's strategy.

While the study has covered the organizational side of BIL's rise, it has done so at the expense of a scrutiny of industrial changes induced or associated with BIL involvement. A focus on attendant industrial restructuring is only possible after the main features of BIL evolution have been sketched. Many issues remain unresolved. These include a long-run view of BIL from inception into the 1980s to gauge whether the company's professed expansionary strategy deviated or altered during earlier business conditions in New Zealand; an investigation of BIL strategy in the late 1970s particularly when the Industries

Development Commission was operating; a detailed analysis of post-acquisition developments in companies acquired by BIL, especially rationalization and divestment moves; and a parallel study of group activity in Australia and New Zealand, particularly with reference to phases of government intervention and industrial policy and in terms of closer economic relations between these two countries.

# 5 Changing Strategies of Financial Corporations in the Federal Republic of Germany

**W. Gaebe**

This chapter investigates the recent expansion of financial services in the Federal Republic of Germany (FRG). Historically, this country's banking and financial system has been characterized by universal banks, dense branch networks and a low degree of internationalization. Indeed, even though the FRG has been an important world industrial power and a large exporter of industrial goods, it occupied only a weak position as an international financial centre. For example, in 1987 the FRG showed the largest foreign trade deficit in financial services (Figure 5.1): the share of banking in GNP was only about 4 per cent (compared to the UK at about 11 per cent and Switzerland with almost 9 per cent). Overall, in 1987 the FRG ranked only tenth in international financial volume as indexed by international banking claims and liabilities (Table 5.1). The country had about one-fifth of the UK's international financial volume and just under one-third of that of Japan and the US. International financial services in the FRG were significantly less important than other international activities such as commerce and tourism.

The development of the financial sector is investigated here in three major sections. The first assesses the extent of the growth of financial services; the second analyzes the factors underlying their growth; and the third considers the consequences of their extension.

## The Growth of Financial Services

Financial services in the FRG have increased substantially. Their expansion has involved new products, new suppliers and new forms of organization. The classical division of labour between banks, commerce and industry has become increasingly obscured (Gerke, 1984). Many new products, including financial innovations such as interest and monetary swaps, and new banking services emerged to support large enterprises in their international financial management decisions (Büschgen, 1986).

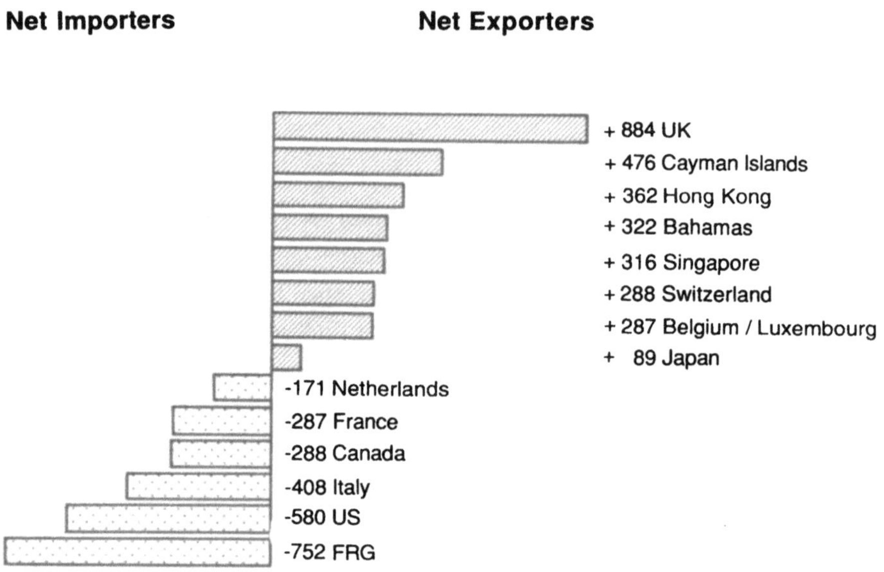


Figure 5.1: Largest net importers and exporters of financial services (US$000 m.), 1987. *Sources:* Thiessen, 1988: 40–1; Kurm, 1989: 12.

As the range of products on FRG financial markets increased so, too, did the number of suppliers, a pattern similar to that which has occurred in other industrial countries such as Japan and the US. In the FRG, market segments and business structures broke up. Banks no longer concentrate solely on asset management and short and medium-term credits, nor building societies on the financing of housing; insurance companies have veered from their focus on long-term or unlimited-time receipt of risks. Customers of the big banks are not now mainly industrial and trading firms and wealthy private households, nor those of savings banks just small savers and municipal authorities. Cooperative banks have extended their clientele beyond craftsmen and farmers (Figure 5.2). All suppliers of financial services have widened their range of products and broadened their client base.

At the heart of the new marketing and sales strategies are banks offering an array of new financial products, including savings agreements with building societies, insurance, and advice for private clients and corporate customers. Although most strive to offer a general package of financial products, some seek to specialize in particular market segments and abandon unprofitable financial services.

Table 5.1: The largest financial centres in 1987 (international banking claims and liabilities)

| Rank | Country | Financial centres 1987 (US$ m.) | Increase 1983 to 1987 (per cent) |
|---|---|---|---|
| 1 | UK | 1,800 | 81 |
| 2 | Japan | 1,167 | 445 |
| 3 | US | 1,121 | 52 |
| 4 | Belgium/Luxembourg | 716 | 109 |
| 5 | Switzerland | 574 | 93 |
| 6 | France | 497 | 83 |
| 7 | Hong Kong | 495 | 293 |
| 8 | Cayman Islands | 476 | 386 |
| 9 | Singapore | 439 | 140 |
| 10 | FRG | 363 | 177 |

*Sources:* Thiessen, 1988: 272; Kurm, 1989: 12.

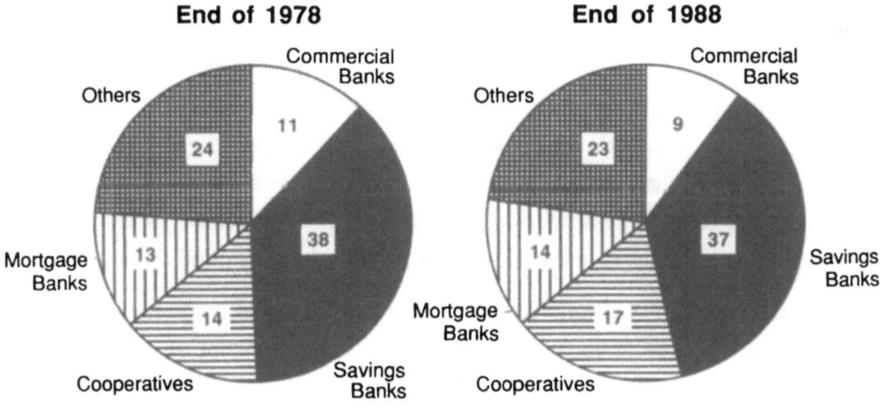


Figure 5.2: Bank groups in the FRG, 1978 and 1988, showing percentage of total business volume. *Source:* Deutsche Bundesbank, 1989: 20.

The process of globalization that has brought about the world-wide integration of capital and money markets and internationalization of financial services not only fostered foreign competition but also increased financial activities abroad. The traditional foreign banking business consisted of the financing of trade which was transacted by correspondent banks abroad. Although FRG banks followed international firms and customers overseas, this expansion path was undertaken much later than was the case with US and Japanese banks, and to a more limited extent. Indeed, only recently have FRG banks begun to purchase branch banks in other countries, to develop their own networks and to co-operate with other financial institutions. Nevertheless, the internationalization of banking is considered a precondition for international cash management, international business financing and financial consulting. For FRG banks, this has had three implications:

(a) they have become involved in international business and can offer electronic systems for payment and capital transactions to clients;

(b) they are represented abroad by branch establishments, subsidiaries or representatives, and gain knowledge of national legal rules, tax laws, regulations and promotion programmes;

(c) they now have at their disposal instruments for transforming their clients' financial policies.

Seemingly today, the concept that 'finance follows trade' is no longer valid. Monetary flows and financial transactions have separated themselves from flows of goods and services and have developed their own world-wide networks and centres. The key issue, therefore, has become the 'commodification' of money and capital markets. For flows of goods, and even more for financial transactions, the 'concept of one world' is increasingly appropriate as banking is undertaken on a 24-hour basis around the world.

Three different organizational concepts may be utilized to understand developing financial services (Figure 5.3). First, there is the concept of integration by agreement + cooperation, good examples of which are the savings banks, regional building societies and public insurance companies, within an overall system based on a division of labour. About half of all banking services for private customers are rendered by the savings banks, one-third of all savings

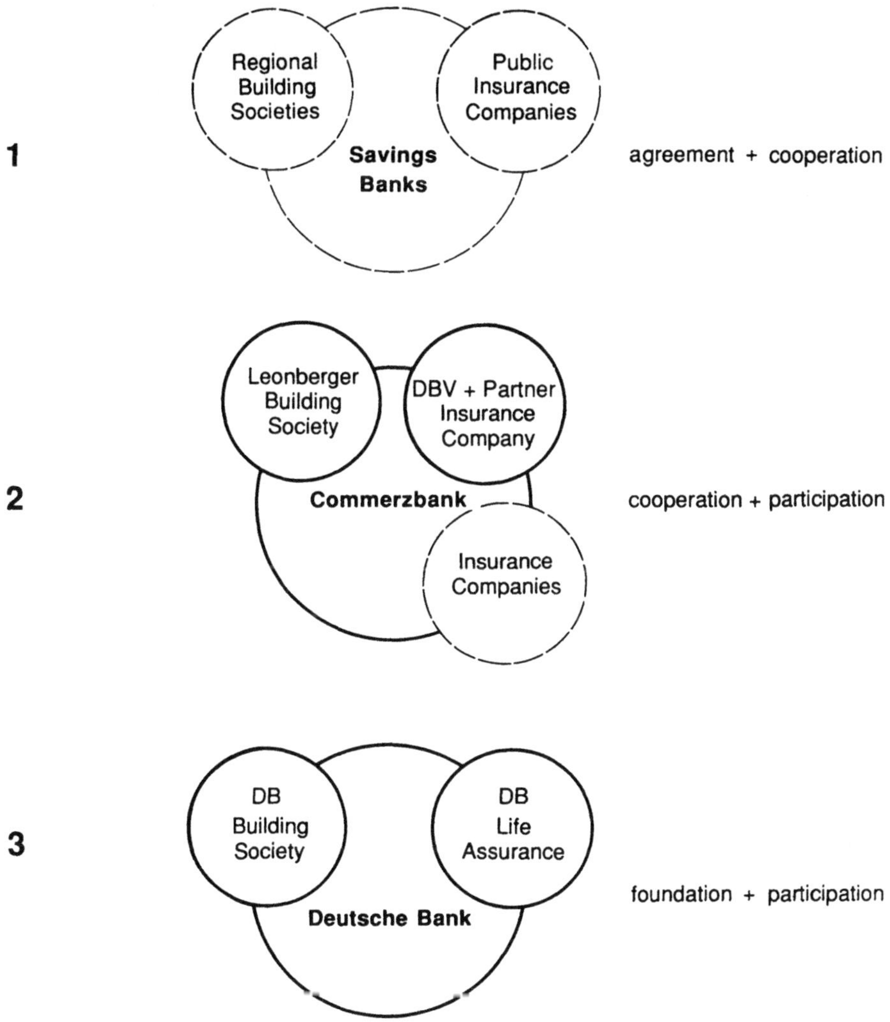


Figure 5.3: Organizational concepts (three examples).

agreements by regional building societies, and one-tenth of the insurance market is covered by public insurance companies. The concept of integration by agreement and cooperation offers both potential benefits and costs. A clear advantage of these groupings is that customer services are decentralized, but this leads to a weak central decision-making structure and competition amongst several enterprises for the same array of products.

The services offered by savings banks, which until recently have been directed towards private households, small and medium-size enterprises (SMEs) and municipal authorities, are now complemented by the corporate financial products offered by the regional banks. These include managing interest and currency risks, financial sharing and takeovers, portfolio management, cross-border leasing arrangements, and issuing shares and securities.

The second concept, that of cooperation + participation, is clearly exemplified by Commerzbank AG — the third biggest bank of the FRG with more than 800 branch offices — which cooperates with 24 life assurance companies and participates in the Leonberger Bausparkasse AG and the DBV & Partner Versicherungs-AG.

The third concept relates to foundation + participation. The Deutsche Bank AG opted for the concept of a multi-corporate enterprise. As own-name products sell better than outside ones and improve market position, a financial multi-corporate enterprise centred around the leading FRG bank (the third largest bank in Europe) was created. This financial group provided a wide range of services through its subsidiaries including a building society and a life assurance company. At the end of 1989, the Deutsche Bank had more than 220,000 corporate customers and more than six million private clients. The bank sought to engage in a diverse range of financial service operations, including participation in the money market, foreign exchange and stock dealing, investment counselling in the European Community (EC), the conduct of private customer business through branch banks, and involvement in global investment banking. Although during the past few years there has been an increase in the Deutsche Bank's international banking and financial service activities, it clearly remains overwhelmingly an FRG bank (Figure 5.4).

Besides the traditional fields of activity such as credit-based commercial banking and service-orientated investment banking, the Deutsche Bank has developed the business of commercial and management consulting. It has entered this new domain of operations by establishing additional subsidiaries and shareholdings, including:

* Roland Berger & Partner Holdings GmbH, Munich (biggest consulting enterprise in the FRG); share of capital: 75.1 per cent;

* Deutsche Gesellschaft für Mittelstandsberatung GmbH, Munich; share of capital: 100 per cent;

* Vaubel & Partners Ltd, Tokyo (consulting for European enterprises which concentrate on the Far East); share of capital: 33.3 per cent;

* DB Mergers & Acquisitions GmbH, Frankfurt (advice and support with the purchase and sale of companies, expansion in the US and establishment of offices in important European countries); share of capital: 100 per cent;

* Deutsche Beteiligungsgesellschaft GmbH, Frankfurt (offer of custom-made participation products for medium-size companies; share of capital: 92.5 per cent.

It is evident that with banks extending the range of services they offer to include payment transactions, credit and savings, investment banking, insurance, building transactions, real estate, shareholdings and consulting services, financial groups are increasingly taking on the character of financial 'supermarkets'.

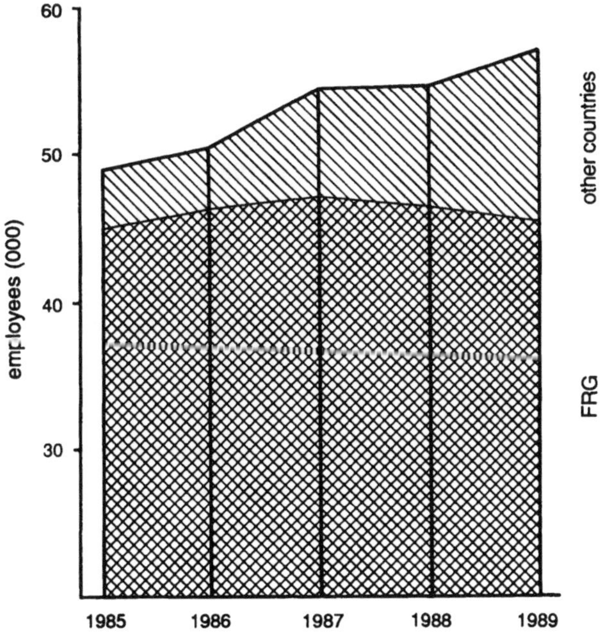


Figure 5.4: Internationalization of personnel of Deutsche Bank, 1985 to 1989. *Source:* Deutsche Bank, 1990: 26.

**Reasons for the Expansion of Financial Services**

Changes in demand, the intensification of competition, and new information and communication technologies have expanded the financial services on offer. During the 1980s, the market for financial services in the FRG changed from a supply market, where selling dominated, to a demand market where (a) more and more wealthy private individuals (private households) and institutional investors required investment counselling and support to organize their assets; and (b) an increasing number of companies needed management consulting as well as advice on issues that included short-term financial strategies, business financing, and broking activities for company shares which are not tradeable on the stock exchange.

At the end of 1989, private assets in the FRG had soared to DM2,805,000 million. Alongside this growing personal prosperity was decreasing confidence in the national pension scheme which triggered escalating demands for professional investment and asset management services. Public and private companies' pension scheme needs were increasingly met by private provision. Accordingly, instead of traditional banking products, such as savings accounts and security deposits, customers gravitated towards such asset alternatives as real estate, fine art and life insurance. It is striking that, as is shown in Figure 5.5, the share of insurances in private wealth formation in the FRG rose dramatically from 13 per cent in 1970 to 30 per cent in 1987; correspondingly, the share of banks in private assets melted from 52 to 42 per cent during the same period. The growing trend towards insurance can be explained by various tax privileges granted by life assurance and annuity contracts. As a result of the new concentration on insurance, banks lost former profitable areas of operation transactions and savings which curtailed their possibilities for low-cost refinancing (Figure 5.6).

Well-informed, yield-conscious private customers not only want advice about investing and managing their assets, negotiating private provisions and risk protection, but also seek help when confronted with particular situations such as when both finance and insurance are needed for buying a house. Business relations between suppliers of financial services and corporate customers expand and surpass short-term financial management, too. In particular, business financing in various guises becomes increasingly important.

Moreover, internal capital markets and investor relations programmes become more international (Pohle, 1986). SMEs, which represent a significant segment of the FRG economy, increasingly require business consulting for foreign and credit transactions, short and medium-term investment and strategic planning to a greater extent than large-scale ones. Because financing has become an important marketing instrument, particularly as far as foreign business is concerned, most SMEs are ill-equipped to meet these challenges because they lack qualified personnel and international experience. Accordingly, the demand exists for banks to supply such firms with financial consulting services, but also advice extending beyond the traditional banking role. In such cases banks begin to undertake the function of external head offices: indeed,

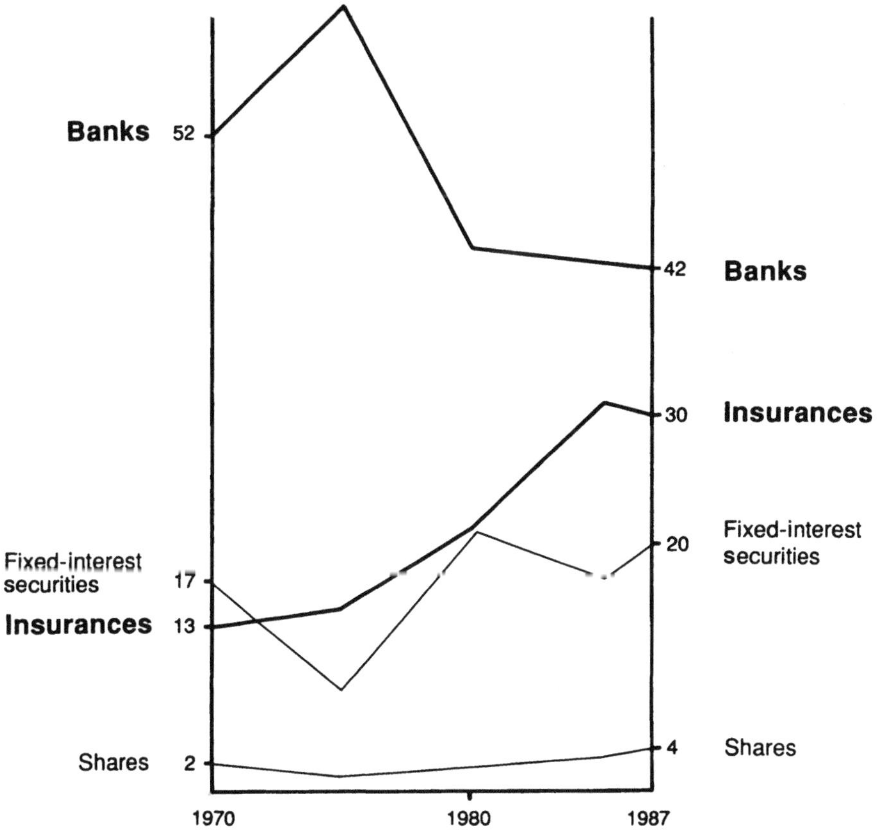


Figure 5.5: Forms of investment in yearly wealth formation of private households in the FRG, 1970 to 1987 (per cent). *Source:* Deutsche Bundesbank, 1989: 20.

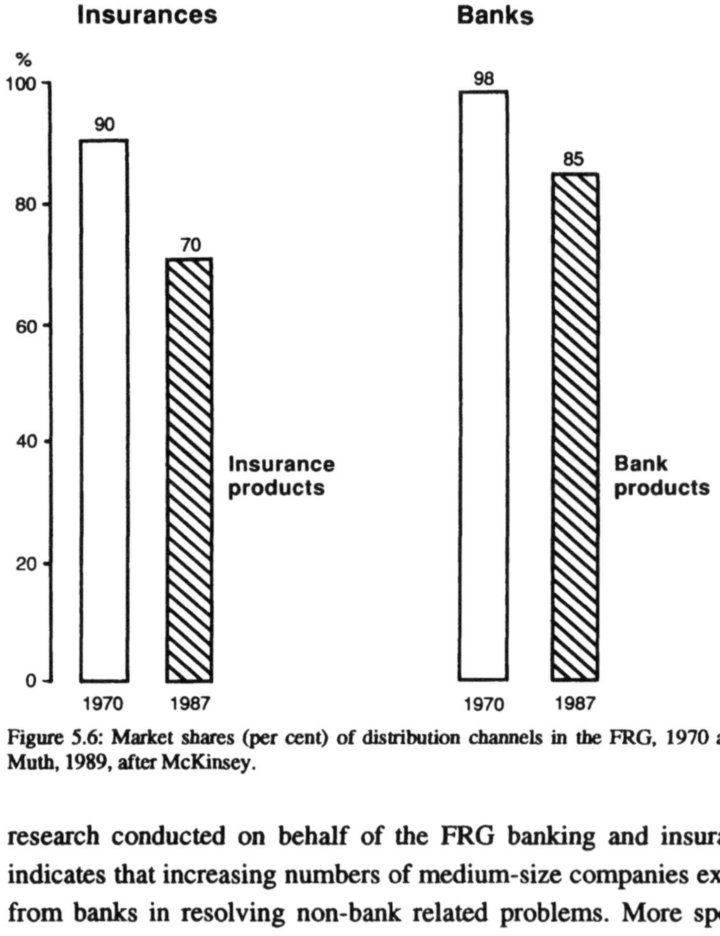


Figure 5.6: Market shares (per cent) of distribution channels in the FRG, 1970 and 1987. *Source:* Muth, 1989, after McKinsey.

research conducted on behalf of the FRG banking and insurance industries indicates that increasing numbers of medium-size companies expect assistance from banks in resolving non-bank related problems. More specifically, they require market analysis and prognoses followed by information concerning technical developments and innovations, advice on financial planning, and assistance with mergers and acquisitions.

Large enterprises show a dual tendency to organize their fields of activities. Whereas purchasing, production and marketing functions tend to become decentralized, financial functions remain centralized, although this is more true of cash management and long-term financing decisions than of capital expenditure management (Zenoff, 1986: 9). Centralized financial services have the advantages of efficiency and economies of scale: decentralized ones have lower costs and regional advantages.

During the 1990s, with the liberalization and deregulation of the EC financial market, new prospects are opening up for the growth of financial services. A homogeneous EC financial market signifies a situation of unhindered access for founding subsidiaries, takeover and merger activities, and competitive conditions comparable with those in domestic markets. Indeed, each authorized bank in an EC country will be permitted to establish affiliates and subsidiaries in other EC countries and offer financial services there. There are two consequences. First, national banks are increasingly going international within Europe which is clearly shown by the growing number of foreign institutions in the FRG. In 1988, 280 foreign institutions from 49 countries held 900 branches, subsidiaries or representative offices there and accounted for 18 per cent of the combined balance-sheet total of all banks (Steinriede, 1989). Second, a significant concentration in EC financial markets, comparable to the concentration processes taking place in The Netherlands and Denmark, will follow. The London consulting firm Lafferty Business Research has suggested that by the year 2000 there may only be 14 large suppliers in the EC including for Germany the Deutsche Landesbank AG, the Allianz Group, the Westdeutsche Landesbank AG and a group consisting of the Dresdner Bank AG, the Banque Nationale de Paris and the Union des Assurances de Paris.

## Consequences of the Growth of Services

Four consequences of the growth of financial services warrant specific attention. These relate, *inter alia*, to the relationships between banks and their corporate clientele, the influence of banks on the economy, the changing composition of bank revenues, and the new staffing requirements.

### Relationships with corporate clientele

Relationships between banks and large firms are both weakening and strengthening. Large firms are becoming less dependent on external economic and financial services, or as Kammer (1986: 112) puts it, 'bankers do not have a monopoly on market knowledge'. They are also by-passing banks by using inter-company clearing systems and in-house banking. The relationship between companies and banks is changing most with regard to routine transactions. House or relationship banking is losing to deal-based or transactional banking (Büschgen, 1990b) because the information position, market orientation and flexibility of firms have all improved. Firms can use their own know-how when looking for the most profitable ways of raising funds and employing capital both at home and abroad. Highly liquid firms whose bargaining power is strong, and those whose own financial management is impeccable, no longer have to rely on house banks.

While relationships to banking in general are declining, it remains important for complex financial products where know-how, creativity and flexibility are more relevant than costs. The large companies, in particular, still maintain close and reliable connections with the international banks and value their efficiency, experience and expertise as well as their advanced technologies and their ability to react quickly to new circumstances (Walter, 1985).

There is no contradiction between companies' efforts to achieve the greatest possible independence for their short-term financial transactions, i.e. transactional banking with selected, specialized banks, and their search for security and advice in relation to longer-term finance and arranging of partnerships that is relationship banking. New information and communication technology allows financial transactions to be transferred to the companies, and large firms, in particular, develop optimization systems for international financial management independently. Companies can therefore compete with banks and management consultants by offering advice on their international operations to other firms, though this is not yet a common practice.

The developing new relationships are exemplified by BASF AG, the second largest chemical concern in the world. It pursues a conservative financial policy and targets the maintenance of financial security, the achievement of an adequate return on total assets and the maintenance of top-rated creditworthiness. For this company, the financial sector is considered a service sector rather than a profit centre. In general, BASF requires the services of international banks which have subsidiaries not only in international financial markets but in all areas where it does business, as this enhances its ability to participate in trade finance and export activities. The enterprise's close relations to international banks are 'based on mutual confidence . . . developed through long-standing cooperation [and principles such as] fairness and a balance of reciprocal advantages and disadvantages' (Kammer, 1986: 112).

BASF needs banks that meet certain performance criteria, which mean credits and loans, banking services on a commission basis (such as foreign exchange dealing and underwriting) and liquid funds including pension funds, and that

> are able to offer a variety of services and take risks as well as to participate in profitable, less risky business. This is BASF's "package-deal" concept. It is a counterpart to the cross-selling activities of the banks and helps to tighten the banking relationship. BASF also cooperates with specialized banks that offer unique services . . . BASF considers its relationship with a bank as an entity on a global basis (Kammer, 1986: 112).

The nascent pattern of bank/corporate relationships is not without its difficulties. In particular, problems may arise if banks betray confidentiality through the knowledge and information at their disposal. For example, information from current account transactions enables banks to gain an insight into their customers' payment habits and business partners. In addition, the relationship between financial business and consulting, a strength of the banks *vis-à-vis* their competitors, becomes problematic if corporate customers perceive a clash of interests between profit and consulting aims. Accordingly, many enterprises refuse to link financial transactions and consulting (Muth, 1989).

**Banks and the economy**

The influence of banks on the broader economy is significant. Despite institutional and legal controls, many banks enjoy a great interest and influence beyond the sphere of banking *per se*. Indeed, the controversial shareholdings of Deutsche Bank illustrate this: by mid-1989 its holdings in non-banking enterprises were estimated to be in excess of DM11,000 million; in Daimler-Benz AG alone they were DM8,300 million (28 per cent of Daimler-Benz shares). This is all the more significant because Daimler-Benz is now by far the largest corporation in Germany (through mergers): among others, it owns Allgemeine Elektricitäts-Gesellschaft AG (AEG), the third largest German electrical enterprise, as well as Dornier GmbH, Motoren- und Turbinen-Union München GmbH (MTU) and Messerschmitt-Bölkow-Blohm GmbH (MBB) which together account for almost all the country's aerospace industry.

A further example of the web of influence of the Deutsche Bank is seen through the example of BASF, in which the share capital is widely spread and no principal shareholder exists. At BASF shareholders' general meetings over past decades, banks held between 78 and 94 per cent of the represented capital — 19 to 24 per cent held by the Deutsche Bank alone — with the assistance of small shareholders' proxy votes and agreements with other institutional investors (Pfeiffer, 1989). Personal linkages and the development of interlocking corporate directorships are also important: for example, the chairman of Deutsche Bank is also chairman of the supervisory board of BASF.

### Changing bank revenues

The third striking consequence of the growing network of financial services in the FRG relates to restructuring the mix of bank income. More specifically, there has been a shift in revenue sourcing from traditional credit transactions to the new significance attached to management services. It is notable that, recently, net fee income has been accelerating at a faster pace than net income from interest.

### New staffing requirements

Finally, the changing milieu of financial service growth in the FRG has precipitated new demands and patterns of staffing. The greater heterogeneity in the range of financial products has created the need for qualified staff, especially highly experienced and professional ones, and those with knowledge of various financial products and the technologies of electronic communications and electronic data processing. These staffing requirements have been met by strengthening their training programmes.

## Conclusion

Changes in both financial markets as well as corporate structure affect the traditional connections between banks and their corporate customers and they are increasingly facing competition from other financial intermediaries and, in certain market segments, from multinationals. Enterprises which are going global to a growing extent need diversified and more sophisticated banking services. Obviously, the traditional influence of banks on the policies of firms is waning thus forcing them to look for new fields of activity. The question remains open, however, as to whether the increasing integration of financial markets and the growing internationalization of financial services and functions will be a necessary condition for the recent trend of German manufacturers to go global.

Deregulation, the introduction of the Second European Banking Directive, and the expansion of the market are generally expected to bring about a considerable increase in competition. About 10,000 banks with 250,000 branches and an increasing number of non-bank financial institutions will be competing for 340 million customers in the EC, including 6,500 large and middle-size firms. The national banking networks will become increasingly integrated and concentration will also increase. Only a few financial groups organized around large banks or insurance companies, which are financially strong, will be able to hold their own. In Germany, the Deutsche Bank is playing a leading role in the reorganization of the supply of financial services. Thus, this 'small regional bank', as it has been called by its Managing Director, is expanding into all the EC countries either on its own account through acquisitions or by establishing branches, or in cooperation with other suppliers of financial services.

# 6 Financial Services, Leasing and Regional Development in the Federal Republic of Germany

E.W. Schamp

Conventional spatial development theory suggests that capital has not limited regional growth. The argument of capital shortage has been accepted only for Third World countries where it has been used to justify, *inter alia*, investments in manufacturing by multinationals. In developed countries, however, there seem to be no spatially defined restrictions to capital access. As Clark et al. (1986: 252) note, 'investment capital is perfectly mobile in space, hence equally available anywhere within a given developed country', although they admit that there are still territorially bound capital markets which can be explained as distortions created by physical distance and the lack of knowledge preventing the even spread of capital across regions. Other distortions may emerge from concentration in the banking sector such as a lack of interest by capital in major urbanized areas of the needs of small firms in remote places.

Recent studies in the US seem to suggest that venture capital is differentially available between regions (Leinbach and Amrhein, 1987; Florida and Kenney, 1988; Thompson, 1989). This is one of the most significant forms of capital supply for small firms, able to foster rapid change in local industrial structure by assisting in the creation and growth of small, high-technology firms. None the less, even in the US, venture capital plays only a minor part in financing industrial change. In Western Europe, and particularly in the Federal Republic of Germany (FRG), industrial change principally seems to take place through investments in existing firms. One recent instrument for financing this process is leasing, which has grown steadily during the past two decades, and thus appears to be an appropriate vehicle to probe the existence of national and regional capital markets in developed countries.

## National Capital Markets and Leasing

The existence of national capital markets cannot be explained by market distortions alone. Rather, they may be accounted for principally by social institutions which govern the limits of the market and its operations. Additionally, a distinction should be drawn between the institutional limits of a market and the economic and historical conditions under which it can function. The national capital market is defined by legislation and established jurisdiction, market barriers, and the character and behaviour of the banks and their clients.

In the FRG, a national market for leasing exists because tax and common law differ considerably from those of most other countries. For example, leased goods are normally entered on the asset side of the lessor, as is also the case in Belgium and France, whereas in other countries, such as the UK and Greece, leased goods are entered on the asset side of the lessee (Pogodda, 1989). Hence, the fiscal conditions for the operation of enterprises are substantially different between nations.

Moreover, given the bank-orientated pattern of private company finance in the FRG (Rothwell and Zegveld, 1985), firms in general face barriers to increasing their equity capital: their equities share is much lower than that of US and UK enterprises. The average proportion of capital and resources in the accounts of FRG enterprises fell from 30 per cent in 1965 to 18 per cent in 1985, thus causing a 'risk-capital gap' (Weichert, 1987). Simultaneously, the ability to self-finance investments decreased. During the 1960s 9 per cent of the national income went towards the accumulation of capital through self-financing by enterprises: this fell to an average of 5.1 per cent in the 1970s, and further to 2.8 per cent between 1980 and 1985 (Weichert, 1987). Accumulation of capital by private households, however, rose constantly, as is shown by the high savings ratio compared with other industrialized nations. The savings share of disposable income of German private households increased from an average of 10.2 per cent in 1961-65 to 12.0 per cent in 1981-85 (Weichert, 1987: 25).

The FRG banking sector developed a characteristically dualistic structure. Large general banking companies operate throughout the FRG, while strong regional systems, principally built up by savings and cooperative banks, emerged as far back as the early nineteenth century. The early Prussian reforms of communal law at that time introduced local self-administration and hence political decentralization. District authorities created savings banks to collect local savings and invest in nearby infrastructure and small-scale industries (Pohl, 1982). Even now these banks are still only permitted to offer their services within a restricted geographical area — normally the county. The 584 independent savings banks (1989) and cooperative banks — the leading collectors of private savings capital and the main lenders to companies — are advantaged by the combination of cheap refinancing through savings capital and exact knowledge of the regional economy. The 'local connection' of these banks is a major part of their success, as bank managers are forced to work intensively in a small regional market. A good example is provided by Sabel et al. (1987), who compared the relationships between 'high-tech and high-finance' in Massachusetts and Baden-Württemberg. In the former case, relationships are almost non-existent as financial services there 'are a world apart' (Sabel et al., 1987: 35). In Baden-Württemberg, however, banks are strongly tied to local companies, including the larger ones which also partly use their services. This particular banking structure is said to have provided a unique advantage in assisting the development of post-Fordist regional structures of production in the FRG (Leborgne and Lipietz, 1989: 18).

There is also a specific client behaviour which turns to the increasing importance of short-term investments and safe profit outlooks (Albach, 1984). Until the early 1980s, small and medium-size enterprises (SMEs) could not be listed on the stock exchange. The main instrument of financing an investment, therefore, was credit from either banks or insurance companies because traditionally in the FRG investment companies taking part in private enterprises have not played a major role as they are controlled by banks which prefer to sell credits (Weichert, 1987). Thus, investment behaviour of companies is not determined by the access to ownership capital but to loan capital, one additional reason being the preference of German manufacturers to maintain their options for strategic decision making through the property of capital. A clear example is provided by SMEs mainly opting to offer only non-voting preference shares to the public.

Leasing was one of the new forms of financing investments that emerged in the FRG in the context of the changing conditions of the national capital market in the 1980s. In comparison to the traditional renting of equipment and premises, leasing offers new opportunities. The duration of a leasing contract may be better adapted to the economic life of an investment, which is usually shorter than the renting period. When the leasing contract expires, the lessee may decide to buy the leased good or share the profit when it is sold to a third party. Furthermore, leasing has been connected with different services. Activities in the investing company, which in the case of renting or purchasing are normally tied to the investment procedure within the firm, will be taken over by the lessor, including purchase of the good; financing; capital allowance; payment of taxes; and sale. In utilizing these services the lessee economizes on its own administrative staff. This is particularly prevalent in a special form of full-service-contract car leasing where the lessor takes over if necessary all costs of the car (insurance, taxes, maintenance and the purchase of new tyres) and also gives a precise cost analysis. Thus, leasing is becoming an instrument to disintegrate the routine services of the administrative organization, which are then purchased from other companies.

There are more advantages in terms of the financial management of the company. Being expenditures, leasing rates diminish the profit on which taxes are paid. Additionally, leased objects do not enter into the balance of accounts which could positively influence negotiations with banks about credit. In contrast to renting or purchasing, the cost of the investment (the leasing rate) can be paid simultaneously with the inflow of profits that result from it. Leasing is, therefore, no longer a financing instrument alone; rather, it must be seen as a range of different services to the enterprise.

## The Growth of the FRG Leasing Market

The first leasing company in the FRG was founded in 1962 as a joint venture with a US enterprise. During the 1960s, leasing activity grew slowly. Although the number of such companies rose from 5 in 1962 to 101 in 1970, their contribution to the total economy remained unimportant. Since 1972, however, their numbers have risen substantially, reaching 1,216 in 1989 (Wassermann, 1989). Furthermore, leasing as a proportion of total investments in the FRG economy increased considerably (Figure 6.1), reaching by 1988 over 10 per cent of total investments, excluding those in the construction sector.

The strong rise of leasing in the 1970s and 1980s resulted from changing conditions and new strategies. First, government regulations altered. In 1971 and 1975, the Federal Ministry of Finance set new regulations to clarify uncertainties about the accounting principles of leasing contracts (Städtler, 1988). The extension of leasing to different sectors of the economy also occurred in response to changes in the legal framework. In the road haulage sector, for example, before 30 September 1986 leased trucks were prohibited from the long-distance movement of goods but this prohibition was then abolished because of the need to harmonize future European Single Market regulations. It remained valid, however, for a firm's own transport to operate over long distances (Wassermann, 1987). The 9,100 long-distance trucking companies (in 1988) were predominantly SMEs. It is expected that the ongoing deregulation of long-distance haulage because of the single market will further intensify competition, and lead to a considerable growth in leasing.

Second, the leasing market steadily expanded in response to the active strategies of leasing companies. Initially, these mainly offered premises which required substantial capital so only a few large companies were involved in this part of the market. Primarily, it was objects known as immovables — plant premises and large items of machinery and equipment, warehouses and office buildings — that were rented. None the less, by 1983 movables' (small equipment) leasing overtook the leasing of immovables, as measured by the annual cost value of leased objects (Wassermann, 1987). The growth of movables' leasing, as well as changes in their composition, increasingly enabled smaller companies to enter the market. Traditionally, office equipment and computers were leased but their share declined in comparison to the growing importance of car leasing for both firms and private households. In 1987, it was estimated that of the total category of leasable movable objects, cars constituted 32 per cent, office equipment 31 per cent and machinery only 9 per cent (Wassermann, 1987).

The emergence of new leasing markets was linked to a diversification of the services: packages of different services and types of contracts evolved. For example, a guarantee of technology exchange was, if necessary, included in leasing contracts even for mini-computers and personal computer systems. A complete offer, including hardware, software and maintenance, was made to

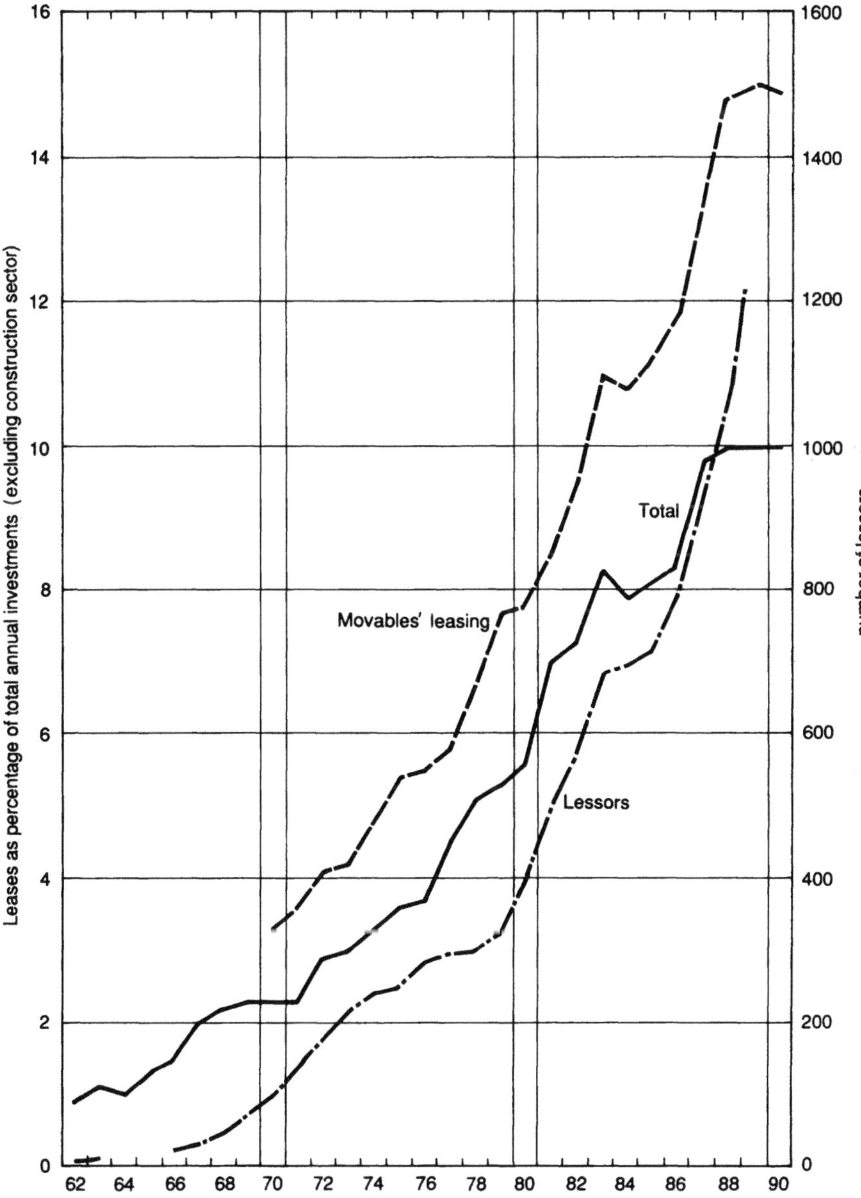


Figure 6.1: Growth of leasing in the FRG, 1962 to 1990. *Sources:* Städtler, 1988, 1990; Wassermann, 1988, 1989, 1990.

smaller companies, notwithstanding the lack of legal clarity about the leasing of software which, because it is not a tangible economic good, cannot be leased on its own.

Finally, structural changes taking place in the world economy have favoured the growth of new financial instruments. One aspect of the emergence of so-called 'flexible specialization' (Piore and Sabel, 1984) and 'post-Fordist' forms of social organization of production is the revived interest in SMEs and new forms of cooperation between small companies. With a trend towards vertical disintegration of industrial production and of new regionally interrelated systems between independent companies (Läpple, 1986; Scott, 1988), favourable circumstances have arisen in which leasing may play a leading role in financing new investments. More particularly, SMEs could use leasing arrangements to rationalize their operations rapidly by taking part in the technical progress of capital goods through leasing movables.

## Regional Distribution and Structural Change of Leasing Companies

In 1961, the US-based Lease Plan International Corporation founded the first European leasing company in London, introducing this new genre of financing into Europe. The following year, the Deutsche Leasing GmbH came into existence in Düsseldorf — also with US participation. The first FRG leasing companies were mainly financed by savings, cooperative, and regional banks. Most were founded in metropolitan areas, especially Düsseldorf, Munich, Frankfurt and Hamburg. Until 1985, the most important part of the market was the leasing of office and computer equipment and this, to some extent, explains why Munich — the centre of the FRG micro-electronic industry — was the initial locus for leasing companies. By the 1990s, however, most of the large ones had nestled in the financial centres of Frankfurt and Düsseldorf.

The distribution of leasing companies in 1988 by economic planning regions (*Raumordnungsregion*) is shown in Figure 6.2. (Such regions consist of either planning regions of the States [*Länder*] or spheres of high-order central places encompassing several counties.) The headquarters of the leasing companies corresponded closely to the hierarchical structure of the city system, with Munich, Stuttgart, Frankfurt, Düsseldorf, Hamburg and Berlin being the chief

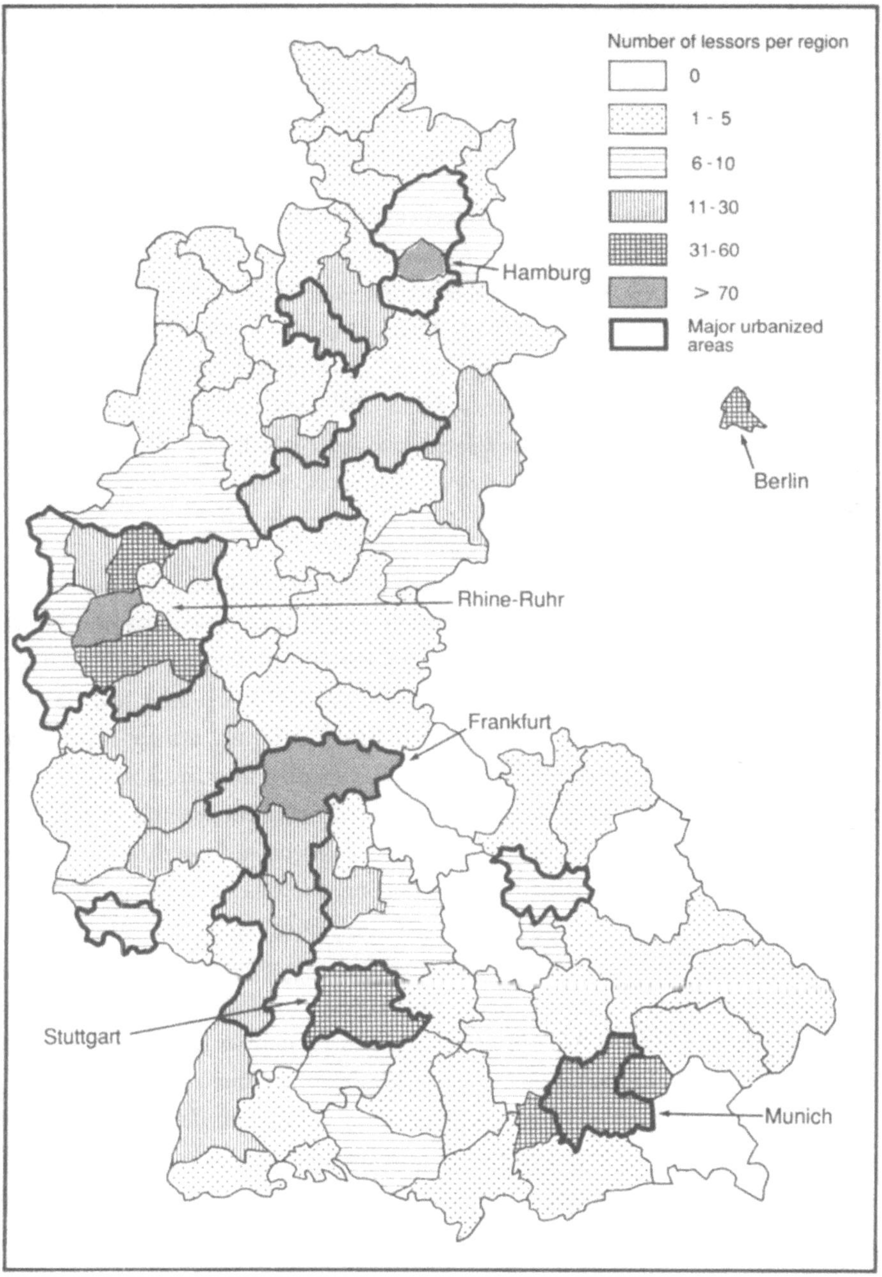


Figure 6.2: Distribution of lessors by economic planning regions in the FRG, 1988.

centres. Branch offices of the largest companies were also clustered in the largest metropolitan areas. Other spatial concentrations of leasing companies were found in densely settled and highly industrialized regions. Few were located outside the main metropolitan centres so that firms in rural areas had to communicate over long distances with the nearest leasing company.

With the growth of the national market, a shift occurred in both the type of suppliers and the goods on offer. Measured by the stock of leased goods, leasing companies of savings and other banks held the most important share in the market, but the companies of trade firms were also significant, albeit small in size. Some banks and savings banks participated in several leasing companies which were orientated towards different market segments. The Dresdner Bank AG, the second largest private FRG bank, exemplifies the influence of such institutions on leasing companies, with its direct and indirect participation being outlined in Figure 6.3 (Wassermann, 1987).

Initially, immovables' leasing was the earliest activity, followed by the leasing of cars, machines and computers. Subsequently, leasing companies began operating in cooperation with manufacturing firms and other banks. Figure 6.3 also indicates the changing type of lessors in the 1970s. At first leasing was purely a financing style of business with banks offering a new instrument through special companies beyond traditional credits and financing through hire purchase. In the 1970s, however, so-called producer leasing evolved as large manufacturing firms began to use it as a sales promotion device. Certain products were exclusively distributed by leasing, such as switchboards and fax and copying machines. Few manufacturing companies had sufficient capital to allow them to establish their own bank or leasing company. None the less, large car producers, such as Volkswagen AG (in 1966) and Bayerische Motoren-Werke (BMW) AG (in 1973) created their own leasing companies and others, such as Ford AG and Opel AG, transferred the leasing business to their credit banks. Medium-size manufacturing companies depended on joint ventures with banks. The FRG's largest leasing company, the Deutsche Leasing GmbH which belongs to savings banks, introduced the so-called 'reference model' for smaller companies: a mechanical engineering company, for example, can negotiate a leasing contract with this lessor when a client is unable or unwilling to purchase a new machine.

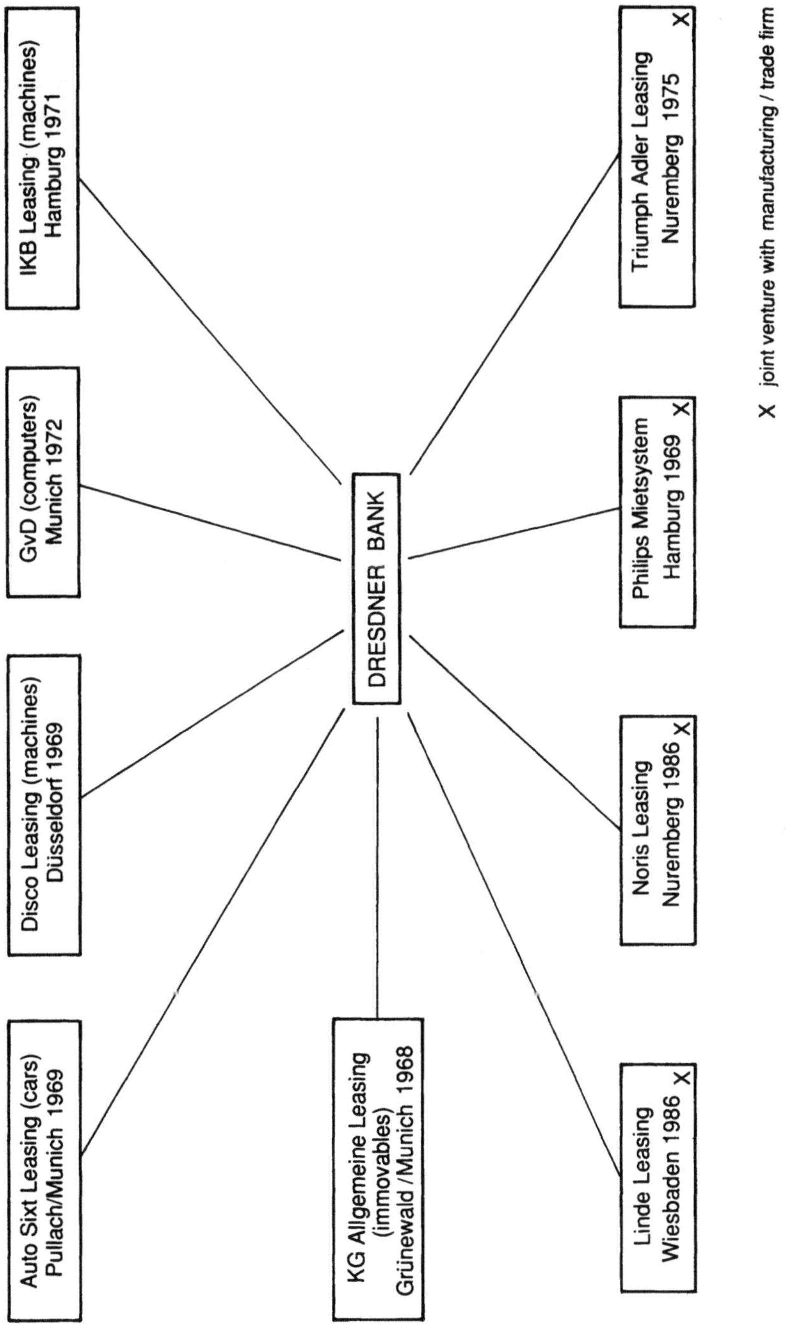


Figure 6.3: Leasing companies owned by Dresdner Bank AG. *Source:* Wassermann, 1987.

## The Growth in Demand for Leasing

Initially, leasing services were mainly used by manufacturers, especially those making capital goods. Whereas in 1970, 52 per cent of all investments in the leasing sector were from the manufacturing industry (Städtler, 1988), the proportion has fallen steadily and by 1985 was less than 35 per cent (Figure 6.4). While manufacturing industry still led, the trade sector, using leasing as a financing tool, increased in importance during the 1970s (Wassermann, 1987). In the 1980s, significant new users emerged in the 'other services' and private households sectors.

Leasing began to diffuse to other sectors of the FRG economy and from large to small companies. During the 1960s and early 1970s, it had been a financing instrument particularly for big manufacturing companies, with the main leased objects being immovables such as plant premises, warehouses, large items of equipment and data-processing machines. Subsequently, miniaturization in the computer sector and falling leasing rates promoted the diffusion of both personal computers and leasing services to SMEs.

Leasing markets do not appear to have been saturated in the FRG as organizations concerned with craft and small-scale industries complain about the low utilization of this facility by their clients. A study in Lower Saxony revealed that over 90 per cent of small industrial companies were in contact only with their local bank. Outside the metropolitan areas, contact was normally with a savings or cooperative bank. Although these were initially the most important suppliers of leasing, such a facility was not offered by all savings banks because they preferred to offer traditional forms of financing such as credit and hire purchase. Moreover, savings and cooperative banks lack competent personnel for offering leasing services of their own which means that they can at best arrange a contract with a lessor. A leasing information gap is discernible among craftsmen and small-scale industry (Hamer, 1988).

During the 1980s, financial market conditions changed. Banks began to guide medium-size companies to the stock exchange, enabling them to find new capital sources for increasing their equity ratio. Hence, fast-growing medium-size firms no longer depended on financing their expansion through leasing premises and machinery but turned to new sources of equity capital and new forms of outside capital. An example is the machine tool company Traub AG, which doubled its turnover to DM300 million during the 1984-87 period. In the early 1980s, the former Traub Company had to lease machinery to finance expansion but in 1986 it was transformed into a joint stock company and listed on the stock exchange. Then, for the first time in the FRG, a company this small raised a loan of DM50 million on the international market for expansion. Subsequently, Traub AG financed all its investments either by equity or long-term outside capital. More recently, leasing has been used for sales promotion, supporting the firm's growth process. Traub AG benefited from the 'references model' of the Deutsche Leasing GmbH, mentioned already.

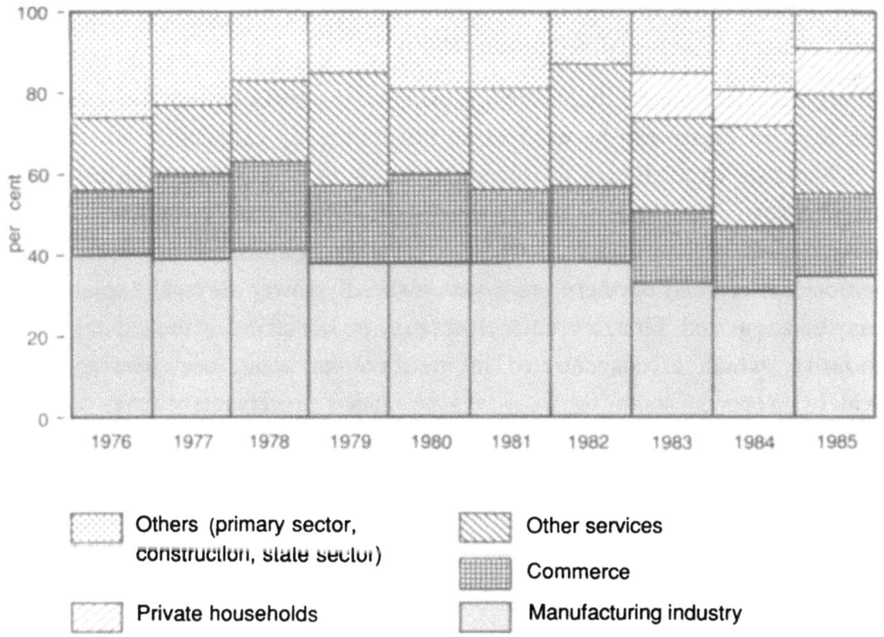


Figure 6.4: Sectoral distribution of lessees as percentage of total leasing in the FRG, 1976 to 1985. *Source:* Wassermann, 1987.

## Regional Development and Leasing

The discussion so far has supported the concept of a national leasing market. Moreover, institutional differences, and hence differences in market behaviour of both lessors and lessees between the FRG and other nations, have been identified. It remains to be considered whether regional leasing markets exist. If legal regulations are the same across the country, the only argument for defining regional markets could be different attitudes of lessors and potential lessees. Although data concerning regional leasing markets are scarce, some preliminary observations are possible.

Applying an innovation theory approach, a top-down diffusion of leasing in relation to both size and region may be identified. Large firms first started this business and lessors initially located in metropolitan areas; subsequently, small firms entered the market and lessors spread spatially. On the demand side, the diffusion process appears to have been similar: small companies in metropolitan areas adopted innovations more rapidly than comparable ones in rural districts (Ewers and Wettmann, 1980).

Composite data on the demand for leasing in the FRG are not available, but the State of Hesse can be used as an illustration by calculating an index of 1987 leasing expenditures in relation to the sum of all gross investments in fixed assets. This clearly shows that leasing was used principally in and around metropolitan Frankfurt whereas, in sharp contrast, its use in the more remote eastern and northern areas was markedly lower. Several explanations may be suggested. First, a branch effect may be occurring as the capital goods industry, which is concentrated in metropolitan areas, uses leasing more widely. Second, some form of agglomeration disadvantage may operate because small companies are forced to spend a much higher proportion of their disposable capital on real estate and personnel, both of which are more expensive in metropolitan areas. Disadvantages faced by manufacturing companies in rural districts, however, include an earlier capital shortage and therefore more need for leasing as a financing mechanism.

The obstacles to the diffusion of leasing to SMEs in rural districts, by both the lessor and the lessee, bring the different behaviour of firms into play. One such difficulty is the mechanics of marketing leasing services. Traditionally, clients were directly contacted by the large companies but because leasing is not generally a standardized service and has to be tailored to the wishes and fiscal possibilities of customers, it demands intimate consultation and face-to-face contact. This requires the maintenance of a costly qualified staff. Small clients, however, tend to use leasing only as a financing tool and often refuse further linked services. This situation, combined with the paucity of customers in rural regions, considerably raises the costs of transactions so that leasing companies have not expanded markets there.

Another obstacle is the behaviour of small companies and local banks. Small-scale entrepreneurs prefer to finance their investments through equity capital. If equity levels are low, they generally attempt to secure outside financing through a local bank and only turn to other sources when they reach credit limits (Hamer, 1988). Leasing is thus considered as a last resort and depends on the entrepreneur's knowledge about it and the information available from local banks which prefer to offer traditional financing instruments. Only if small savings banks themselves reach Federal Credit Control Authority limits do they utilize leasing in an attempt to keep clientele.

This situation may change with the growth of competition from non-local banks. During the 1980s, the supply of leasing facilities has been decentralized through the indirect sale of such services. Specifically, only since 1988 have leasing companies owned by savings banks sold their products over the counter. Because of this, local banks have been pressured to improve their offer in leasing facilities and this, in turn, has strengthened local bank-entrepreneur ties. A further stimulus to decentralized leasing has been the new sales policies adopted by many medium-size capital goods companies which have increasingly used producer leasing to promote sales.

In remote areas, a regional market for leasing may remain because of the specific behaviour of entrepreneurs, given the strong ties between smaller companies and local banks, and the strict regulatory barriers to regional expansion manifested in the territorial principles of savings and cooperative banks. It remains to be seen whether this situation offers a potential for regional development in the FRG or a liability in the face of increasing competitive pressures of the world economy (Bonus and Schmidt, 1990).

**Towards a Redefinition of the Market?**

As the national market for leasing services is clearly defined by social institutions, questions may arise surrounding its permanence in times of rapid institutional changes in the world economy. In terms of the leasing market, two different trends could alter its spatial boundaries, namely the increasing internationalization of medium-size manufacturing companies and the increasing integration of the EC.

Since 1985, there has been a considerable growth in foreign direct investments, by both large and medium-size FRG companies, in neighbouring EC countries, and the US (Schamp, 1988). Large FRG lessors could follow their clients into foreign countries either directly through exports or 'going international' or indirectly through cooperation. Lessors could directly export their services through cross-border leasing, by offering them to a foreign subsidiary of a German firm from their German bases. In view of the great difference between national laws and jurisdictions, however, this manoeuvre has many risks. Although FRG leasing companies, having had some bad experiences, now limit this activity to extremely large projects, they have rarely internationalized through direct means (Eckstein, 1988; Büschgen, 1990a).

The majority of FRG leasing companies have preferred an indirect route to international business by cooperating with foreign partners. Such an arrangement appears an appropriate strategy designed to lower transaction costs, given the substantial national differences in taxation laws and common law. So-called lease clubs have been formed among firms from different countries where members negotiate and execute transactions on a commission basis: the largest of these are Multilease (headquartered in Frankfurt), the International Finance and Leasing Association (UK), Leaseclub (France), and Ebiclease and Interlease (Belgium).

Overall, it is clear that the market for leasing services remains overwhelmingly national, a feature underlined by several authors. According to Pogodda (1989) and Büschgen (1990a), an integrated European Financial Area will not emerge for many years. Different tax legislation, common law, languages and attitudes towards leasing appear to consolidate the national markets. Foreign leasing companies, however, have increasingly created subsidiaries in the FRG since 1985; indeed, by 1987, a third of all new establishments were foreign leasing companies and, in 1989, foreign subsidiaries constituted nearly 8 per cent of all such companies operating there. These deal exclusively with movables, particularly motor vehicles. Among foreign companies, banks and large finance companies dominate, with most coming from the US, Switzerland, UK, Sweden, The Netherlands and France. Foreign companies rarely take over German leasing firms, preferring instead to form new subsidiary operations in the financial centres of Frankfurt and Düsseldorf.

Recent decisions of the European Court to foster the liberal transfer of services within the EC has opened up national markets to a limited extent. Further deregulation concerning the formation of foreign subsidiaries and attempts to harmonize national laws in anticipation of the single market are likely to intensify competition among large leasing firms in Europe. Indeed, an accelerated concentration process towards more international leasing firms is probable. With the liberalization in 1990 of capital transfer within the EC, large leasing firms can refinance internationally. Thus, even given permanent national markets for the sale of leasing services, there will be a growing link to global finance markets.

# 7 Property Development and the Industrial Built Environment in the United Kingdom

**A.C. Pratt**

This chapter emphasizes the production of the built environment in the analysis of the location and form of industrial activities. The dominant theoretical traditions of industrial location and development commonly ignore the production of the built environment. Where it is considered, as in neo-classical theories, it is assumed to be the unproblematic result of the operation of supply and demand as determined by the individual firm. Moreover, in Marxian theories the production of the built environment is commonly subsumed within a functionalist reductionism: in effect such an explanation reduces it to a means of circulation rather than acknowledging its role in production. Thus, little attention has been paid by researchers working in either theoretical framework as to how, why and if the 'demand' or 'need' for property is achieved, and what the material consequences of its provision are.

The contradictory position which has emerged in the UK's industrial built environment, where it is simultaneously a commodity and a means of production, is illustrated in this chapter. As a consequence, the industrial built environment should be seen as both potentially enabling and constraining the location and activity of firms. More generally, the wider importance of considering the production of the industrial built environment in explaining the social and economic reproduction of localities is stressed.

The first section of the chapter argues the case for a rigorous theoretical context for the study of production and the built environment, it being suggested that reliance upon positivism has led to an over-emphasis by researchers on the firm as an unconstrained actor. Then follows a critical realist reformulation of the problem, which stresses the variety of forms of provision of the industrial built environment. Empirical evidence from the UK is drawn upon to demonstrate how financial organizations (retail and wholesale banks, pension funds and insurance companies) have come to dominate the provision of property. It is argued that this restructuring has had particular consequences for the location, form and utilization of industrial property.

## Methodological Framework: Critical Realism

It may seem unusual to discuss issues such as methodology in a consideration of such a concrete phenomenon as property development. However, it is contended here that adherence to 'traditional' methodologies, primarily positivism, has led to the lack, or inadequacy, of research on this topic. It is important to recognize why and how critical realism is different from positivism in order to grasp fully the argument being put forward.

Space permits only a sketch of the nature of critical realism, although further elaboration can be found in Sayer (1984). Basically, the critical realist position has been developed out of work within the philosophy of science as a critique of the positivist position. Critical realists are, like empiricists, epistemologically opposed to idealism. The main dimension of critical realists' opposition to empiricism is in terms of ontology. Empiricists hold a nominalist position, believing that reality is solely what it appears to be. In terms of industrial location, this view leads one to a concern with patterns of industrial activity. The tendency is to look for correlations *between* patterns and to infer causes. This highlights another characteristic of empiricism, namely the atomistic view of the world, in which cause and effect are simply inferred from the constant conjunction of events. There can be no conception of a fundamental interrelationship between things in empiricism as this implies that there is something 'beyond' appearances.

Critical realists argue in favour of the 'ontological depth' of reality. They would be, in the industrial location case, more concerned with what *caused* the patterns of industry rather than the patterns *per se*. Thus, critical realists have a relational conception of the world. This is not to imply a facile position of considering everything being related to everything else. Rather, critical realists argue that some relationships are more important than others by virtue of their necessity in sustaining events.

One example might be the relationship between the worker and the factory owner in capitalist society. Both rely upon the other in order to sustain the causal process of production. However, as is quite obvious, the same causal process can give rise to many different events under different contingent conditions, in this case a variety of empirical forms of organization of production ranging from cooperatives to transnational corporations. Simply identifying a causal relationship is not sufficient for critical realists. Explanations only come from applying this abstract reasoning to particular empirical conditions, the understanding of which may cause the researcher to reconsider the initial conceptualization of the causal process. Thus, the different philosophical positions outlined above have important consequences for the mode of study and analysis of phenomena.

Whilst critical realist methodology may avoid some of the problems of positivist science, it must be stressed that it does not offer ready-made solutions to the theoretical problem of the adequate explanation of social action. Attempts to develop such an understanding have come most notably from recent developments within the field of social theory, particularly structuration. Perhaps the best-known representative of this position is Giddens (1984), although views that are more closely compatible with critical realism have also been put forward (Bhaskar, 1979). The crux of structuration theory is that producing and reproducing social life is the accomplishment of skilled and knowledgeable actors living in society. Furthermore, no unitary meaning can be given to constraint in social analysis; structure is both the medium and the outcome of practices which constitute social systems. The following section considers the application of this methodological and theoretical framework to the production of the industrial built environment.

## Explaining the Production of Industrial Property

While there has been some interest in the interrelationship between financial investment and industrial production (Boddy, 1981; Walker and Storper, 1981; Faegin, 1987; Harvey, 1989), it has often fallen foul of the economic reductionism and functionalism inherent in the Marxian thesis. Useful pointers to a way out of these difficulties have come from those who have concentrated upon the empirical analysis of the property and investment sector itself (Thrift, 1986b, 1987). However, conceptualization of the causal processes has, as yet, remained underdeveloped. Thrift's (1986b: 145) analysis of property services, for example, draws upon Faegin's conception of property actors but, as Faegin (1982: 41) notes, such a taxonomy can be misleading in that property actors often subsume other activities, such as construction or banking, which might otherwise be separately categorized. What is lacking is a more comprehensive conceptualization of the process of property development.

The issue can be clarified by taking one case. An individual firm has to be accommodated and located in space. There, labour, the means of production, commodities, and finance are structured together to create surplus value. As such, locations can be considered to be a nexus of relationships, both socially produced and socially producing. Any *particular* location may, for example, make some firms more 'central' to other areas of production, or workers more 'peripheral'. There is a necessary relationship between industrial production and industrial accommodation. However, the particular resolution of this relationship will depend upon the distribution of power and resources between the firm on one hand, and those responsible for accommodation on the other. These issues are contingent upon specific spatial and temporal contexts related to the particular social and economic structures that exist. Before exploring these further, it is important to comment on the consideration of space and its relationship to the issue of wider social and economic reproduction.

Recent critical realist accounts have reconsidered the conceptualization of space, emphasizing its socially created nature. The significance of space is not unitary or universal; it can, and does, change by virtue of causal powers and liabilities that constitute it *in situ* (Sayer, 1985: 52). Theories that utilize absolute concepts of space in their explanations, such as is found in Harvey (1989: 33) (i.e. the 'spatial fix'), must be problematized. It is not simply enough to be satisfied that space is a social creation; instead it is necessary to inquire into *how* it is created.

The ability to control concrete spaces is contingent upon the 'rights' related to it, for example, the system of land-ownership. Such rights are not trans-historical but firmly rooted in time and space, and, furthermore, they are the result of social struggle. In this case, the struggle is over the form and process of property production which 'creates' new spaces. Thus, the nature of space is an integral part of ongoing social and economic struggles.

Urry (1981: 37) considers the issue of land-ownership to be crucial as it is necessary for maintaining and reproducing capitalist society, yet the capitalist means of production do not create the necessary conditions for its existence. This is a basic problem in the evolution of, and change in, society: how capitalism is reproduced. The relationship between production and the rest of society has not yet been properly articulated. A favoured solution to this problem is achieved through an analysis of specific organizations and sectors in the context of space and time. Arguably, a central actor in this process is the state.

While industrial geographers have long considered the state in studies of industrial location, it has predominantly been either as a further factor in location, or in terms of economic or class reductionism. Some of the most useful attempts to develop non-reductionist accounts of the state are to be found in studies seeking to apply the work of Gramsci to economic geography (Cooke, 1983). An important argument offered by these approaches is that civil society — that is activities not directly related to production — has relative autonomy from both the state and capital. Thus, it is suggested that the particular nature of social relations in civil society at any one time or in any particular place will relate to the development of forms of domination and legitimation by the state, particular forms of production by capital, and degrees of fragmentation and organization within civil society itself. The changing relationships between the state and civil society take the 'concrete' form of new laws which are enacted by the state, whilst the mediation between capital and civil society takes the form of changing monetary relationships.

It is not just social structures that result from this process of reproducing everyday life but the 'created spaces' of the built environment. These forms can both determine, and be determined by, wider social and economic relationships. The exact nature of these will be contingent upon the specific relations of production which exist at any one time as a result of previous transformations of space and society. In short, the specificity of all the previous time and space interrelationships that 'make up' a locality. It must be concluded that an understanding of the articulation of power and control within and between the actors involved in the property development process at any one time, and their relationship to the rest of society, is a key to explaining the form and nature of uneven development. Due to their specificity, their exact form can only be elaborated by theoretically informed empirical enquiry.

## The Property Development Sector in the UK in the 1980s

This section begins with an explanation of some of the wider changes which form the context for producing industrial property in the UK in the 1980s. Thereafter, the forms of provision of the industrial built environment and their relationship with the firms occupying them and those organizations funding the developments are considered.

The key characteristics of restructuring property provision in the UK in the 1980s were, first, the dominance by large financial organizations; second, the segmentation of markets by property type and location; and third, the greater control over the form and location of property developed for investors. After the British property market crash of 1973, caused by over-inflated expectations of returns and the oil crisis, investors lost confidence in property as a safe investment. The little development that did take place during the next five years was a mopping up of the surplus property on the market by the remaining developers and funders (in 1975 there were £2,000 million-worth of unsold property in all sectors of the commercial market). The Property Advisory Group (1975) noted that the number of property companies fell from 129 to 98 between 1970 and 1975. Although restructuring of the property sector had occurred on a large scale following taxation changes in the mid-1960s, the concentration of interests in property development was primarily in favour of size of property company. The 1970s restructuring led to a dramatic shift towards concentrating ownership, as the dominant beneficiaries of the collapse of property companies and their funders (merchant or wholesale banks) were the large pension funds and the insurance companies.

The financial sector in general, but pension funds and insurance companies in particular, have experienced substantial growth in the UK during the past 20 years. The reasons are diverse. Partly, they relate to the increase in the personal savings ratio but, more substantially, they result from the introduction of legal requirements on British public-sector workers in 1974 to invest in occupational pension schemes. Further legislative changes promoting private home ownership after 1980, and the commencement of 'portable' pension schemes from 1988, have continued to increase the volume of receipts for the financial sector.

There have been some interesting shifts in the proportion of deposits held in retail banks, falling from 43 per cent in 1962 to 38 per cent in 1982; over the same period building societies took 20 per cent and 46 per cent, respectively, of the total savings market (Greater London Council, 1986: 27). The most significant growth occurred in the pension fund and insurance segment of the market where total assets were estimated to be £7,000 million in 1957 and £200,000 million in 1984.

As a consequence, funds were searching for new investments at an increasing rate. The Coal Board pension fund, the largest, had assets of £5,730 million (Philipp, 1985: 133). A graphic example of the consequence of holding such huge amounts is illustrated by the case of the Post Office pension fund, another very large fund, which had to find sites for £3 million investment finance *every day* (James, 1984: 13). Since exchange controls were abolished by the British Government in 1979, a substantial amount of British investment has gone abroad (estimated at £40,000 million between 1979 and 1984 (Greater London Council, 1986: 26). Likewise, foreign investment has recently come to play a substantial role in British markets.

Financial organizations spread their investments between gilts, equities and property. Pension funds and insurance companies, via their investments, controlled just under 13 per cent of the equity of all British companies quoted on the London Stock Exchange in 1957, compared with just over 47 per cent in 1988. During this period, personal shareholdings fell from over 65 per cent to just 20 per cent (International Stock Exchange, 1990). Such trends, despite the much-publicized privatization programmes of the Conservative administration and the consequential increase of personal shareholding from three million to twelve million people (International Stock Exchange, 1990), have caused much concern about the concentration and control of ownership of companies. However, the focus here is on the property aspects of the finance sector's investment. Insurance companies typically dedicate between 15 and 20 per cent of the values of their investment portfolios to property. Between 1978 and 1987, the commitment of pension funds and insurance companies to property investment grew from £15,000 million to nearly £60,000 million (Debenham, Tewson and Chinnocks, 1989: 15–16) so that by the early 1980s the funds controlled an estimated 83 per cent of the property investment market.

In terms of overseas interest in the British property investment market, US investment was significant in the early 1970s, but by the late 1980s Japanese, and to a lesser extent Australian, banks had become key lenders (Debenham, Tewson and Chinnocks, 1989: 5). Changes to the investment rules by the Swedish and Dutch governments gave rise to increased participation in the British market by funds originating in those countries. The relaxation of British exchange controls in 1979 and the liberalization of the stock market (the 'big bang') in October 1986 created the conditions for global investment markets; early evidence suggests that British property advisers, such as Jones Lang Wootton, will be key actors (see Thrift, 1986b).

Within its property investments, a typical pension or insurance fund portfolio might comprise 15 per cent industrials, 30 per cent retail, 5 per cent agriculture and 50 per cent offices (Sim, 1983: 106). Thus, the value of industrial property held by the funds at any one time can be estimated at £9,000 million. However, it is misleading to view the property market in such a static manner.

The turnover rates for different types of investment holdings vary. Debenham, Tewson and Chinnocks (1982: 7) estimate that, on average, 45.5 per cent of government securities, 14.2 per cent of company securities and 1.8 per cent of property is turned over annually. However, recent figures suggest that by 1989, turnover for property had increased to 10 per cent for pension funds and 6 per cent for insurance companies (Debenham, Tewson and Chinnocks, 1989: 15). Even conservatively estimated, it is likely that funds turn over £3,600 million-worth of property annually, of which some £540 million would be industrials. The proportion of property held by financial organizations recently has registered an increase, first because of the stock-market crash of 1987 and, second, because of the effects of monetarist policies pursued by the Conservative government in the 1980s which have cut public spending and hence eroded the market in government securities.

## The Forms of Provision of Industrial Property

It is not enough simply to plot the growth of pension funds and insurance companies and their increasing involvement in property development; what is required is an understanding of how this has translated into industrial buildings. This section draws upon an intensive analysis of the development of industrial property (Pratt, 1989) which focused not on individual actors but on the process involved and the changing role that the actors take in it. Concern here is with the causal processes and how they give rise to different events.

The easiest way to convey the breadth of activity and complexity of processes is to consider a range of relations that result in the production of property. The simplest and most direct relationship would be that of a firm directly purchasing land and itself building a factory. Possible variations are that intermediaries may be engaged to arrange the transaction and/or to construct the factory. There is also a financial consideration. The firm may have money available, or may have to arrange a loan from a third party, usually a financial institution. Conditions could be set on such a loan, as they could on the property transaction by, for example, the state in the form of taxation or planning control. Thus, even within an apparently simple transaction there are a multiplicity of outcomes dependent upon local contingencies.

The latter may be viewed differently by firms depending on their organization and relative economic power. For instance, a transnational corporation may well be able to secure a loan at a reduced rate compared with a newly established one-person business which might be considered a greater risk. In fact, the concept of risk is far more useful in explaining the range of outcomes than that of 'supply and demand'.

If this analysis is extended, more complex situations can be considered. If the firm has decided to lease property, possibly to reduce its exposure to risk, then clearly it will become dependent on the providers of industrial property. The simplest situation would be where the factory is purpose-built for the firm, although even in this case the project would be contingent upon the developer being prepared to act. Such action might depend on the property developer's perception of the risk of the potential tenants' not paying rent, and/or the risks involved in securing a loan. The wider context, such as the changing nature of interest rates and the relative performance of other competing potential investments, must also be taken into account.

The hypothesized causal relations presented here illustrate that providing property is a complex process. Although capital may flow into the property sector, what happens when it gets there cannot simply be 'read off', but rather will be closely dependent on the contingencies of place, time and particular actors. This is not to deny a deeper underlying structure, but rather to emphasize the variability of outcomes. There are three key points in this process: the property sale, the tenure of property, and the availability of finance. The concept of supply and demand is doubly contested, first in terms of an oversimplified process and, second, in the implication of a one-way causal relation. For example, the 'demand' of investors for property may influence the 'supply' of property constructed. The exact form can only be explained by reference to the specific historical circumstances.

## The Location and Form of Industrial Property

Even the specifications of industrial accommodation that is not constructed for rental are influenced by the investment rules of the financial organizations. As they have become dominant in the market, those adopted by pension funds and insurance companies have become the 'bench-mark'. The standards for 'prime' property (the 'blue-chip' investments) are proximity to a motorway interchange, construction using high-quality materials (usually brick), and a flexible design which can accommodate a wide range of potential users. A key rule of investment advisers is to spread risks, and a variety of investment types have been created to satisfy this need. In short, the industrial property market itself has become segmented.

A separate industrial property sector emerged in the early 1960s with an expanding rented industrial property market. In the 1970s, a blue-chip funded investment in industrial property focused on warehousing developments; there has been a further segmentation of this sector recently with the modification of planning regulations regarding alternative uses of property. These changes in the 'use classes order' have liberalized land-use controls giving rise to 'mixed use' developments. The resultant buildings often combine manufacturing, warehousing and office functions. Hi-tech and retail warehouse developments, which are manifestations of reorganization at both ends of the production process (new product development and new consumption patterns), have been the key foci of investment. Both are the backbone of many new industrial estate and science park developments. Significantly, in many cases capital returns on investment in these developments have out-performed even some office developments, whereas those of the remaining industrial property sector have been less impressive. The yields of different types of commercial properties are shown in Table 7.1. The percentage yield of an investment is related to the rental income and the market value of property:

$$\text{Market price} = \frac{\text{Annual rental income x 100}}{\text{Yield (\%)}}$$

The lower the yield per cent, the less exposure to risk.

Table 7.1: Prime investment yields on commercial property by type, Great Britain, 1990

| Property type | Yield (per cent) |
|---|---|
| Shops | 5.00 |
| Food stores | 7.75 |
| Retail warehouses | 7.75 |
| Industrial and warehouse | 7.75 |
| Mixed-use business space | 6.50 |
| Central London offices | 5.00 |
| Provincial offices | 6.50 |

*Source:* Healey and Baker, 1990.

An historic barrier to involvement in property-market investment and trading has been illiquidity and size of investments. There are indications that this situation may be changing with the emergence of new financial instruments, namely Property Unit Trusts. The consequence may well be a more liquid investment market in property, greater diversification, and an expansion of the total size of the market as new investors are drawn in.

The segmentation of the property investment market is not only by user type, but also by size of property and by location. Smaller properties imply more users, more rents to collect, less reliable companies, and hence more risk and administration costs for the owner. In terms of location, the greater the distance from both London and the M4 motorway corridor (linking London and Bristol), the more the risk to investors (Figure 7.1). Locationally, 45 per cent of the capital value of the property portfolio is likely to be in London (little of which will be industrials), 20 per cent in the rest of the South and 10 per cent in the Midlands. The remaining 25 per cent, where industrials will be over-represented, are scattered through the prosperous parts of the country (Sim, 1983: 109). Property development that does occur in remoter areas or sectors can only do so, if at all, at considerable risk to developers. It is in these localities and sectors that state intervention has occurred to provide rental accommodation.

Another strategy of risk-minimization has affected the nature of leases. The structure and length of leases on premises have been modified in recent years; during the early post-war period leases were commonly of 20 years duration with rental reviews only at the end of that period. Recently, the five-year review has become standard with three-year reviews not unknown. Furthermore, rental payments are written into leases so that they are a prior charge on bankruptcy, a clear indication of a shift of risk from developer to tenant.

Whilst science parks have become very popular with economic development agencies and corporate investors, financial organizations have been cautious in their approach. There is a strong feeling among both investment advisers and tenants (Evans and Plumb, 1984) that much of the development is investor-led. Two factors account for this. First, there is the nature of hi-tech property development: basically, science parks are buildings with a high percentage of office space constructed on industrially zoned land. As office space commands a far higher rental than industrials, and industrial land is far cheaper than at normal office locations, there is potentially a bigger return to be made on investments. Furthermore, the premium attached to science park locations has led, in some cases, to rental levels outstripping even neighbouring urban office levels (Evans and Plumb, 1984). Second, there is strong pressure on financial organizations with mounting funds to acquire new property to balance their existing portfolios. Clearly, these sectors of the market with more favourable yields are key targets for investment, whether or not there is a 'real' demand for them.

Figure 7.1: Industrial yield contour map of Great Britain. *Source:* Hillier Parker Research, 1987.

## Changes in the Tenure of Industrial Property

The restructuring of the market and its products (industrial property) described above is not necessarily in the interests of industrial users. Indeed, it can lead to a fundamental conflict of interest between users and developers. As Fothergill et al. (1987: 79) point out, inappropriate industrial buildings can have a deleterious effect on productive capacity and efficiency.

There have been substantial changes in the nature of provision and availability of industrial property in the UK in recent years, an important consequence being a shift away from owner occupation to rental or leasehold occupation. As noted, this has coincided with a dramatic concentration of control and expansion in the number and proportion of leasehold industrial properties owned by financial organizations. The statistical basis for monitoring change in tenure is extremely poor: the most comprehensive national survey to date (a sample of just 632 firms carried out by the Department of Trade and Industry) suggested that 34 per cent of all industrial properties are leased or rented (United Kingdom, 1973: 651). However, only 59 per cent of those properties purchased by firms were specifically built by or for them, 27 per cent were previously occupied, and 14 per cent had been speculatively built. Thus, at a conservative estimate, 48 per cent of properties are speculatively built. A survey of 800 industrial units in Cornwall in 1984 revealed that 72 per cent of all properties were either speculatively built, or not specifically built for their present occupants (Pratt, 1989: 277). Prior to 1945 most industrial property was owner-occupied (Henneberry, 1988), as is still the norm in the FRG.

The exact reasons for a trend towards rented accommodation are not clear. Apart from the changing structure of the development process, three factors can be highlighted as significant; these relate to the conceptualization of the development process outlined above. The first is that, on average, industrial firms annually direct some 15 per cent of their fixed investment into property (Fothergill et al., 1987: 17). One option for a firm, in order to release more capital for research and development, is to lease their property. A related factor is the cost and rapidity of change in production technology which has different space requirements, and thus creates the need for more appropriate premises, or flexibility in terms of their design and location.

Second, as a consequence, while interest rates are low — as they were until the mid-1970s — development of premises by individual firms was not too problematic. However, high interest rates characteristic of the late 1970s and 1980s created funding problems. Another factor is the increasing complexity of the property market. There are now considerable risks associated with developments; while land is an appreciating asset, buildings are not. In addition, there is the risk involved in estimating whether the development will achieve a predicted resale value in the long term, thereby justifying the initial investment. Not surprisingly, given this increased complexity and risk, industrialists might want to shift responsibility for development to an expert property developer, or move out of freehold property altogether thereby leaving the owner of the property with all the risk of reletting. Third, changes in legislation have made property leasing a more secure proposal since the *Landlord and Tenant Act* 1954 which secured tenancy for industrial occupants.

## Conclusion

The restructuring of financial organizations, such as insurance companies and pension funds, has led to their dominance in the UK commercial property market, but their property development activities are closely linked to the needs of investors, not industrial firms. Furthermore, changes in production techniques and the internal balance of investment within industrial firms, have led to a demand for leasehold accommodation. A consequence of these two trends is the dominance of the location and form of industrial property by investment needs, and whereas core areas of the economy and growth sectors have benefited from these trends, many others have been less well served.

The restructuring of the property sector has led to two profound consequences for industrial users. First, it has enabled flexibility in terms of firms' capital use but, second, it has also constrained them in terms of location or the productive use of factory space. The relationship between these two impacts in any particular case depends on the relative economic resources available to the industrial property users, investors and developers.

# 8 Financial Reorganization in Hungary and the Role of Joint Ventures

G. Barta, G. Csáki and E. Poszmik

Since September 1989 radical political changes have swept through Central and Eastern Europe, first in Poland and Hungary, later in the German Democratic Republic (GDR) which unified with West Germany in October 1990, Czechoslovakia, Bulgaria and Rumania, and more recently in the Soviet Union which formally became the Commonwealth of Independent States (CIS) in December 1991. During the current transition from socialist to capitalist economies the organization and performance of the financial sector, a prerequisite to industrial restructuring, is constantly changing.

It is still very difficult to provide a comprehensive picture of possible future trends in Central and Eastern Europe so that this chapter concentrates on explaining recent events in the light of the long-term processes that emerged during the 1980s. Because of the various attempts to effect economic reforms in Hungary and Yugoslavia, these economies differed substantially from the original Soviet-type economic model. Moreover, Poland and Hungary were severely retarded by general economic crises aggravated by massive indebtedness, while Rumania also suffered shortages of food, fuel and energy reminiscent of the 1939-45 period. The economic, social and political situation in each of these countries, of course, differed. It is suggested here that 'pre-revolutionary' circumstances and processes will greatly influence future trends in the transition to a market economy and shape the particular character it will take in each nation.

## Political Limits to Early Reform Movements

The Soviet model was characterized basically by a total absence of the regulatory role of the market, by the steering of economic processes through central government commands, and by the state and cooperative ownership of assets. This model, which seems to have been adequate for effectively mobilizing, accumulating and redistributing the scarce resources of the economy to achieve the goals of the state, produced outstanding results at the beginning of the 1920s, but its inadequacies soon became increasingly obvious.

A long and diversified history of reform efforts in the Central and East European countries has involved many modifications and policy zigzags. This could explain the diversity of judgements on their effectiveness. According to Nove (1983) and Kornai (1989), only four countries — Yugoslavia, Hungary, People's Republic of China (PRC) and Poland — can be considered to have introduced real reforms, while others argue that only a few countries, of which the GDR was the prime example, insisted explicitly on the traditional Soviet model. Reforms were aimed at limiting the bureaucratic commands within the economy and at increasing the role of the market.

Apart from these four countries, the others only toyed with the idea of reforms by changing one or two elements of the socialist economic system but without modifying its substance. The efforts of reform movements were always contained or cancelled whenever they would have touched basic political or social issues. Efforts at social change, for example, systematically avoided the institutional structure. Prior to the recent transition, Poland had just begun to experiment with reforms, while in Yugoslavia the original idea of enterprise self-management mostly failed.

## The Hungarian Case

The most comprehensive reform programme that matured in any real sense occurred in Hungary where a special mixture of bureaucratic command and market coordination emerged (Kornai, 1989). Certainly, the state intervenes in substantial ways in capitalist economies but is usually careful not to weaken the effectiveness of the market. In Hungary, even after the introduction of reforms, the state extensively interfered in enterprise-level activity, but the bureaucracy had to bargain with state enterprises and this eventually changed their relative power positions. A horizontal interdependence began to emerge between the enterprises and their suppliers and consumers.

In agriculture, cooperative ownership was dominant. An outcome of the reforms was the abolition of the compulsory delivery of commodities. The growing autonomy of large-scale cooperatives led to freedom in decision making about, for instance, production structures and use of profits. Consequently, cooperatives diversified into other activities so that by the beginning of the 1980s about one-third of their income came from non-agricultural pursuits.

Among the socialist countries Hungary was the first to introduce the household plot system with its private control. Cooperatives were instructed to allocate limited size plots among their members who were free to dispose of the produce. This increased agricultural production used minimal private investment and the spare time of rural households. Finally, the system of family plots boosted rural living standards as they generated about half the average household income.

In non-agricultural activities, small-scale entrepreneurs were allowed to emerge during the early 1980s yet by mid-decade, despite the growth of the formal private sector, only about 4 per cent of the active population and 5 to 6 per cent of the national income were accounted for by this part of the economy. Furthermore, it was strictly limited by the state: a private entrepreneur could employ no more than seven people and had great difficulty in obtaining state loans. Even though the income of private entrepreneurs exceeded most personal incomes, the changing official ideology with respect to the private sector caused considerable uncertainty and short-term thinking.

Consequently, a partly sanctioned and partly tolerated second economy had emerged by the late 1980s. As understood in Hungary, the 'second economy' included both the formal and informal private sectors without regard to their legality. The fact that it involved 70 to 80 per cent of the population and generated an estimated 30 per cent of the national income, explained the higher Hungarian living standards compared to the other socialist countries. However, the extended and exhausting working time for a considerable proportion of the society caused serious social problems, including large numbers of suicides and divorces, a high level of alcoholism and lower male life-expectancy.

The move away from the classical system of the 'shortage economy' can be regarded as a great success in Hungary, with agricultural supplies increasing in both quality and variety and shortages of industrial goods decreasing. The growing role of the private sector in both the first and second economies helped to spread entrepreneurship, the positive effects of which will probably be felt in the future. These changes increased personal freedom but, none the less, reforms left basic problems unsolved while creating new social and political tensions.

The socialist economy, even in its reformed modes that intended to incorporate market mechanisms, has never been shaped by market forces. Competition, prices and other manifestations of the market existed only in simulated forms. State intervention was hardly reduced, while state enterprises retained their monopolistic position and could not become innovative. Reforms actually mobilized the last stocks of under-utilized physical resources, thus enabling further extensive forms of economic development, but failed to capture the creative and innovative capacity of people. After exhausting all the available resources, the economy began to stagnate.

To some extent accelerated inflation can be attributed to the reform movement releasing the strict fixing of prices and wages but without at the same time creating a real market system. Inflation caused increasing social differences between segments of the society and, moreover, absolute impoverishment of large strata within it, particularly young people starting their careers, pensioners and big families.

Further evidence of the weakness of the reform movement is shown by the unbalanced foreign trade. The Hungarian economy, even in a modified form, was unable to accommodate the changing circumstances of the global market or compensate for the worsening terms of trade. Efforts to keep the rigid and obsolete structure of the economy — which meant that even consumer goods' manufacturers that did not pay their way were supported — led to the tragic indebtedness of the country and, hence, to the economic crisis.

The reforms can be considered as a series of so-called non-socialistic elements introduced into the traditional socialist economy. This has led to the appearance of a dual system, made up of the first and second economies, the parts of which are unable to join organically but only exist in parallel in a legal or semi-legal way. Arguably there are limits to the development of this dual system, and substantial political changes are needed to break through the barriers. Even so, the reforms were at best a postponement of the essential need for more substantial economic and political change.

## The Open Door Policy in Central and Eastern Europe

To form new connections with the developed world, Central and East European countries formerly based their strategies on bilateral commerce and credit transactions. Efforts to attract foreign working capital were neglected. The East-West relationship was necessarily limited by insufficiently developed business arrangements, different political systems, and fluctuations in economic prosperity and recession. The somewhat hesitant steps towards opening these economies during the 1980s can be encapsulated by developments in three different but related areas of finance: the rise of external credits, the emergence of an internal system of financial services, and the increase of direct foreign investment by Joint Ventures (JVs). After briefly discussing the first two of these, the chapter then turns to a more detailed elaboration of the role of JVs, especially in Hungary.

## External Debts

During the early 1970s some Central and East European socialist countries tried to modernize their economies by raising external credits. Western countries, especially the Federal Republic of Germany (FRG) and Japan, in addition to the World Bank gave credits to those countries which seemed to have financially reliable and stable political systems. Instead of the intended purposes, however, this finance mainly served to maintain the increasingly ineffective economic systems and macro-economic structures. Finally, the East European countries became indebted to various degrees (Table 8.1). Poland and Hungary almost became bankrupt, while Rumania paid back its debt at the expense of horrible deprivation to its population.

Indebtedness created an awkward dependency on Western countries and paralysed steps towards economic modernization. Yet even after the revolutionary changes, the Central and East European countries are still tending to run into debt because the comprehensive restructuring of the economic system is overtaking the necessary radical political changes. Western bankers are extremely cautious about new credits for East European countries because enterprises rather than governments have become their partners in credit transactions. Thus, Western bankers are reluctant to finance the *status quo*, to increase credits or to finance large-scale infrastructural investments. Hungary probably has the best credit rating because of its relatively long-standing openness to market-orientated countries and its demonstrable progress in undertaking economic and private-sector reforms.

Table 8.1: Estimates of USSR and East European convertible gross currency debt, 1982 to 1989 (US$000 m.)

| Country | 1982 | 1983 | 1984 | 1985 | 1986 | 1987 | 1988[a] | 1989 |
|---|---|---|---|---|---|---|---|---|
| Bulgaria | 2.9 | 2.4 | 2.1 | 3.5 | 4.9 | 6.2 | 7.6 | 9.5 |
| Czechoslovakia | 3.7 | 3.5 | 3.1 | 3.3 | 3.9 | 5.1 | 5.1 | 6.9 |
| GDR | 12.6 | 12.1 | 11.6 | 13.6 | 16.1 | 19.1 | 19.9 | 21.2 |
| Hungary | 7.7 | 8.3 | 8.8 | 11.8 | 15.1 | 17.7 | 17.3 | 20.6 |
| Poland | 25.9 | 26.3 | 26.9 | 29.7 | 33.5 | 39.2 | 38.9 | 41.0 |
| Rumania | 9.8 | 8.9 | 7.2 | 6.6 | 6.4 | 5.7 | 2.7 | 1.0 |
| *Eastern Europe* | *62.6* | *61.5* | *59.7* | *68.5* | *79.9* | *93.0* | *91.5* | *100.2* |
| USSR | 28.6 | 26.8 | 25.6 | 31.4 | 37.3 | 40.3 | 40.0 | 48.0 |
| **Total** | **91.2** | **88.3** | **85.3** | **99.9** | **117.2** | **133.3** | **131.5** | **148.2** |

[a] Estimated.

*Sources:* Comecon Reports, 6(1), 1989; *Heti Világgazdaság*, 5 May 1990: 76.

## Emergence of Financial Services

The banking sector is pivotal in the process of enabling industrial and other activities to develop and operate on a fully free-market basis. Governments, anxious to restructure collapsed economies, hope that the banks will force firms to become efficient by restricting the availability of finance. As the former monolithic and omnipotent state institutions devolve functions and responsibilities, the banks have their own problems including limited liquidity and a lack of trained and competent staff. Because of the critical role of banks and the essential need to maintain financial services, governments clearly must control the banks while taking care not to destroy newly born ones with 'too much competition' from foreign banks and especially not 'too early' (Dugan, 1990). This will probably necessitate a transitional period of a decade because the state sector will be privatized only slowly on account of the great indebtedness in Poland and Hungary, as well as the people's wishes for a rapid rise in living standards. It is feared, however, that some countries will not have this time.

## New Banking System in Hungary

The emergence of the Hungarian banking sector warrants special attention because the list of the 'Top 50 East European Banks' (Gallagher, 1990) is dominated by the 25 Hungarian banks, as against those in Poland (11), Bulgaria (7), Czechoslovakia (6) and Rumania (1). During the 1980s several financial institutions, mostly small banks that specialize in developing a given sector or technical innovation, were established. An outstanding example of the step-by-step expansion of financial services is provided by the National Bank of Hungary (NBH) that became increasingly active internationally. It established the Hungarian International Bank, now one of the most profitable in the City of London and one of the world's largest banks specializing in forfaiting operations (the purchase, without recourse to any previous holder, of debt instruments due to mature in the future and arising from the provision of goods and services — see Guild and Harris, 1985).

As early as 1979 the NBH set up an 'offshore' bank in Budapest, the Central European International Bank (CIB), with the shares held by the NBH and six major banks from Austria, Italy, the FRG, France and Japan, and which was only allowed to conduct business denominated in hard currency. In 1987, after the establishment of the two-level banking system, the CIB decided to operate also in the Hungarian domestic market through a wholly owned branch, the Central European Credit Bank (CCB). Two years later, in order to follow the rapid changes in the Hungarian foreign trade system brought about by liberalization, CIB and CCB also created a foreign trade company (Cibintra). Recently CIB entered into portfolio management and broking at the reopened Budapest Stock Exchange. The CIB now handles about 40 per cent of Hungary's export-related transactions.

The second offshore bank, Citibank Budapest, was established in 1985 as a JV of the Citibank N. A. New York (COIC) and the Central Bank of Exchange and Credit Ltd (CBEC), which is fully owned by the NBH. The following year, the International Financial Corporation (a World Bank affiliate) organized Unicbank, Rt, a new fully fledged commercial bank to promote non-state-owned companies. A JV of Hungarian, Austrian and FRG cooperative banks and Hungarian cooperative associations, this focuses mainly on cooperative and private sector profitable medium-size domestic companies even though it possesses the general foreign exchange authority of the NBH in respect of transactions that would otherwise require special permission.

While mixed offshore and domestic banks were established in Hungary in the mid-1980s, the traditionally centralized state socialist banking system remained, although in 1986 the government agreed to allow a decentralized, two-tier system (National Bank of Hungary, 1988, 1989).

In June 1990 the Budapest Stock Exchange, which was established in 1884, was reopened after a 42-year interval. Preparations for this step included trading bonds to private individuals and establishing limited companies (1984), the beginning of a secondary bond market (1985), and the opening of a secondary equity market (1987). As no regulatory framework existed, 23 banks agreed about how the market would operate.

Consulting as a financial service is of growing importance in Hungary. Privatization, foreign portfolio investment and the establishment of mixed companies are prominent issues so that asset evaluation, auditing and assistance in both domestic and international marketing activities are very important. The market for consultancy services has spawned many new local limited companies and attracted the attention of some foreign leasing firms which, assisted by the local ones, have been able to penetrate the Hungarian market without any preliminary knowledge of it.

## Joint Ventures

JVs and Foreign Direct Investment (FDI) are now the most popular economic and political terms in Central and Eastern Europe because most political forces and social pressure groups believe that these seem to be the only way out of the current socio-economic crisis and the only means of joining the world economy in the early stages of privatization (Charap and Dyba, 1991; Cruszecki, 1991; Newberry, 1991).

Prior to the 1980s foreign capital was not welcomed in the socialist economies. Certain types of economic cooperation existed but these were no more than relatively long-term trade agreements with some buy-back elements. The almost complete prohibition of JVs was purely ideological as it was argued that the capitalist partner directly 'exploited' the domestic ones and, eventually, the country. Repatriating profits — obviously a precondition of the establishment and the operation of any JV — was seen as the expression of this exploitation.

The politico-economic situation is now totally different almost everywhere in Central and Eastern Europe. The only solution to the high indebtedness of all the countries, the need for modern technology, marketing and organizational skills, and the chronic shortage of working capital, seems to be a massive inflow of foreign funds. The current political situation appears favourable for the establishment of JVs as the major and most fruitful way of achieving effective East-West cooperation. As El-Rifai (1990) commented:

> Experience through the world shows that foreign investment can play an important positive role in any country's economy. It brings risk capital, technology, management skills and access to export markets and thus supports the restructuring of the economy. Likewise, the foreign exchange earned and the taxes derived from foreign investment, can play an important part in increasing domestic savings and reducing a country's debt burden.
>
> In addition, modern technology that is often transferred through foreign investment is now more important than ever before. As the global marketplace becomes more and more of a reality, business firms and countries need to constantly reinvest in technology to remain competitive.
>
> In the same time, effective management skills are also important, especially in the competitive, cost- and quality-conscious exporting world. Furthermore,

specific export skills and access to international markets are becoming more and more crucial. Business needs access to distribution channels. They need accuracy and sensitivity in knowing just what these markets want, and in predicting what they will require in the near future. All these factors are of growing importance and foreign investment is often the best vehicle to bring them about.

JVs first attracted interest in East European countries in the 1980s, but the new economic attitude came up against difficulties stemming from the rigid traditional economic mechanism in the unchanged political situation. Even the most agreeable political background was not enough to achieve a rapid major breakthrough (Table 8.2).

Table 8.2: Number of JVs with equity participation in market economy firms

| Country | pre-1980 | 1984 | 1987 | 1990 | 1991[a] | |
|---|---|---|---|---|---|---|
| | | | | | no. | equity (US$m.) |
| Bulgaria | — | 8 | 10 | 6 | 900 | 300 |
| Czechoslovakia | — | — | 2 | 85 | 4,000 | 480 |
| Hungary | 4 | 32 | 107 | 1,600 | 11,000 | 2,089 |
| Poland [b] | 30 | 633 | 700 | 1,550 | 5,100 | 670 |
| Rumania | 9 | 7 | 5 | 5 | 8,022 | 231 |
| USSR | — | — | 7 | 1,800 | 5,400 | 5,650 |
| **Total** | **43** | **680** | **831** | **5,046** | **34,422** | **9,420** |

[a] Foreign investment registrations as at 1 October.
[b] The figures for Poland include the 'Polonia' investments (see Chapter 9).

*Sources:* United Nations Centre on Transnational Corporations, 1988: 301; *Népszabadság*, 7 November 1990; United Nations Transnational Corporations and Management Division, 1992.

Foreign enterprises can only operate successfully if the economic policy and circumstances of the host nation make the proposed use of foreign capital mutually advantageous. Countries wanting to import working capital must first change their economic system and also introduce a favourable and stimulating regulatory environment.

Following the fundamental changes in the political systems of East European countries, companies in the industrialized world have been taking a growing interest in JVs.

**Joint Ventures in Hungary**

Hungary has some advantages that are facilitating the transition to a market economy. Restructuring, organizational changes and privatization have already shown some positive results, the stock exchange is operating, and the real estate market is improving. The establishment of JVs is supported by government bodies, including the Investment Agency, the Hungarian Chamber of Commerce, the Joint Venture Union, and Investcenter. In addition, the regulations for founding and operating JVs are the most favourable of all East European countries as there are no limitations on licensing and majority ownership, no tax differentials between Hungarian and foreign companies, and no restrictions on repatriating profits.

Table 8.3: Number of foreign JVs in Hungary and capital invested

| Year | Number | Capital (US$ m.) |
|---|---|---|
| 1987 | 130 | n.a. |
| 1988 | 227 | 125 |
| 1989 | 1,357 | 425 |
| 1991 | 9,117 | 2,688 |

*Sources:* Központi Statisztikai Hivatal, 1991: 4; 1992: 18.

The spectacular increase in the number of JVs in Hungary is shown in Table 8.3. In March 1991 the registered capital of newly established JVs amounted to some US$1,400 million, of which the foreign share was about 38 per cent (Table 8.4). Most are small with 43 per cent having a registered capital of less than US$15,000 and 75 per cent of less than US$150,000. Over 96 per cent of the operating foreign capital was thus concentrated in only a quarter of the JVs. The relatively high proportion of small companies arises because, initially, it was mainly *émigré* Hungarians who invested capital, and because of the chaotic ownership arrangements and the stagnation or decline of the economy.

Domestic and foreign trading activities occupy nearly half the JVs: the initial capital outlay is relatively low, the knowledge of foreign markets is better, existing business and personal contacts can be exploited, and additional profits are available as a result of the continuing shortages. JVs have a leading role in foreign trade, earning about 10 per cent of the national total.

Table 8.4: Activity of foreign JVs, Hungary, 1991

| Activity | Number of enterprises | Foreign Investment (US$ m.) |
|---|---|---|
| Mining | 3 | 9 |
| Electricity | 3 | — |
| Metallurgy | 32 | 25 |
| Machinery | 979 | 541 |
| Building materials | 108 | 170 |
| Light industry | 528 | 195 |
| Food | 216 | 427 |
| Others | 302 | 167 |
| *Industry sub-total* | *2,171* | *1,534* |
| Construction | 811 | 167 |
| Agriculture | 142 | 15 |
| Transport and communications | 198 | 41 |
| Trade | 4,203 | 440 |
| Others | 242 | 37 |
| *Total* | *7,767* | *2,234* |
| *Other activities* | *1,350* | *454* |
| ***Total*** | ***9,117*** | ***2,688*** |

*Source:* Központi Statisztikai Hivatal, 1992: 19.

In 1990, JVs employed over 218,000, or some 4.5 per cent of all employed persons. Significantly at a time of rising unemployment, these figures are increasing, as are the numbers of such enterprises themselves. The 33:67 ratio of white to blue-collar workers in enterprises with foreign capital invested compares with the 42:58 ratio for all firms in Hungary. Moreover, wages in JVs were 18 per cent higher and, even more significantly, those of white-collar workers in JVs were 35 per cent higher. Such data point up both the generally low level of the national wage structure but as well as the greater efficiency of this kind of enterprise. However, while labour is cheap in Hungary by Western standards, it is now comparable with other East European countries and has no particular advantages over them in terms of skills, qualifications, language abilities or attitudes to work. Thus, the idea of Hungary forming a 'bridge' between East and West is no longer tenable.

## Towards a New Role in Europe

What has been labelled a revolutionary transition process from socialist to capitalist economic systems in Central and Eastern Europe is continuing. Change in these systems is still in an embryonic stage as the necessary fundamental shifts in the political environment are yet to be realised and the new democratic system settled. Many of the legal regulations necessary for a market economy are only slowly emerging and the future shape of national market economies has yet to be seen. This is clearly shown with the ongoing debate as to how to proceed with privatization of the formerly socialist assets both in production and services like the banking sector (Charap and Dyba, 1991; Cruszecki, 1991; Newberry, 1991). Central and East Europeans are ambiguous towards the opening of their economies. Foreign capital is desperately needed but, at the same time, there is a commonly held opinion that a 'sale of national economies' is taking place, at present, both in Hungary and [former] Czechoslovakia (Ash, 1991:12).

What happens in Central and Eastern Europe has major implications for the new economic order emerging in Western Europe following the introduction of the Single Market on 1 January 1993. As a result there is a rising self-interest for the European Community to help reconstruct the eastern parts of Europe. This is clearly pointed out by Johnson and Ash (1990:26).

> first . . . without sufficient help, Eastern Europe could become a nasty, threatening mess. Second, if the aid works, it could provide a positive example for the Soviet Union [now the Commonwealth of Independent States], even through a period of conservative reversal in Moscow. The third argument is that what we spend on helping the reconstruction, we may save on defense.

Hungary is in the most favourable situation of the former socialist countries of Eastern Europe: for instance, almost as many JVs have been founded here as in all the East European countries combined. Yet it is becoming increasingly evident that Hungary can no longer sustain the idea that it can act as a 'bridge' between East and West. On the one hand, the Eastern and Western partners are able to establish direct relationships and do not need intermediaries while, on the other, the Eastern partners are moving into an ever-deepening economic crisis and are in no position to join the international economy.

# 9 Foreign Enterprises in an 'Economy in Transition': The Example of Poland

**R. Matykowski and T. Stryjakiewicz**

Eastern Europe in the early 1980s could be characterized as 'a global region in the melting pot' (Hamilton, 1990); now it is a region in what may be termed 'post-communist' transition. Accompanying the changing politico-economic systems are fundamental alterations in the operating conditions of economic enterprises. Under the former socialist economic systems their functioning was determined by several factors which are absent in a free-market capitalist economy. These included:

(a) the centralization of investment decisions and the absence of capital markets;

(b) a political character to the location of many investments;

(c) lack of operational independence of enterprises (for example in setting prices and wages);

(d) an unequal treatment of economic actors with the state-run sector having a privileged position and restrictions on the operation of private firms and foreign capital;

(e) a warped price system in relation to the world system and exorbitant government subsidies;

(f) the inconvertibility of currencies and the artificial character of exchange rates (at one time in Poland 17 official dollar rates were counted);

(g) the appointment of managers other than by the criteria of professional qualifications and competence.

The functioning of the socialist economic system, based on such 'principles', led to a crisis and the disappearance of competitive business behaviour among individuals and firms. Some of its manifestations were the permanent shortage of both consumer goods and investment funds, serious debts, and the 'falling out' from the international division of labour (Kornai, 1980). The Polish economy is a glaring example of regulatory mechanisms thrown out of gear:

what exists at the beginning of the 1990s can be called an 'economy in transition'. More specifically, the country is striving to put the regulatory mechanisms in order again, but currently faces a situation in which the old determinants have stopped functioning while the new ones have yet to become consolidated. The reforms carried out in the early 1990s in Poland and in other countries of Eastern Europe aimed to facilitate a transition from the former socialist centralized economic system to a free-market one (or at least its approximation) allowing foreign capital to participate. This transition requires many barriers to be overcome, one of the most difficult being the transformation of ownership and sector structures. A serious obstacle to such changes is the scarcity of capital and this has prompted efforts to encourage foreign investment. The potential role of foreign investors, however, is not simply to fill the gaps in the utilization of state-owned production assets. As the President of the Foreign Investment Agency, stated in February 1989 in an interview with the weekly *Wprost* (Skajuj, 1989: 4):

> We have squeezed everything possible out of the economy as it is now. What it needs is a general restructuring . . . Our torpid state capital is incapable, of itself, without a stimulus from outside, of restructuring the economy quickly and efficiently. What we need is an aggressive . . . foreign capital. It is expected to force dynamic market behaviour on state-run firms.

The goals set foreign investors by the government differ, however, from the goals of the other actors involved, as Table 9.1 shows.

The 'state of transition' across Eastern Europe in the early 1990s offers interesting research opportunities about the behaviour of industrial organizations. The fundamental determinant of behaviour is uncertainty following, among other things, from the instability of the legal and financial systems. This chapter investigates the roles of foreign enterprises, capital and joint ventures (JVs) in the transitional Polish economy. First, it reviews the nature of foreign investment in post-communist Eastern Europe; second, it analyzes the 'rules' in the Polish legal and financial systems which control the functioning and performance of foreign enterprises; and, third, it considers the role of foreign firms in the national economy and the directions of foreign links. Finally, attention turns to the locational trends of foreign firms.

Table 9.1: Goals set Joint Ventures by various actors

***Government***

Access to advanced technologies
Additional source of investment capital
Increasing exports and resources of convertible currencies
Enriching the home market
Improving management, quality and effectiveness of production
Restructuring the economy (including ownership transformation)

***Domestic enterprises***

Possibility of free fixing of wages and their growth
Source of financing investment and import of materials
Promotion of exports
Possibility of tax exemption

***Foreign co-partners***

Quick and relatively easy profit even with small initial capital
Minimizing investment costs and/or production costs
Exploring new sources of materials and new markets
Providing against competition and economic fluctuations

*Source:* Authors' research.

## Foreign Investment in Post-Communist Eastern Europe

Across post-communist Eastern Europe there are differential possibilities for foreign investment with the scope of such activities being defined by special legislation. The comparison of the 'key rules' for such investment in selected socialist countries which created the institutional environment at the end of the 1980s (Table 9.2) shows that Hungary offered the most advantageous legal and financial conditions. Indeed, as it had the most advanced economic reforms in Eastern Europe, Hungary was also the most successful country in attracting foreign business during the 1980s as is indicated by the fact that at the end of 1988 there were over 220 foreign firms (including JVs) with assets of some US$200 million (Tarnowski, 1989; Hungary, Ministry of Foreign Affairs, 1991). During the 1980s, an increase in the number of foreign enterprises also took place in Poland where by the end of 1988 there were 52 JVs with a capital of US$40 million, as well as 787 small manufacturing enterprises (often called *Polonia* firms) set up by foreigners of Polish origin which had invested about US$120 million. In the USSR, the process of establishing enterprises with foreign capital involvement only began in 1987, much later than in other East European countries. Nevertheless, some progress occurred: during the first year of the new regulations, in 1987-88, 19 foreign firms were established and several hundred additional proposals were under consideration. These three countries showed the greatest interest in wooing foreign investors. By contrast, in the former German Democratic Republic (GDR), foreign firms were non-existent; in Czechoslovakia there were only two JVs; and in Rumania there were only five foreign-linked enterprises by 1987. The example of Bulgaria is interesting because, despite liberal regulations such as low income tax (at 20 per cent), only 15 companies had been established after seven years of trying to garner foreign investors.

Table 9.2: Rules applying to JVs in selected socialist countries, 1989

**Poland**

*Scope of activity*
Profit-orientated production, construction, trade and services

*Agency giving permission to set up Joint Ventures*
Foreign Investment Agency

*Share of foreign partner*
Maximum up to 100 per cent; minimum 20 per cent of initial capital

*Taxation of profits/income tax*
40 per cent. Exemption for first 3 years with possibility of prolonging to 6 years; tax reduction by 0.4 per cent for each 1 per cent of goods and services exported; tax reductions for reinvestment of profits

*Transfer of profits abroad*
Only from excess of exports over imports after selling Polish bank 15 per cent of export proceeds

*Managerial positions not available to foreigners*
No limitations

*Table 9.2 continued*

**Hungary**

*Scope of activity*
No limitations on any economic sector

*Agency giving permission to set up Joint Ventures*
Minister of Finance if foreign partner has most shares; otherwise simple registration

*Share of foreign partner*
No limitations

*Taxation of profits/income tax*
40 per cent. In priority sectors (e.g. tourism and hotels) 20 per cent for first 5 years then 30 per cent; in branches of special importance for economy, exemption for first 5 years then 20 per cent

*Transfer of profits abroad*
Without limitations through National Hungarian Bank in currency agreed on in memorandum

*Managerial positions not available to foreigners*
No limitations

**USSR**

*Scope of activity*
Not defined

*Agency giving permission to set up Joint Ventures*
Multi-level system of decision making; final decision taken by Council of Ministers

*Share of foreign partner*
Less than 100 per cent

*Taxation of profits/income tax*
30 per cent of total profit after deduction of means for reserve fund; exemption during first 2 years, later possible reductions

*Transfer of profits abroad*
Possible after payment of additional 20 per cent tax

*Managerial positions not available to foreigners*
Chairman of supervisory board, general manager (the possibility exists of these restrictions being lifted)

*Table 9.2 continued*

**Bulgaria**

*Scope of activity*
All branches of production and services except banking, insurance and telecommunications

*Agency giving permission to set up Joint Ventures*
Council of Ministers

*Share of foreign partner*
No limitations

*Taxation of profits/income tax*
20 per cent. Possibility of full or partial exemption for 3 years

*Transfer of profits abroad*
Possible after payment of additional 10 per cent tax

*Managerial positions not available to foreigners*
Chairman of supervisory board, general manager

**Czechoslovakia**

*Scope of activity*
Industrial production

*Agency giving permission to set up Joint Ventures*
Appropriate ministry in agreement with Planning Committee, Ministry of Finance, Ministry of Foreign Trade and national bank

*Share of foreign partner*
Maximum 49 per cent

*Taxation of profits/income tax*
50 per cent

*Transfer of profits abroad*
Possible after payment of additional 25 per cent tax

*Managerial positions not available to foreigners*
Key positions in company

*Table 9.2 continued*

**Rumania**

*Scope of activity*
All branches of production and services except banking, insurance and telecommunications

*Agency giving permission to set up Joint Ventures*
Council of Ministers

*Share of foreign partner*
Maximum 49 per cent

*Taxation of profits/income tax*
30 per cent. Right to yearly exemption and 2-year 50 per cent reduction

*Transfer of profits abroad*
Possible after payment of additional 10 per cent tax

*Managerial positions not available to foreigners*
Director of company

*Sources:* Economic and Social Council Economic Commission for Europe, 1988; Tarnowski, 1989; authors' research.

According to the Economic and Social Council Economic Commission for Europe (1988), the major sources of foreign investment in post-communist Eastern Europe have been the Federal Republic of Germany (FRG) and Austria, which accounted for 25 and 22 per cent, respectively, of the total number of companies. About half of all the enterprises are producing investment and consumer goods; in addition there are many trading, building, tourist, consulting and technical-service firms. The typical investment path begins with a trading, cooperation or licence-related contract. Despite many bureaucratic obstacles, only 5 per cent of all JVs have ended in bankruptcy or the dissolution of the partnership, which may reflect the great caution with which partners enter such businesses.

Recent data show a rapid growth of enterprises with foreign participation not only in Hungary and Poland but also in the [former] USSR and Czechoslovakia. This has been facilitated by legislative liberalization, detailed by Vukmir (1989) and Buhl and Schulz (1991). The new, frequently changing, laws in most countries not only provide more favourable taxation and abolish many of the restrictions set out in Table 9.2 (especially those relating to the scope of permissible activity of foreign firms, share of foreign partners, and transfer of profits) but also merge foreign investments with the programmes of privatization. It is difficult to give a precise up-to-date number of foreign enterprises, because not all firms registered are actually operating (a difference particularly marked in the USSR). The Economic Commission for Europe estimates there were 6,836 JVs in October 1990, whereas the Austrian Ministry of Economics puts their number early in 1991 at about 13,000 of which about 5,000 were in Hungary, 3,000 in Poland, 2,600 in the former Soviet Union, 1,700 in Czechoslovakia and 700 in other countries (Buhl and Schulz, 1991: 81). The leading role of Germany and Austria as the main sources of capital in Eastern Europe has not been changing. Although from the point of view of international business, the volume of foreign capital involved is small — for example in 1989-90 US$800 million entered Hungary, the most successful country — and small JVs still predominate, there are some indications of an influx of larger companies such as Volkswagen AG, General Motors Corp., General Electric Company, Philips Electronics NV, Siemens AG, Hyundai Ltd and Levi Strauss International.

A second feature of East European foreign investment relates to JVs formed and operating in the West (Lebkowski and Monkiewicz, 1987; McMillan, 1987, 1989; Economic and Social Council Economic Commission for Europe, 1988; Economou, 1990). In 1977, East European socialist countries were involved in 283 such enterprises, in 1987 in 416, and at the end of 1989 in 579. These mostly came from Hungary (152 JVs in 1988), Poland (143), and the USSR (135) and were mainly located in the FRG (109), the UK (71) and Austria (61). The character of these enterprises differs from parallel JVs in the socialist countries as they were created mainly to promote their exports. Only in Hungary were any attempts made to establish production operations in the West but even then only on a modest scale. Towards the end of the 1980s a number of marketing and trade enterprises, however, gradually began to engage in activities beyond export promotion. The larger of them became involved in transport, distribution, technical servicing and manufacturing in order to ensure flexibility of supplies and to modify products according to Western specifications and tastes (Economou, 1990: 46).

Despite these efforts, the role of JVs involved in manufacturing, extraction, processing and assembling in the developed countries remains insignificant (accounting for only 6 per cent of all JVs at the end of 1988). In contrast, East European JVs operating in the developing countries, estimated to number 268 at the end of 1989 (98 in Africa, 60 in the Middle East, 59 in Latin America and 51 in Asia), are directed more towards primary and manufacturing production as well as providing engineering and construction services.

The final dimension relates to the establishment of JVs between the East European countries themselves, although this occurred slowly. For example, in Poland at the close of 1988, there were only three JVs with Soviet enterprises and one with a Hungarian firm. Sadzikowski (1989) suggests several reasons for the lack of such developments:

(a) the incomparability of prices, which were contracted and did not reflect world pricing;

(b) the artificiality of exchange rates and the 'fictitious' nature of the common currency of the socialist countries, namely the transferable rouble;

(c) the lack of surplus goods and services over domestic demand;

(d) the similarity of technological levels reducing the interests of partners;

(e) the history of government isolation of enterprises from participation in the international division of labour.

With political and economic changes gaining momentum in Eastern Europe, a key research issue is the impacts of the evolution of the legal and financial systems for foreign investment. Attention now turns to the experiences gathered in Poland where foreign firms have been operating for almost 15 years.

## Polish Legal and Financial Rules for Foreign Enterprises

In the socialist political and economic system that began to take root in Poland after the Second World War there was little place for foreign investment. Indeed, a 1946 law limited the possibility of this kind of involvement. Hence, during the 1950s and 1960s, only a trickle of enterprises with foreign participation appeared in Poland, mainly from socialist countries as a result of bilateral inter-governmental agreements. One such enterprise, intended to be a model of socialist cooperation, was the Polish-Hungarian Mining Stock Company 'Haldex' in Katowice which recovers hard coal from mine dumps.

The foundations of a changing politico-economic environment about foreign investment were laid by the ordinance of the Council of Ministers of 14 May 1976. This set out principles according to which various agencies could grant permission for foreign legal and natural persons to operate in Poland. In particular, it provided for foreign firms to set up in the crafts, trade, catering and hotel sectors. Behind this new legislative environment were political rather than economic motivations. The first foreign small manufacturing enterprises (those employing fewer than 50 people) were founded in 1977 and were of Polish ethnic origin: by the end of 1981 they numbered about 130. The imposition of martial law on 13 December 1981 drastically reduced the flow of foreign capital in the form of loans, thereby diminishing home market supplies. Against this background, a law was passed in July 1982 setting down rules for economic activity in the domain of small manufacturing undertaken by foreigners. Owners of firms were obliged to place on deposit at the Polish Bank an equivalent of a fixed minimum investment capital in convertible currency, an amount of about 0.8 to 4 million złotys or US$10,000 to US$50,000 at the then official rate. Such enterprises were exempt from income tax for the first three years of their operation. It was envisaged that they would contribute towards enriching the domestic market (e.g. with cosmetics, toilet articles and chocolates); transferring advanced technologies to the local economy (e.g. personal computers); and promoting exports.

The new legal regulations aroused interest among several small businesses in Western Europe and North America and, despite official political and economic boycotts against Polish authorities by the governments of these countries, 565 had been established by March 1984. The office of the Government Plenipotentiary for Foreign Firms of Small Manufacture was created in 1982 to coordinate and control their operation but in fact permission to establish a foreign business was granted by a voivodeship office (a regional level). This usually also involved obtaining the opinion of local commune authorities about the benefits that such a firm would bring. Furthermore, the voivodeship office defined the maximum number of people to be employed. In some cases, granting permission also involved the Ministry of Communications or other ministries. Most of these foreign enterprises characteristically had a good labour organization, high efficiency levels, reasonably modern technologies and relatively high wages. Small foreign firms also played an important role in fostering exports (Table 9.3). In 1985, however, the legislative environment facing foreign investors in Poland was made less attractive when the government amended the 1982 law. The new regulations involved, *inter alia*, increasing income and turnover taxes, stipulating that firms had to sell half their export proceeds to the Polish Bank, and raising the founder's deposit in convertible currency to US$50,000. Such regulations led to a considerable decrease in the formation of new foreign businesses and a change in the behaviour of existing ones, many of which focused on risk minimization.

Table 9.3: Production and exports of small manufacturing enterprises in Poznań voivodeship, 1985

| Type of enterprise | Production | | Exports | |
|---|---|---|---|---|
| | złotys (000m.) | per cent | złotys (000m.) | per cent |
| Polish private workshops/crafts | 28.3 | 40 | 0.36 | 20 |
| Foreign firms | 15.6 | 22 | 0.77 | 43 |
| Cooperatives | 26.9 | 38 | 0.67 | 37 |
| Total | 70.8 | 100 | 1.80 | 100 |

*Source:* Hauser, 1987.

The 1982 law, with the 1985 amendments, allowed foreigners to create ventures with Polish enterprises under various forms of ownership. By 1986, however, a mere 14 JVs had been established, and these only with private firms. As a result, further legislation enacted on 23 April 1986 clarified the conditions surrounding the financing of mixed-capital enterprises with state-run or cooperative enterprises as co-partners holding at least 51 per cent of the capital. In contrast to the 1985 law, conveniences in taxation and export settlements were introduced. Permits to establish JVs were to be issued by a central agency — the Ministry of Foreign Trade — in agreement with the Ministry of Finance. The new legislative regime was intended to secure conditions for establishing strong companies with the participation of some large and relatively modern state-run and cooperative enterprises (e.g. to increase export possibilities), and to create competition between these new companies and existing small foreign firms operating on the basis of the 1982 law. During the 1986-88 period, 52 of these Polish-foreign companies were spawned in the context of this shifting legislative milieu.

An attempt to unify the rules affecting the operations of foreign investors in Poland was made on 23 December 1988 with laws providing that foreign investment activity could be conducted in the form of a limited liability or a joint stock company established jointly by Polish and foreign parties, or solely by foreign parties, or even a one-person business. The Foreign Investment Agency became the sole central administrative authority empowered to issue permits for foreign businesses. The minimum initial capital was set at 25 million złotys (equivalent to US$50,000 at the official rate) and the income tax level at 40 per cent. Moreover, companies had to sell 15 per cent of their foreign currency export proceeds to a Polish foreign exchange bank. When provision was made in December 1989 for the internal convertibility of the złoty, the financial rules governing the functioning of foreign firms, as of all the enterprises in Poland, were changed, one of the most significant being the cancellation of most restrictions about the transfer of profits abroad. Legislation passed on 14 June 1991 lifted the 'automatic' three-year tax holiday but abolished many bureaucratic obstacles, simplified registration procedures, and guaranteed repatriation of all after-tax profits and capital invested as well as compensation for all losses resulting from expropriation or similar events. Moreover, it merged foreign investment law with the legislation of 13 July 1990 that privatized state-owned enterprises, thus stressing the potential role of foreign capital in transforming the ownership of the Polish economy.

Thus during the 15-year period of foreign investment operations in Poland, the legal and financial system has shown much instability. Indeed, regulations have been altered six times during this relatively short time-span and the average duration of laws was, therefore, only 30 months. In recognition of this situation, the 1989 Act guaranteed a five-year period of stable regulations about income tax and the transfer of profits.

## Foreign Firms in the Polish Economy and Their Foreign Links

Given this shifting environment, by 1990 foreign involvement in Poland took place under various layers of legal measures, two being particularly important.

(a) The 1982 law (amended in 1985): Type A, embraced 787 small manufacturing enterprises established by 31 December 1988, and will operate on the basis of this law until the expiry of their permits, valid for 20 years.

(b) The 1988 law: Type B, embraced 52 companies in which foreign (and local Polish) capital participated that were established during the 1986-88 period and all foreign firms set up after 1 January 1989. In November 1989 there were 657 Type B firms and in March 1990 1,145; by the end of September 1991 4,808 licences had been granted with foreign shares amounting to US$670 million.

In June 1988, small foreign Type A manufacturing businesses employed 73,300 workers of whom 83 per cent were in industry and 16 per cent in construction. The spheres of industry attracting most foreign investment were light industry (24,700 employees or 34 per cent), electrical equipment (10,500 or 14 per cent), chemicals (7,400 or 10 per cent) and food (6,900 or 9 per cent). This investment came from more than 40 countries but especially from the FRG, the US and Sweden (Figure 9.1).

The territorial origin of the owners has remained much the same since 1984 (Manikowska et al., 1985): during the 1984-89 period, the largest increase was in the shares of firms originating in the FRG (+3 per cent) and Switzerland (+1.4 per cent), while the major decreases were those in the UK (–1.6 per cent) and the Arabic countries (–1.3 per cent). One ownership feature was its geographical diversity and range of links: beyond Europe and North America, it included Turkey, Syria, Lebanon, Jordan, Israel, Egypt, Kuwait, India, Afghanistan, Tunisia, Morocco, Venezuela, Panama, Brazil and Australia.

**Type A**

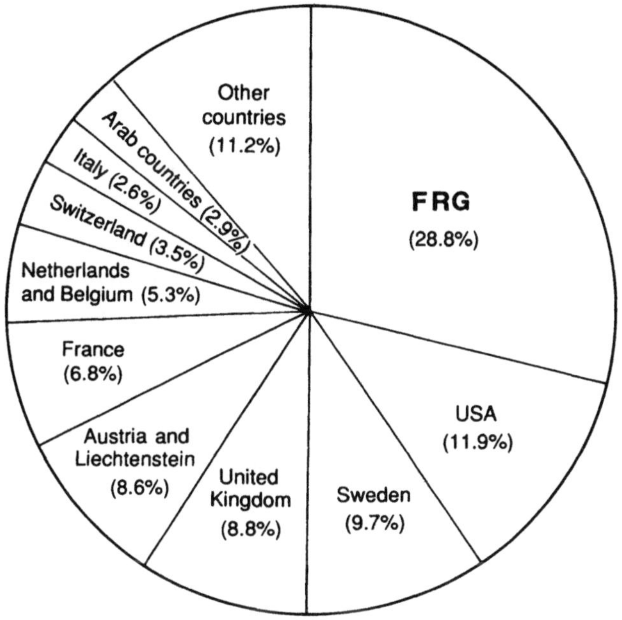


**Type B**

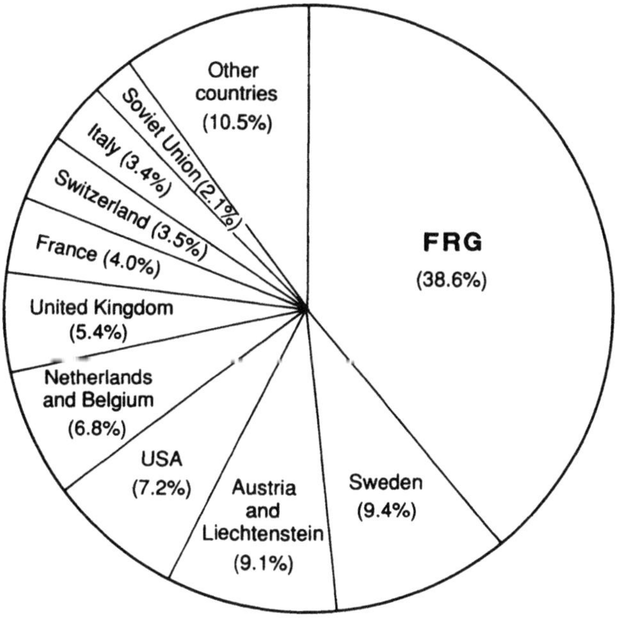


Figure 9.1: Countries of origin of owners of foreign firms in Poland, 1989. *Source:* unpublished data from the Foreign Investment Agency.

Among the 657 Type B firms, capital from the FRG was well ahead of that from Sweden, Austria, the US and the UK (Figure 9.1). Moreover, FRG firms had invested the largest amount — US$43 million — by April 1990, followed by Sweden with US$20 million. Of note was the establishment of the first 14 companies in which Soviet enterprises participated (involving printing machinery, clutches and mini-computer systems). Overall, foreign capital involvement in Type B enterprises was relatively small: in over half the companies it did not exceed US$50,000 and in only five concerns was it greater than US$5 million. This clearly reflects the cautious character of foreign investment. Data from the Foreign Investment Agency in Warsaw indicate that as at 30 September 1991 the average capital share amounted to US$139,200. German capital is still predominant but simultaneously a growing role for American, Dutch and multinational capital is noted. A partial list of some of the largest and most promising JVs in Poland (Ryniewicz, 1991; Poland, Information and Negotiating Centre of the Ministry of Privatization, 1991) is:

(a) Furnel International Ltd (a multi-plant JV with the British firm International Computer Ltd);

(b) Intercell (a JV of the Ostrołeka Cellulose and Paper Plant with a Swedish cellulose company);

(c) Gdynia Shipyard – Kvaerney (Norway);

(d) Polam Piła – Philips Electronics NV (The Netherlands);

(e) Paper Machinery Factory 'Fampa' in Jelenia Góra – Beloit Corporation (which is a subsidiary of the American concern Harnishfeger Industries Inc.);

(f) Polcolor Piaseczno (TV tube manufacturer) – Thomson Consumer Electronic (France);

(g) Telkom-Teletra Poznań (telecommunication systems) – Alcatel CIT (France);

(h) Warsaw Telecommunication Works – Siemens AG (Germany).

## The Location and Changing Dynamics of Foreign Enterprises

### Type A firms

The location and changing dynamics of Type A firms in Poland can be outlined in two phases. During the 1977-84 period, the strong influence of bureaucratized administration on economic activity (even at a local level) emphasized investor perception of the locational advantages of major decision centres. Their locational advantages included the accessibility of information which permitted firms to respond and successfully adapt to changes in their external operating environment. Consequently, the risk-minimizing clustering of firms around such places, especially Warsaw, occurred: in 1984 some 34 per cent of all foreign enterprises in Poland were concentrated in the Warsaw voivodeship as compared to 5 per cent of population. This may also reflect a lack of 'locational confidence' among investors in other areas of Poland, especially the 'new' voivodeships (i.e. those established because of the administrative reform in 1975) which attracted only 25 per cent of all the enterprises even though they embraced 60 per cent of the country's area (Table 9.4). Indeed, it is striking that, until 1984, no foreign firms were established in 8 out of the 32 'new' voivodeships.

Table 9.4: Changing role of 'new' and 'old' voivodeships as locations of foreign enterprises in Poland: percentage of foreign firms, area and population, 1984 and 1988

| Criterion | Years | Voivodeships | |
|---|---|---|---|
| | | 'new'(post 1975) | 'old' |
| Total foreign firms in Poland | 1984 | 24.8 | 75.2 |
| | 1988 | 33.3 | 66.7 |
| Area of Poland | 1984 | 59.6 | 40.4 |
| | 1988 | 59.6 | 40.4 |
| Population of Poland | 1984 | 44.1 | 55.9 |
| | 1988 | 44.2 | 55.8 |

*Source:* Authors' calculations.

Two further issues underpinning the location and functioning of foreign enterprises in Poland warrant attention — the territorial origin of the proprietors, and the distribution of crafts and the current economic regional specialization. Business people usually locate their first firms in regions from which they or their families have emigrated; such preferences can be attributed to the maintenance of individual contacts and greater 'confidence' in familiar areas. In turn, interweaving the location of foreign businesses with regional economic specialization and the spatial distribution of crafts follows from the possibility of cooperation in production, the procurement of materials and the availability of skilled labour, as well as from the specific 'social climate' in regions with well-developed crafts favourable to small-scale production. Thus the Katowice voivodeship has only a few foreign firms despite its large local market, while the neighbouring Bielsko-Biała voivodeship has many because its economic profile better suits the needs of foreign investors.

During the second stage of the development of foreign firms after 1984, the most important locational factor was the availability of production premises. This had played a role during the first period, particularly in 1982 and 1983 when many new businesses were located initially in villages surrounding major cities where there was more chance of obtaining premises. Subsequently, after the existing 'location gaps' had been identified and suitable financial means gathered, these firms relocated to major urban centres. During the second stage this latter tendency was reversed as increased land prices and rents made it more difficult to obtain or build factories. In addition, with the stabilization of the legislative environment governing the functioning of foreign enterprises, the need for access to a decision centre became less significant. Moreover, investors were more willing to locate their firms in the 'new' voivodeships as is clearly demonstrated in Table 9.4.

Currently, two spatial regularities can be identified. One is the stagnation of foreign enterprises in the initial foci, such as the 'old' voivodeships of Warsaw, Poznań, Kraków and Łódź, and the other is the high level of growth in some of the 'new' voivodeships, especially those near Warsaw (Figure 9.2). Consequently, in terms of the overall geography of investment, there was a relative decline in the importance of the urban agglomerations, especially Warsaw, and thus less contrast between them, the neighbouring voivodeships and the remaining areas of the country. A location quotient index for the 1984-88 period, presented in Table 9.5, shows a marked shift of foreign investors from the capital to the surrounding voivodeships which offered lower labour costs and available accommodation.

Table 9.5: Development dynamics of foreign firms in the Warsaw and adjacent voivodeships, 1984 and 1988

| Criterion | Date | Warsaw | Adjacent voivodeships |
|---|---|---|---|
| Number of firms | 15/03/84 | 65 | 191 |
| | 31/12/86 | 107 | 181 |
| | 31/12/88 | 112 | 179 |
| Location quotient | 1984 | 1.4 | 5.2 |
| | 1988 | 1.8 | 3.8 |
| Index of dynamics 1984 to 1988 (1984=100) | | 172 | 94 |
| Mean pay (złotys 000) 1988 (first half) | | 58.1 | 64.5 |

*Source:* Authors' calculations.

## Type B firms

Type B firms, embracing mostly companies of socialized Polish enterprises and foreign investors, evinced differing start and operating conditions. Factors influencing their establishment and locational choice included (a) a permit to set up a company issued by the central authorities; (b) the great efficiency and elasticity shown by Polish shareholders in searching for foreign firms willing to cooperate; and (c) Polish enterprises offering their foreign partners the use of their immovables and part of the staff. Because Type B foreign enterprises have been functioning for only a short period, their precise loca-ional dynamics are difficult to discern. Nevertheless, data for November 1989 show that in common with Type A firms in the initial stage of their development, Type B firms were concentrated mainly in Warsaw, Poznań, Szczecin, the Gdańsk-Gdynia-Sopot agglomeration, Kraków, Wrocław, and Łódź (Figure 9.3). These cities host nearly half the Type B enterprises. However, some Type B firms are scattered in small towns or villages because their Polish co-partners are state-run or are cooperative farms.

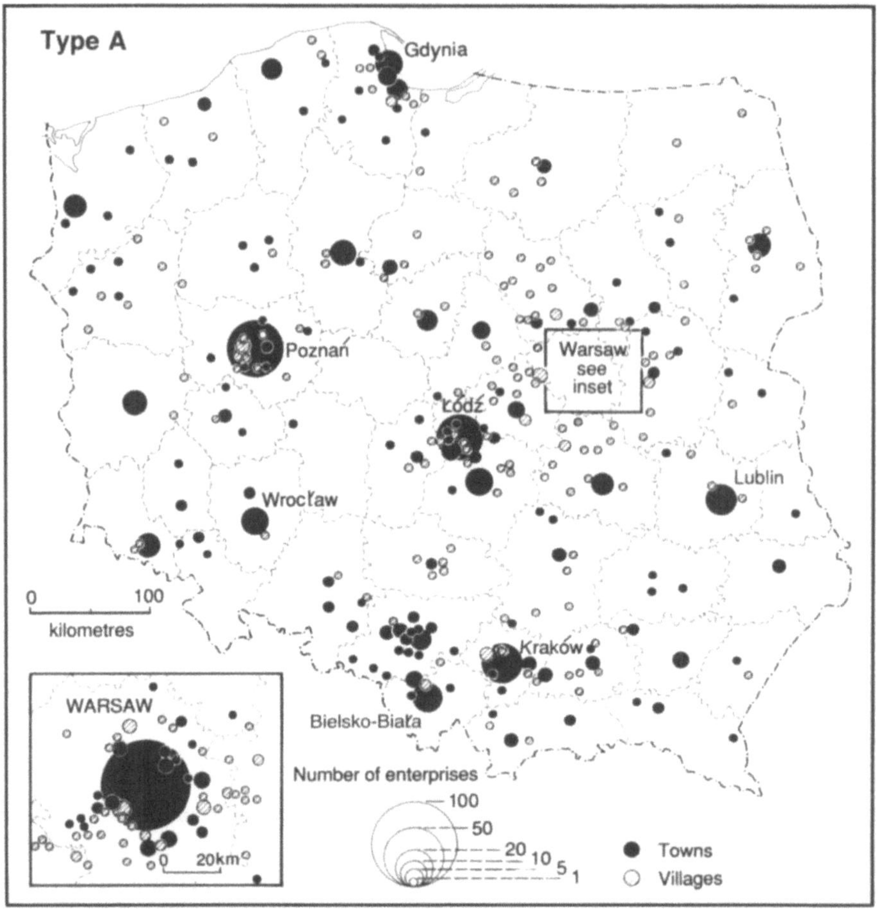


Figure 9.2: Spatial distribution of Type A foreign enterprises in Poland, 1989. *Source:* unpublished data from the Foreign Investment Agency.

## Research Directions

This paper has sought to shed light on the nuances of foreign enterprises in an economy in transition, using the example of Poland. As emphasized earlier, the transitional state of Eastern Europe in the late 1980s and early 1990s offers a vital set of research issues for geographers about the behaviour of industrial organizations. A recent survey carried out among more than 100 German-Polish JVs (Heiduk et al., 1991: 44–8) shows that 48.5 per cent of them

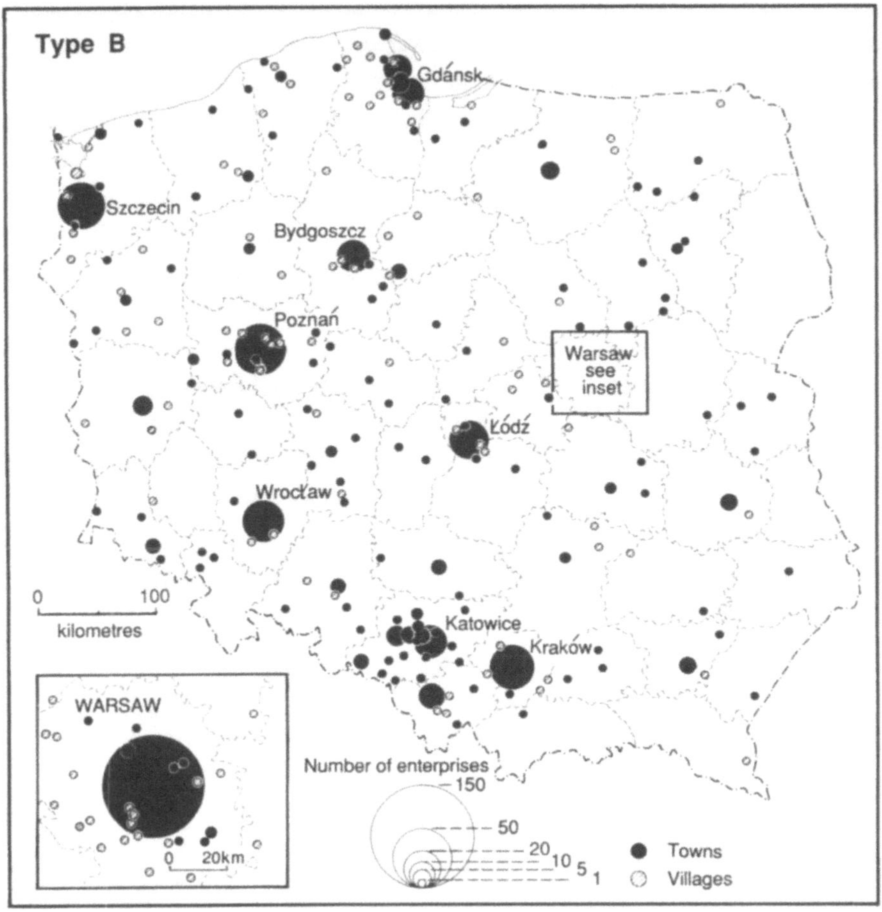


Figure 9.3: Spatial distribution of Type B foreign enterprises in Poland, 1989. *Source:* unpublished data from the Foreign Investment Agency.

considered location advantages as very important or important reasons for their decision to found a JV. Simultaneously the same research proves that — apart from communication difficulties — the main obstacles to their establishment and functioning are associated with the institutional context (63.2 per cent of the firms pointed out this problem). Hence, of particular significance in interpreting the changing geographies of foreign enterprises is their response and adaptation to the shifting legislative milieu. This is even more important in the light of recent legislative changes which break with the earlier policy of having no formal spatial preferences for foreign investments; these changes are exemplified by the lower than average 20 per cent tax and five-year tax holidays in the Bulgarian free-trade zones, and by the possibility of tax exemption in Polish regions with high unemployment. On the other hand, legislation in some countries, especially in Poland (where the 'automatic' tax exemption provision was abandoned), is beginning to reflect a more selective approach towards foreign investments. This takes into consideration the initial experience — many small firms engaged in simple processing or the distribution of goods, and the limited entry of companies introducing new forms of production (especially those involving more advanced technologies) — and thus gives preference to larger export and high-tech orientated JVs. Geographers must be aware of the evolving institutional context of the melting pot of Eastern Europe which will condition the future spatial organization of foreign industrial activity. Moreover, the spatial consequences of growing legislative competition among East European countries to encourage foreign investors are another emerging problem for future studies.

# 10 Business Behaviour and the Restructuring of the Turkish Economy

**A. Eraydin**

The world economy has been undergoing dramatic changes. In particular, the internationalization of production and capital, and world-wide economic restructuring have gained momentum. Major steps have included greater reliance on market forces and export-orientated trade policies, increased foreign investment, mergers between domestic and foreign firms, and the privatization of industrial and service enterprises. Together, these have increased multinational flows of goods and capital. Consistent with the new economic climate, political relations have been diversified. This has induced radical changes in financial systems and business relations — even those of countries like Turkey which have 'traditionally' remained 'semi-closed' systems in the world economy. In addition, the changing character of international relations has prompted fresh foreign trade linkages which, in turn, have encouraged private business to search for new institutional arrangements and to adopt innovative business attitudes.

Business behaviour is examined here in the context of the restructuring of the Turkish economy. By the 1980s, Turkey had shed its status as a semi-closed system, and was moving into the global economic and financial systems. This process is considered through three main sections. After first presenting an analytical framework, the Turkish experience is outlined with particular emphasis on the restructuring of external trade relations and capital movements. Finally, changes in the structure and business behaviour of Turkish firms involved in foreign trade activities are scrutinized.

## Analytical Framework

Changes in business behaviour, in terms of organizational forms and productive methods, are evident in Turkey's attempts to integrate into the world economy. This chapter focuses specifically on macro-policy changes under various external and internal forces, the restructuring of productive activities, the emergence of new financial and institutional structures, the development of new external relations and the improvement of channels for capital flows (Figure 10.1).

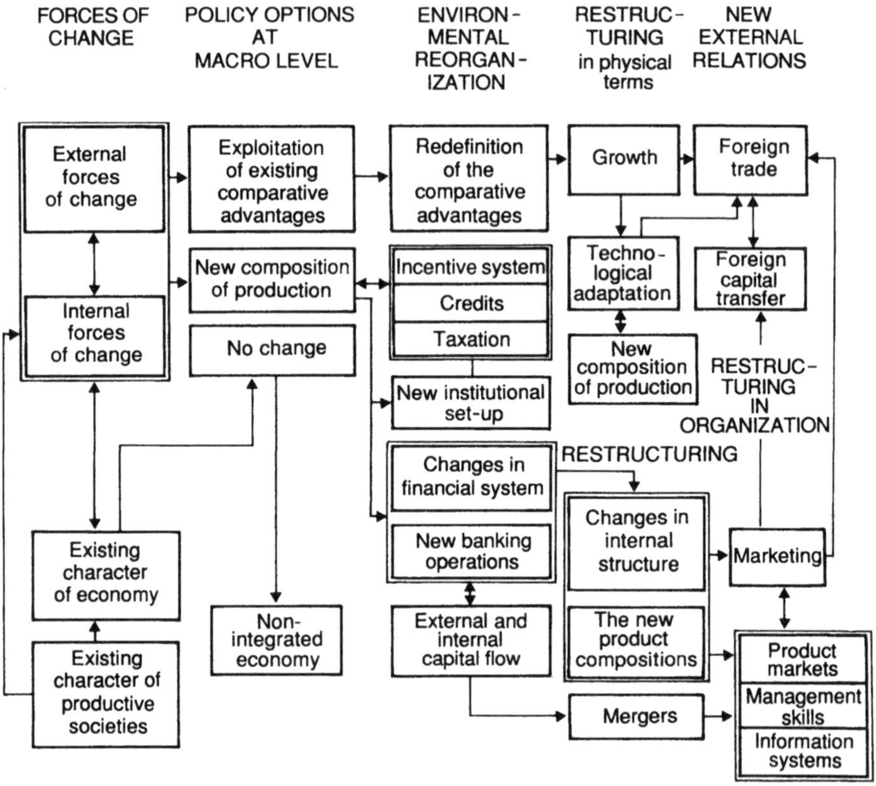


Figure 10.1: Framework of transformation during Turkey's integration with the world economy (author's compilation).

The decision to integrate with the world economy is not arbitrary; rather, it is made under the impact of both external and internal factors (Balassa, 1978). Major external forces leading to the reorganization of the world production system have been identified as economic crises in advanced countries and their foreign trade policies (Bhagwati, 1964; Evans, 1979; Adelman, 1984; Tussie, 1987), the attitudes of international finance institutions, relationships with foreign capital and multinational firms (Taylor and Thrift, 1981), and the needs of a new international division of labour. Important internal factors include industrialization strategies, levels of development, the proportions of different factors of production, foreign deficit problems (Alpar, 1982), and socio-political forces.

Whether forced by external factors, induced by internal factors, or both, the economic integration process requires the restructuring of productive activities and of the organizational forms of parts of the economic system. Restructuring at the level of business behaviour involves changes in operational scale and organization, marketing, communication with other agents and enterprises, labour relations, product markets, and managerial skills and strategic priorities.

Economic restructuring is directly related to introducing and adapting new technologies to create and maintain comparative advantage, or to improve the utilization of the factors of production. At the macro-level, this prompts change in the composition of production and hence *growth* in some sectors and *decline* in others. The process is also affected by domestic and international market conditions, the investment behaviour of multinational enterprises, the availability of domestic funds, and the inflow of foreign capital. Thus, new external relations emerge, as in foreign trade and global capital movements. To accelerate the restructuring process, governments usually define the financial support systems so as to temporarily improve and protect the comparative advantage of certain sectors (Balassa, 1977). Moreover, governments involve themselves in measures to develop financial and banking systems, foreign trade services and infrastructure activities.

At the level of the firm, attempts are made to adapt to new conditions by changing production systems. This can take the form of growth in the scale of operations; alteration of the product mix and the technological basis of production; increases in capacity utilization; and new or renewed investment to increase capacity. At this time, the economy's ability to adopt flexible specialization methods becomes a major determinant of change in the productive system (Piore and Sabel, 1984) as poor flexibility will increase the need for new sources of capital. Physically adapting the productive system is not sufficient, however, to enable it to compete on external markets: new marketing information systems, management skills, and linkages with domestic and outside firms are also necessary.

Changes at the level of the firm are directly influenced by attempts to reorganize the general economic environment including adjustments to institutional arrangements, banking, the financial system and capital mobility. The first of these involves establishing new public institutions, semi-public organizations, or locally initiated bodies by various interest groups. Their formation often reflects the conflicting interests of small, medium and large enterprises (Steed, 1968). The banking and financial systems also need to be shifted away from an introverted to an extroverted outlook so as to improve external relations, create strong communication networks, and enhance cooperation with the financial institutions of other countries. To achieve this, the financial system has to gain foreign experience so that it can compete with external banks and financial institutions. Among the agents improving the external linkages of the economy, the flow of capital is particularly important. New channels of capital flow include multinational firms, foreign direct and portfolio investment, mergers with foreign firms, bilateral credits, and loans from international organizations or commercial banks.

New trade relations are characterized by changed production activities and institutional and financial arrangements. In developing countries (and in certain advanced countries), organizations emerge to provide access to external markets for small, low-technology firms and to assist small and medium-size enterprises (SMEs) to find markets and export products. These intermediaries include large trading houses and industrial enterprises that have succeeded on the domestic market and have set up cooperative and other export ventures, state-owned organizations, and export outlets connected with multinationals (International Trade Centre, 1987).

Oligopolistic firms have different strategies as they tend to adopt a specific set of corporate policies and competitive behaviours directly linked to foreign enterprises (Markusen, 1985; Suarez-Villa, 1987). Moreover, relations between manufacturing firms and their networks of financial, trading and transport enterprises tend to change as new economic structures evolve. The internal organization of enterprises can also be altered in response to the growing concern for international relationships by extending foreign trade departments and overseas contact offices. The internal reorganization of SMEs is, however, not the same as it reflects the dualistic character of production. As a new economic milieu emerges, with business pursuing a different development strategy, the human factor gains special importance not only during the production stage but also in terms of marketing. The staffing of departments evolves and management skills become of central importance.

## The Turkish Experience

This section summarizes the Turkish experience since 1980 and highlights several central themes within the process of this country's integration into the world economy. Restructuring foreign trade relations and capital movements deserve specific attention because they have undergone important changes.

### Integration into the world economy and external economic relations

Apart from some short-lived liberalization attempts, protectionist attitudes dominated Turkish economic policy prior to the 1980s (Akat, 1984; Kazgan, 1985; Togan et al., 1988), with import substitution being the main force driving the industrialization process during the 1950-79 period (Aktan and Baysan, 1985; Boratav, 1988). However, the economic crisis beginning in the mid-1970s caused the current account deficit to increase considerably while short-term foreign debt rose from 6 to 56 per cent of the country's total debt burden. This, in turn, led to reductions in foreign borrowing. Stabilization programmes in 1978 and 1979 failed to check the declining per capita income or the rising rate of inflation, thus prompting a re-evaluation of Turkish economic policies and the adoption in 1980 of several initiatives placing increased reliance on market forces.

This new programme greatly freed up foreign trade and exchange (Togan et al., 1988). In 1984, major structural changes further liberalized trade and payments by dismantling foreign exchange controls and quotas on imports, and by revising tariffs (Olgun and Togan, 1984; İhracaatı Geliştirme ve Destekleme Merkezi, 1988a). This liberalization initiative has continued (Türkiye Sanayici ve İş Adamları Derneği, 1986; Şenses, 1988). Exports have been encouraged by depreciating exchange rates and by direct support (Şenses, 1988). Total direct subsidy reached 23 per cent in 1983 and averaged 20 per cent during the 1980-84 period. New policies were promulgated to increase inflows of foreign loans and investment. Market-orientated policies increased Turkey's rating and thereby improved its access to medium and short-term credit.

## Foreign trade relations since 1980

Foreign trade, encouraged by macro-policies, gained momentum in Turkey after 1980 with total trade volume increasing by some 136 per cent between 1980 and 1988, and exports and imports by 18 and 8 per cent, respectively. Exports of industrial goods rose spectacularly from US$1,074 million in 1980 to US$11,683 million in 1990 (current prices), primarily as a result of improved competitiveness, export incentives, and subdued domestic demand (Kazgan, 1985; Şenses, 1989). This occurred during a period when world trade was growing only slowly (Patton, 1988). Exports rose by 62 per cent in 1981 and 22 per cent in 1982, almost stagnated in 1983, and then increased again in 1984 and 1985 by 25 and 12 per cent (reflecting problems in exporting to Middle East countries). Subsequent rises of 37 and 14 per cent in 1987 and 1988 reflected diversification into new markets.

The increase in foreign trade can further be traced from the rising proportions of exports and imports in total GNP. Exports accounted for less than 5 per cent of GNP in 1979 but for 15 per cent in 1987, almost matching European averages (Türkiye Sanayici ve İş Adamları Derneği, 1986). Similarly, the share of imports in GNP grew during the same period from 16 to 21 per cent (Devlet Planlama Teşkilatı, 1988).

In 1980 only 36 per cent of the total value of exports consisted of industrial goods, including processed agricultural and petroleum products, but by 1990 the ratio had altered to 90 per cent with non-agricultural manufactured products now contributing about 77 per cent (Table 10.1). However, exports of agricultural products — in which Turkey is usually considered to have a comparative advantage — failed to increase rapidly after liberalization (Akder, 1988). Exports became more diverse, with the share of the three most important categories dropping from 59 per cent in 1980 to 41 per cent in 1985 (Türkiye Sanayici ve İş Adamları Derneği, 1986), while the number of commodities sent abroad more than doubled during the 1970-83 period (Togan et al., 1988). In 1988, the relatively higher share of textile goods (36 per cent), iron and steel products (16 per cent) and food products (10 per cent) echoed the situation in various developing countries and reflected Turkish specialization in textile, leather, glassware and food products, and its tendency to become a net importer of engineering goods (Türel, 1987).

Table 10.1: Percentage share of industrial goods in total exports and imports, Turkey, 1980 to 1990

| Year | Exports | | | Imports | | |
|---|---|---|---|---|---|---|
| | all industrial | agro-industrial products | other industrial | all industrial | oil | other goods |
| 1980 | 36.0 | 8.5 | 27.5 | 47.5 | 47.5 | 5.0 |
| 1981 | 48.7 | 11.0 | 37.7 | 52.0 | 43.4 | 4.6 |
| 1982 | 59.7 | 15.9 | 43.8 | 52.7 | 42.4 | 4.9 |
| 1983 | 63.9 | 15.8 | 48.1 | 56.1 | 39.7 | 4.2 |
| 1984 | 72.1 | 17.1 | 55.0 | 59.8 | 33.8 | 6.4 |
| 1985 | 75.3 | 12.8 | 62.5 | 62.2 | 31.8 | 6.0 |
| 1986 | 71.4 | 11.3 | 60.1 | 74.8 | 18.1 | 7.1 |
| 1987 | 79.1 | 11.6 | 67.5 | 71.3 | 20.9 | 7.8 |
| 1988 | 76.7 | 10.4 | 66.3 | 76.6 | 17.0 | 6.4 |
| 1989 | 88.2 | 8.1 | 80.1 | 74.9 | 16.4 | 8.7 |
| 1990 | 89.9 | 7.3 | 82.6 | 76.1 | 14.0 | 9.9 |
| 1980-90 annual increase (per cent) | 25.7 | 16.2 | 27.5 | 13.6 | 2.5 | 16.0 |

*Sources:* Turkey, State Planning Organization, 1985; 1985 to 1991 annual.

Studies of the composition of exports to the European market using the 'similarity' index (concordance of the shares of the various product groups of foreign trade at the base year and the particular year taken into account), show that between 1981 and 1986 the index dropped to 62 per cent, and the similarity index within the types of textiles exported fell to 51 per cent (Alkaçar, 1988). Business people claim that quotas imposed by some countries — especially the Federal Republic of Germany, UK, US and Canada — on various textile products induced this diversification (Alptekin, 1988). The increase in total exports and more diverse product mix improved the position but even so, due to terms-of-trade distortions, Turkey had to sell more to compensate for the small increases in export prices. During the 1973-84 period, for example, import prices increased about three times more than those of exports (Türkiye Sanayici ve İş Adamları Derneği, 1986).

In the face of the trade liberalization, the growth of imports remained lower than that of exports. In particular, the reduction in oil prices led to a fall in the share of crude oil in imports from 48 per cent in 1980 to 14 per cent in 1990. Turkey's imports are now dominated by industrial goods, especially chemicals, machinery and iron and steel products. Between 1980 and 1988 the balance of trade improved and the trade deficit declined from US$4,999 million to US$2,678 million (Devlet Planlama Teşkilatı, 1988) but grew in 1989 to US$4,162 million and in 1990 to US$9,341 million. As has been the experience of other Newly Industrializing Countries (NICs), a positive trade balance is difficult to achieve, primarily because of the enhanced demand for imports and for raw materials for conversion into exports (World Bank, 1988).

Prior to 1980 the OECD countries were the main markets for Turkish exports with the share of Middle Eastern and North African countries totalling little more than 20 per cent. Then, during the early 1980s when exports increased sharply, these countries became the major markets: the Middle East alone absorbed over 48 per cent of Turkey's exports in 1982 and 42 per cent in 1984 (Akder, 1987). When oil prices declined, however, the share of Middle Eastern countries dwindled, thus causing a reduction in Turkey's overall exports. Alternative markets were soon developed in OECD countries, which increased their share of Turkish exports during the 1980-86 period from 45 to 66 per cent. Almost all exports to the European Community (EC) in 1984 were labour-intensive products, whereas mainly capital-intensive goods went to Middle Eastern countries (Şenses, 1988).

**Foreign capital movements**

After adopting new economic policies in 1980, the Turkish authorities revised their attitude towards foreign investment and made several legal and institutional reforms (Baban, 1987). Foreign capital invested then increased rapidly from a mere US$228 million at the end of 1979 to US$2,902 million in 1990. Permissions for foreign capital inflow reached US$5,583 million in 1990 with over 1,800 foreign companies being involved (Table 10.2).

Table 10.2: Turkey: foreign capital inflow, 1980 to 1990 (US$ m.)

| Year | Number of firms | Permissions | | Actual inflow |
|---|---|---|---|---|
| | | total foreign capital | annual inflow | |
| 1980 | 100 | 325 | 97 | 35 |
| 1981 | 127 | 663 | 338 | 141 |
| 1982 | 170 | 830 | 167 | 103 |
| 1983 | 185 | 932 | 103 | 87 |
| 1984 | 267 | 1,204 | 271 | 162 |
| 1985 | 421 | 1,438 | 235 | 158 |
| 1986 | 610 | 1,802 | 364 | 170 |
| 1987 | 839 | 2,338 | 536 | 171 |
| 1988 | 1,109 | 3,163 | 825 | 406 |
| 1989 | 1,542 | 4,633 | 1,470 | 738 |
| 1990 | 1,813 | 5,583 | 950 | 503 |

*Sources:* Turkey, State Planning Organization, 1987, 1989, 1990.

In 1990, 508 foreign firms were engaged in manufacturing, 52 in agriculture and 29 in mining, as well as 1,224 in trade, tourism and banking services, transport and other activities which together showed the highest rate of growth (Table 10.3). The numbers of firms involved in trade, tourism and banking in 1983 (7, 13 and 5 respectively) rose considerably by the end of 1987 (to 303, 80 and 23) but, given their nature, considerably less foreign capital was involved in manufacturing.

The development of financial markets in Turkey was long retarded by government regulations which obstructed the growth of portfolio investments. In March 1986, however, these were clarified, thus actively attracting new foreign capital even though lengthy procedures were introduced (Table 10.4).

Table 10.3: Sectoral distribution of foreign firms and investment, Turkey, 1983 to 1990 (US$ m.)

| Year | Industry | | Agriculture | | Mining | | Services[a] | | Total | |
|---|---|---|---|---|---|---|---|---|---|---|
| | firms | foreign capital | firms | foreign capital | firms | foreign capital | firms | foreign capital | firms | foreign capital |
| 1983 | 148 | 186 | 3 | 7 | 2 | 2 | 32 | 79 | 185 | 274 |
| 1984 | 167 | 197 | 3 | 6 | 3 | 2 | 94 | 118 | 267 | 323 |
| 1985 | 202 | 227 | 7 | 12 | 4 | 2 | 208 | 161 | 421 | 401 |
| 1986 | 235 | 232 | 12 | 13 | 6 | 5 | 357 | 203 | 610 | 453 |
| 1987 | 263 | 290 | 33 | 28 | 10 | 7 | 533 | 184 | 839 | 509 |
| 1988 | 323 | 295 | 41 | 28 | 17 | 6 | 728 | 223 | 1,109 | 552 |
| 1989 | 427 | 578 | 46 | 25 | 23 | 12 | 1,046 | 521 | 1,542 | 1,135 |
| 1990 | 508 | 774 | 52 | 31 | 29 | 15 | 1,224 | 663 | 1,813 | 1,484 |

[a] Banking, trade, tourism, transport, other services.

*Sources:* Turkey, State Planning Organization, 1987, 1990 and unpublished data.

Whereas in 1983 only US$4 million of the capital inflow was in the form of portfolio investments, this had risen to US$341 million by 1989 (although falling again to US$94 million in 1990), much of which went into manufacturing (especially chemical products, textiles and ready-made clothing), trade and tourism.

Table 10.4: Annual permissions by type of foreign investment in the manufacturing sector, Turkey, 1983 to 1990 (US$ m.)

| Year | Number of firms | Type of investment | | | | Total foreign capital |
|---|---|---|---|---|---|---|
| | | extension increase | new investment | capital | portfolio | |
| 1983 | 124 | 44.6 | 16.2 | 24.2 | 3.9 | 88.9 |
| 1984 | 98 | 27.4 | 130.1 | 24.3 | 4.1 | 185.9 |
| 1985 | 115 | 7.1 | 77.7 | 37.1 | 21.0 | 142.9 |
| 1986 | 179 | 18.6 | 95.8 | 54.1 | 25.0 | 193.5 |
| 1987 | 220 | 26.9 | 67.5 | 127.7 | 51.6 | 273.7 |
| 1988 | 292 | 53.9 | 149.8 | 147.5 | 132.9 | 484.1 |
| 1989 | 327 | 122.1 | 192.8 | 246.1 | 340.5 | 901.5 |
| 1990 | 376 | 90.8 | 411.5 | 544.3 | 94.4 | 1,143.0 |

*Sources:* Turkey, State Planning Organization, 1987, 1990 and unpublished data.

Firms whose shares have been sold to foreign enterprises fall into two distinct groups. The first consists of leading Turkish firms, including those with short-term capital problems arising from rising interest rates on domestic credit and mounting foreign debt because of fluctuating exchange rates (*Ekonomik Panorama*, 2 October 1988: 27–31), and those which tried to enlarge their international trade activities. The second group includes medium-size companies where the main motivations for foreign share sales are to increase the scale of production and to form direct links with outside firms.

## The Growth of Turkey's Foreign Trade

Although the value of Turkish foreign trade is less than that of some NICs and the most recent EC members, it represents a rapid growth in the nation's foreign relations (World Bank, 1988). The type and intensity of such linkages can be evaluated by examining the comparative advantages of the various sectors. The picture is distorted, however, by tariffs, quotas, exchange rates and subsidies. If these are excluded, agricultural, animal, mineral and quarry products, iron and steel, ceramics and, especially, textiles and clothing are clearly competitive. Metal and forest products industries owe their comparative advantage to the new capital flowing into these activities which are also major sources of exports (Aktan, 1985; Kazgan, 1987; Togan et al., 1988). Industries, such as electrical and other machinery, transport equipment, metal products, and chemicals, had a 10 to 70 per cent disadvantage on EC markets (Aktan and Baysan, 1985).

Sectors with a comparative advantage, and marginal ones whose positions improved through increased capital stock and various financial incentives, were mainly labour-intensive (Yeşilada and Füsunoğlu, 1988). Capital-intensive sectors were greatly disadvantaged, a situation difficult to remedy even with strong incentive schemes.

### Policies and instruments aiding export performance and capital inflow

Export incentives, tax and tariff reductions, investment allowances, low-cost credits, and tariff exemptions on imported capital goods and material inputs, have operated in Turkey since 1963, mainly to try to increase domestic investment. Thus, direct financial incentives were provided for investment in industry, while tariffs and quantitative restrictions discouraged imports. Furthermore, the overvalued exchange rate played a leading role in dampening trade. Domestic conditions, such as the rapidly increasing demand resulting from the relatively high purchasing-power of the middle-income class, also eliminated the need to search for new markets.

The revised economic policy introduced in 1980, mentioned earlier, aimed to change the development strategy of the economy by emphasizing market forces, financial schemes and improved cost/price ratios, thus reducing distortions (Togan et al., 1988). The initial measures enabled exporters to import intermediary and packaging goods without customs duties and take advantage of extended foreign-exchange retention schemes. The liberalization attempts led to the replacement of the fixed exchange system and the growing competitiveness of exports (Erdal, 1986). Existing export incentives were supplemented by new ones, of which two were important. First, during the early years of the stabilization programme, cheap and abundant export credit played a significant role in expanding exports (İhracaatı Geliştirme ve Destekleme Merkezi, 1988b). Until 1985, traders had access to preferential credit through the export promotion fund which, after a period of stagnation, was revitalized in 1989. Second, tax rebates stimulated concerns both within the country at the phase of implementation (because of such problems as 'fictitious' exports), and in terms of foreign trade relations. Financial incentives provided after export (rather than during production or marketing) led to disputes with international bodies which claimed that these created unfair competition (Balkır, 1987). For example, all indirect dues on exporters' inputs were rebated to eliminate the tax on products sent abroad. However, rebates in excess of the indirect taxes constituted a subsidy, and during the early 1980s these were considerable. In 1984 direct financial incentives were eliminated, and the export rebate scheme was phased out early in 1989 after Turkey had signed the GATT subsidy code (Alpar, 1989). Eximbank, the first official export credit institution, was then established.

The early attempts to liberalize imports continued during the 1981-84 period (Şenses, 1988), and were then strengthened by reducing import guarantee deposit rates, eliminating a production tax on imports, and abolishing a 5 per cent surcharge on imports from EC countries. Imports were categorized into prohibited goods (weapons and narcotics), imports with permission, and liberalized goods. Items on the second list declined from 1,000 in 1984 to 245 in 1988 and formed only about 10 per cent of all imports.

After foreign exchange controls were dismantled, Turkish citizens were allowed to hold foreign exchange in banks operating in Turkey and other countries and to invest abroad. All banks could carry foreign exchange positions, foreigners could invest freely in real estate, citizens were allowed to exchange money in commercial bureaux and take US$1,000 on each journey abroad plus an additional US$2,000 annually in foreign currency (Türkiye Ticaret, Sanayi, Deniz Ticaret Odaları ve Borsaları Birliği, 1987). These rights were extended in August 1989 and the monetary limits increased.

A further effect was a change in the nominal and effective rates of protection. By 1984, the former had gone from 74 to 49 per cent and the weighted average from 228 to 65 per cent. These reductions took place in processed tobacco, ginning and textiles, plastics, and cement and paper products (Togan et al., 1988). Negative effective protection rates even occurred in slaughtering, sugar refining, chemical products, petroleum extraction and refining, non-metallic mineral products, cement, iron and steel, and non-ferrous metals (Türkiye Sanayici ve İş Adamları Derneği, 1986). These falls did not, however, lead to a rapid increase in imports mainly because the purchasing power of middle-income earners was seriously eroded. Two trends were important. First, some manufacturing firms, with the help of existing distribution channels, turned to importing some of the goods they had previously made. Second, increased imports of some consumer goods (even though making up only a small proportion of total imports) led to shifts in consumption patterns.

In 1986 the direct financial export incentives were removed and replaced by Eximbank facilities. Among other measures adopted after 1986 were rediscount facilities for short-term export credits and subsidies for specific commodities from the Price Stability and Support Fund. The incentive scheme was again changed in 1989 so that instead of encouraging export activities during the last phase, production support was given, for example, by discounting the cost of energy to the firms concerned.

Eximbank instituted two short-term credit programmes. One involved a rediscount facility for exporters having annual sales of over US$100 million and the opportunity for them to obtain additional credit of up to 5 per cent of the value of their sales during the subsequent twelve months. The other programme was formulated for small traders and restricted to industrial goods: to qualify, exporters had to achieve total sales of only US$25,000. Pre-shipment credits with an interest rate of 35 per cent have been made available since 1989 in addition to a global insurance system with lower premium rates. A further liberalization occurred in 1989 when foreigners and citizens were able to transfer capital freely, and restrictions were removed on exchanges of assets of foreign and domestic firms.

Following the 1980 stabilization programme, and especially after 1983, new policies on foreign capital inflow were implemented. Responsibility for authorizing foreign investment was concentrated in a newly established Foreign Investment Department (FID) within the State Planning Organization (SPO). This was empowered to permit, and provide incentives for, projects with foreign capital participation of up to US$50 million. Applications for larger projects had to be submitted for preliminary investigation to the SPO and then presented to the Council of Ministers for approval (Yabancı Sermaye Derneği, 1988). In December 1983, a new decree extended the authority of the FID and ensured the repatriation of earnings. Law 2634 on the Encouragement of Tourism (1982) and Law 3218 on Free Trade Zones (1985) identified new areas of foreign capital inflow and provided several incentives. Following this, Decree 86/10353 of 1986 eliminated restrictions on investment in Joint Ventures (JVs) with domestic firms and allowed 100 per cent ownership by foreign investors. In addition, non-resident taxpayers became eligible for investment credits, tax rates were reduced, corporate tax liability by foreign investors (in addition to regular taxes) was abolished, and the after-tax transfer of profits by foreign partners was allowed. Foreign investors in Turkey were able to utilize the financial incentives provided for domestic investments and, like domestic firms, were exempted from taxes, fees and duties if they guaranteed a minimum level of export earnings. These changes increased foreign investment and stimulated new patterns of capital inflow, much of which came from multilateral agencies and bilateral and private lenders (Table 10.4). It took various forms including project and programme credit,

Eurocurrency loans, rescheduled debt, bankers' credit, overdrafts and acceptance and pre-export credits. After 1983, commercial banks also contributed increasingly to the availability of credit.

## Emerging Organizational Arrangements and Export Performance

A country with a semi-closed economy and limited foreign trade experience has to learn the rules and institutionalize its trade activities by establishing new organizations. An important influence is the dualistic production structure. On one side, relatively large firms using modern production techniques form oligopolies in some manufacturing sectors; on the other, SMEs mainly use traditional methods. The former are usually organized within large corporations enjoying access to international market information and are thus able to form contacts in the foreign markets; the numerous small enterprises, however, have to overcome a range of problems to engage in foreign trade.

Export activities can be expanded in several ways. One is to set up a manufacturing facility abroad; another is to use or establish a trading agency (sometimes on a cooperative basis). State-owned organizations can mobilize small handicraft producers (Vos and Zurawicki, 1984; International Trade Centre, 1987), but the means will differ according to the power of interest groups, the social structures, the characteristics of the country, and the production structure. Countries adopting export-orientated policies have been impressed by successful examples in advanced countries such as the USA and Japan, and recently the Republic of Korea (Yonekawa, 1983; Cho, 1987).

Institutions specializing in export activities have recently developed in Turkey (Figure 10.2). These include foreign trade companies (FTCs), associations of small exporters, sectoral associations, and semi-public exporter associations. FTCs, legally introduced by a 1980 decree (Türktrade, 1988), were inspired by the Japanese and Korean models (Özel, 1988a). Firms which specialized in marketing for large manufacturing corporations before 1980 adapted themselves to gain the various privileges and incentives offered. The annually defined conditions for gaining FTC status were based on capital, the preceding year's export performance, and the fulfilment of a required level of industrial exports.

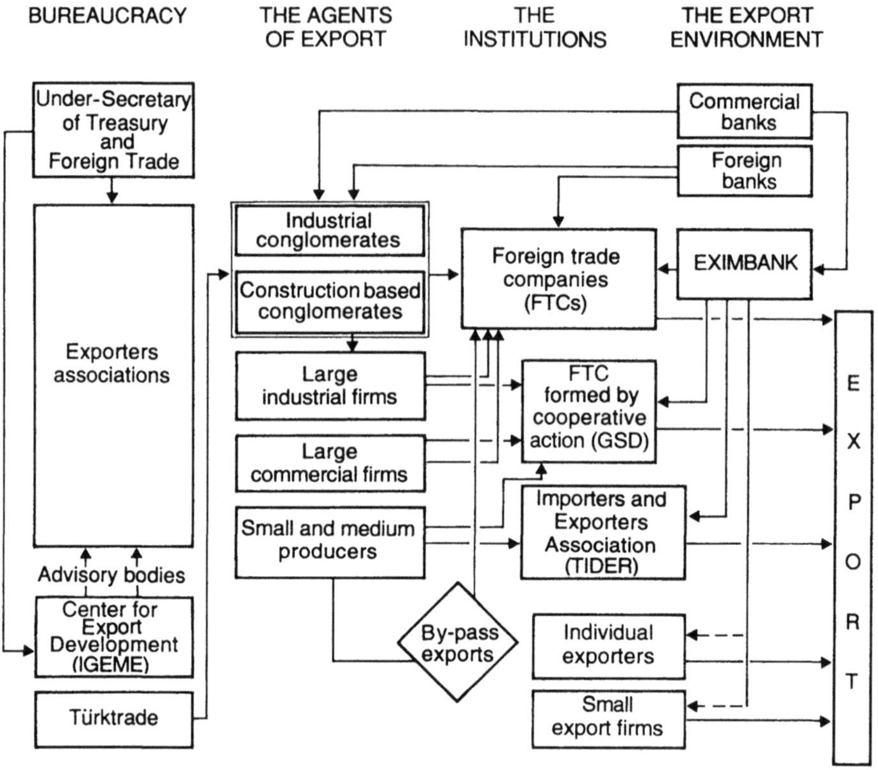


Figure 10.2: Institutional arrangements for Turkish foreign trade activities (author's compilation).

Unlike specialized companies in advanced countries, Turkish FTCs handled a wide range of goods and services to gain economies of scale and minimize the risks associated with fluctuating world prices. Most were affiliated with local industrial and business conglomerates and primarily exported their products, or acted as middlemen for others (Özel, 1988b). Because of the additional incentive premium available to FTCs, SMEs also tried to use them as agents but the FTCs were reluctant to handle this type of business because the turnover was not commensurate with the time, money and effort involved.

The 28 FTCs (1988) increased their share of total exports from US$427 million in 1981 (9 per cent) to US$4,335 million in 1987 (46 per cent). In the latter year one FTC alone handled exports value at US$357 million (Balkır,

1987). Compared with Japan, the Republic of Korea and Taiwan, the number of Turkish FTCs is large, although the average scale of activity is smaller (Korum, 1987). Tax changes in 1989 reduced their export advantages.

The Giyim Sanayicileri Derneği (Union of Ready-Made Clothing Manufacturers) represents a different FTC model. Several textile makers, who believed that the main purpose of FTCs was to deal with the bureaucracy rather than give financial, technological and marketing assistance to SMEs, formed a cooperative export firm that attained FTC status without the support of a large conglomerate (Benzes, 1988). This illustrates the potential for cooperation when common interests exist among small firms.

Some traders, not wanting to work with large companies, have formed separate bodies, a recent example being the Importers and Exporters Association of Turkey (TIDER). This has 820 members and aims to bring together small foreign traders under an umbrella association that can represent their collective interests. One goal is to establish a research unit to undertake market and product research for members and provide information on foreign trade legislation by cooperating with international organizations (Türkiye İhracaat ve İthalatçılar Derneği, 1989).

Another type of organization is the semi-public Exporters Association formed by the Under-Secretary of Foreign Trade and Treasury (UFTT) and the private sector. Among other functions this is responsible for allocating quotas to existing firms according to their past performance as well as to new firms. The private sector, however, is critical of the structure of the organization which permits extensive government control but allows it only a relatively passive role (Coşkun, 1988). Besides the institutions directly related to exports, there are sectoral advisory bodies, such as the Center for Export Development which is connected to the UFTT, and Türktrade formed by FTC entrepreneurs.

## Changing Structure and Business Relations

Previous sections discussed Turkey's macro-policies and various financial schemes involved in transforming development, as well as the emergence of intermediary institutions concerned with arranging export relations. It is appropriate now to define the changes in the structure and business behaviour of large enterprises and SMEs, the two distinct groups involved in foreign trade activities.

**Structural and organizational changes in large enterprises**

A study by the İstanbul Chamber of Industry (İstanbul Sanayi Odası, 1988) covering 288 firms which in 1988 were responsible for 21 per cent of total exports, provides some data on recent structural change and the growth of large enterprises. Exports made up 40 per cent of total sales among 60 per cent of these firms. About 69 per cent have restructured and grown, by investing in new capacity (25 per cent), modernizing existing plant (34 per cent), renewal (21 per cent), establishing a new plant (15 per cent), or other methods (5 per cent). Their main difficulty lay in obtaining finance rather than in technology transfer. While satisfied with their record of growth and restructuring, the firms admitted that their ability to find new outlets and their marketing strategies were inadequate. Previous studies (İstanbul Sanayi Odası, 1984), which examined similar samples of large industrial firms, indicated that they had at least an intention to adapt to the changing world industrial structure. However, later research produced little evidence that structural transformation had occurred other than in a few individual cases (Türel, 1987).

These analyses did not provide information about organizational change and emerging relations with other producers or trading, services, finance and other agents. Yet the changing make-up of conglomerates and the addition of new units to them are very important results of Turkey's extroverted development policies. Conglomerates have become more dominant in the economy. Before 1980, most consisted of several industrial firms with limited export capacity, domestic trade firms, and JVs with foreign enterprises. Liberalization and outward-orientated economic policies led conglomerates to become leading partners in the process of Turkey's integration into the world economy. By forming new structural relations, a different type of conglomerate has appeared. In addition to factories and domestic firms distributing their products, these include a commercial bank, a foreign trade firm in the image of an FTC, and tourist investments such as hotels and tourist villages (Eraydin and Eraydin, 1989). Furthermore, a tendency to form mergers with foreign enterprises has been noted (Devecioğlu, 1988; Kırım, 1989).

As already outlined, the leading FTCs are directly related to conglomerates. Although they have begun to develop offices abroad, their foreign representation is rather weak compared to that of Southeast Asian firms (Özel, 1988a). None the less, conglomerates specializing in international construction, for example, have used their existing offices abroad to gain an important initial advantage (International Trade Centre, 1987). Or again, conglomerates already owning a commercial bank have established offices in Europe, the US and, very recently, in the Commonwealth of Independent States, and use these as overseas contact points for foreign trade.

Even before 1980, two of Turkey's largest conglomerates incorporated a commercial bank but generally access to private banks was limited in a financial system dominated by public institutions. With the adoption of an extroverted development strategy, the country's large production groups became involved in financial institutions because of increased interest rates and the difficulty of obtaining cheap credit, and also because of changes in the legal framework. Groups with bank connections were advantaged. In addition, growing trade relations and moves towards liberalization attracted foreign banks which by 1987 had established 20 branches engaging in foreign rather than domestic trade (Aras, 1987). The entry of foreign banks and the growing number of private ones introduced a competitive climate, forcing these institutions to expand their financial resources and become more active in external relations.

Finally, the increasing importance of tourism in Turkey and the foreign currency it generates attracted both large conglomerates and industrial and construction entrepreneurs. This emphasis on tourism, however, reduced the volume of capital moving into the manufacturing sector.

Capital movements between firms in conglomerates and foreign enterprises were motivated by the desire of manufacturers to adopt new technologies, enlarge production capacity to enter world markets, and increase export earnings. Foreign firms were seen to provide a ready market for at least some types of production and to create a partnership sensitive to domestic market conditions. However, some of the industrial mergers were probably due to financial difficulties being experienced by Turkish firms (*Ekonomik Panorama*, 28 May 1989: 11; Kırım, 1989; Tonak, 1989).

## The changing attitude and structure of SMEs

Informal interviews with SME entrepreneurs and various case studies (Ayata, 1989; Kazgan, 1989; Orta Doğu Teknik Üniversitesi, 1989a,b) revealed how small entrepreneurs with no foreign experience can export their products into well-organized markets. A central problem in developing external trade is the changing quality and type of products being demanded. SMEs working as subcontractors as well as larger enterprises that use trading firms, complain about the inaccessibility of up-to-date information about market structures and new regulations. These basic factors, along with the instability of foreign demand for some products, largely account for the discontinuity in the exports of these firms. Attaining compatibility between demand and existing production thus becomes a major concern for SMEs. The FTCs have a critical role in overcoming these problems.

A study at Bursa (Orta Doğu Teknik Üniversitesi, 1989a) indicated that almost a third of the small and medium-size textile firms exported their goods directly to a foreign firm, assisted by their previous contacts. None the less, their relationships with the FTCs had some advantages. About half mainly relied on FTCs and only temporarily exported their products directly. This occurs because SMEs, in particular, come under pressure from FTCs when they are unable to fulfil their quotas (Orta Doğu Teknik Üniversitesi, 1989a).

In some instances, contact between production units and export firms or FTCs takes place through middlemen — usually tradesmen experienced in import activities — who often organize both subcontracting activities and foreign contacts. These agents are particularly active in small-scale labour-intensive production where subcontracting is prevalent. Locally important tradesmen (usually members of the local Chamber of Commerce) play a leading role in initiating exports of agricultural produce. Trade firms operating on the domestic market may also organize the export of products made by SMEs alongside the FTCs established specifically for this purpose. Direct individual contacts, such as friends or relatives living abroad, also have an important role in developing foreign trade.

Overall, the redirection from domestic to foreign markets necessitates restructuring physical capacity, technological change and a reassessment of the scale of production. SMEs frequently have links with the external world through informal channels, contacts and sources: scrutinizing the existing literature and attending trade fairs are more common practices than licence agreements, partnerships with foreign firms or branch plant relationships (Orta Doğu Teknik Üniversitesi, 1989a).

## Summary

The Turkish experience in attempting to integrate with the world economic system emphasizes several points. First, much more important than the physical restructuring of production activities are changes in attitude, both at the macro-level and at the level of the firm. The integration process can only take place after the transformation of the financial system and the emergence of new organizational structures that create contact patterns. Thus, while limited restructuring of the productive base is important, it is not possible to adopt a new production system without improving the entire economic milieu.

Second, introducing a more open economy leads to certain inevitable transformations, both positive and negative. The state mechanism must be reorganized to cope with changing conditions, and must support the integration process while considering existing production structures and business organization. It must recognize, however, that the production sphere creates its own means, relations and institutions. Large conglomerates with oligopolistic characteristics tend to emphasize corporate behaviour, minimize competition among their members, organize to create pressure groups, and capture additional support from political powers.

Finally, during the adaptation process, a new institutional arrangement evolves, reflecting the interests of newly emerging agents of the integration process. Under these conditions, SMEs are organized by means ranging from more traditional middlemen arranging exports and capital inflows, to firms responsible for foreign capital and trade relations. These intermediary mechanisms facilitate low-technology, labour-intensive, low-wage SMEs to take part in foreign trade while acting as a buffer supplying the domestic market. As such, they play a positive role in the extroverted development process.

# 11 Dynamics of Integrating Foreign Direct Investment into the ASEAN Economy

M. Santokh Singh

During the 1960s and 1970s Japanese, US and West European manufacturing firms began investing abroad, mainly to secure the domestic markets of newly independent nations. Their goal of replacing imports with domestic production complemented these countries' policies of import substitution and encouraging manufacturing. In most cases, plentiful cheap, semi-skilled, non-unionized labour and inexpensive but developed industrial land, as well as attractive incentives (for example, fiscal incentives and relaxed pollution laws) encouraged firms to establish facilities overseas. Besides capturing domestic markets, foreign direct investment (FDI) served to secure a stable supply of tropical raw materials (Singh and Chi, 1981).

The rising costs of labour, energy and raw materials in Japan, the US and the European Community (EC) countries during the 1970s, as well as the need to strengthen their national balance of payments, led to the globalization of industrialization so firms could capitalize on the comparative advantages of manufacturing in Third World countries. The 1980s, in particular, saw a rise in the international economy of a greater emphasis on FDI and the expansion of intra-firm trade. These factors have introduced a new facet to the globalization of industry that challenges existing international trade theories and industrial location theory (Douglass, 1990).

The success of the Asian newly industrializing countries (NICs) — the Republic of Korea (RoK), Taiwan, Hong Kong and Singapore (known as the 'four dragons') — in changing to export-orientated industrialization and service industries is well documented. This chapter examines four of the six developing countries (listed in Table 11.1) making up the Association of South-East Asian Nations (ASEAN). These economies — Thailand, Indonesia, Malaysia and, to some extent, the Philippines — are experiencing faster industrial expansion following several decades of modest growth (Table 11.1). They have become major exporters of a limited, but expanding, range of manufactured goods similar to those of the Asian NICs at an early phase in their industrial development (O'Connor, 1989). In fact, to some extent, exports from these four ASEAN countries compete on world markets with those from the other Asian NICs.

Table 11.1: ASEAN countries: selected economic indicators[a]

| Indicator | Indonesia | Malaysia | Philippines | Thailand | Singapore |
|---|---|---|---|---|---|
| **Area** (000 km$^2$) | 1,905 | 330 | 300 | 513 | 1 |
| **Population** (m.), mid-1990 | 178.2 | 17.9 | 61.5 | 55.8 | 3.0 |
| **GNP per capita** (US$) | | | | | |
| 1979 | 370 | 1,450 | 640 | 600 | 3,770 |
| 1986 | 490 | 1,830 | 560 | 810 | 7,410 |
| 1990 | 570 | 2,320 | 730 | 1,420 | 11,160 |
| 1991 | n.a. | 2,700 | n.a. | 1,620 | 15,000 |
| **Real GDP growth**[b] | | | | | |
| 1965-80 | 7.0 | 7.4 | 5.7 | 7.3 | 10.0 |
| 1980-86 | 3.4 | 4.8 | −1.0 | 4.8 | 5.3 |
| 1980-90 | 5.5 | 5.2 | 0.9 | 7.6 | 6.4 |
| 1989 | 6.5 | 7.6 | 6.0 | 10.5 | 9.2 |
| 1990 | 7.5 | 8.3 | 5.6 | 7.5 | 9.0 |
| 1991 | 7.2 | 8.6 | 4.7 | 7.9 | 6.7 |
| 1992(est.) | 5.5 | 8.6 | 3.5 | 8.0 | 6.0 |
| **Net FDI** (US$ m.) | | | | | |
| 1970 | 83 | 94 | −25 | 43 | n.a. |
| 1990 | 964 | 2,902 | 530 | 2,376 | 4,808 |
| 1986-90 (cumulative) | 2,865 | 6,201 | 2,463 | 5,873 | 17,213 |
| **Manufacturing share of GDP** (per cent) | | | | | |
| 1965 | 8 | 9 | 20 | 14 | 15 |
| 1986 | 14 | 21 | 25 | 21 | 27 |
| 1990 | 20 | n.a. | 25 | 26 | 29 |
| **Manufacturing growth** (per cent, per annum) | | | | | |
| 1965-80 | 12.0 | 12.5 | 6.8 | 11.2 | 13.2 |
| 1980-86 | 7.7 | 5.8 | −1.7 | 5.2 | 2.2 |
| 1980-90 | 12.5 | 8.8 | 0.1 | 8.9 | 6.6 |
| 1989 | 12.2 | 11.6 | 6.6 | 13.1 | 9.8 |
| 1990 | 13.7 | 11.8 | 6.1 | 9.3 | 10.2 |
| 1991 | 13.2 | 10.2 | 5.0 | 9.5 | 10.7 |
| **Value added in manufacturing** (US$ m.) | | | | | |
| 1970 | 994 | 500 | 1,625 | 1,130 | 379 |
| 1985 | 13,447 | 4,896 | 8,048 | 7,696 | 4,311 |
| 1989 | 17,272 | n.a. | 10,728 | 17,635 | 8,463 |

[a] Brunei excluded because of lack of data.
[b] Average annual rate.

*Sources:* World Bank, 1988: *passim*; 1992: *passim*.

The topic reviewed here is the process by which some developing countries move from low-skilled labour-intensive production to more skilled and technology and capital-intensive output by adopting improved labour processes and reorganizing and automating manufacturing. The roles of FDI and national policies deliberately designed to foster it and to build up the national resource environment must be closely examined. These factors have induced significant structural changes at the global scale in key industries such as electronics, telecommunications, computer software, textiles and automotive components. Specifically, the 'territorial framework within which the parts of the division of labour can be sensibly focused upon' (Walker, 1988: 401) has been adopted by foreign capitalists, either alone or assisted by local government and/or local capitalists. These developments foster new learning processes and the possibility of deepening linkages in the regional economy, and therefore have implications for its future. This chapter discusses the dynamics of integrating FDI into the regional economy of these four ASEAN countries by analyzing the regionalized relationships in the manufacturing sector between investment, public policy, and a new socio-political environment for 'modes of production and spatial division of labour' (Walker, 1988: 398).

## ASEAN Nations Within the Global Economy

There is intense competition between these four ASEAN countries in relation to the manufacture of labour-intensive products for export. Each tries to outshine the others in developing a package of incentives to attract foreign investors. In general, their comparative advantage in low-cost production is quickly being eroded by many other developing countries that offer cheaper labour. The People's Republic of China and India, for example, have large markets and offer low labour costs, a factor-mix that enables them to carve out shares of the world market for products like textiles and apparel. Furthermore, attempts by these four ASEAN countries to combat high labour costs by moving into a range of products that command greater value based on the intensity of capital and skill involved in their production are, likewise, confronted by similar attempts by other NICs (Singh, 1989: 2).

A further aggravation is the protective stance adopted by OECD countries (O'Connor, 1989) which shields their domestic markets from low-cost imports by the Multi-Fibre Arrangements regulating trade in textiles and garments. Of more immediate concern and impact, however, has been the effort of these countries to restore their own competitive advantage by automating production and applying innovations based on micro-electronics to product manufacturing, design and testing. Such innovations have also aided coordination problems involved in multi-stage, materials and component-intensive production processes (Rowley, 1988). In general, these developments have had the effect of removing or drastically reducing the labour cost advantages enjoyed by NICs, and have serious implications for the future prosperity of those Asian countries that have already assimilated such innovations in the manufacture of more sophisticated products (O'Connor, 1989: 2).

Neither the OECD countries nor the NICs have applied the new technological developments within an organized geographical production network. Recent changes in the four ASEAN countries, however, point towards the emergence of such a framework, nurtured by foreign and local capitalists in countries at rather different levels of manufacturing ability, skill and economic development. Attention has to focus on connections between this globalization of capital and the extent to which national policies have served to maximize benefits from forging links with the global economy and using them to help induce capital accumulation, industrial transformation and regional development in ASEAN.

## The New Wave of Foreign Direct Investment

The realignment of international exchange rates following the Plaza Agreement in September 1985, and the appreciation of the yen against the US dollar (Figures 2.2 and 2.4), led to an increase in foreign investment in the Asia-Pacific region. Moreover, OECD protectionist policies caused outflows of US, European and Japanese investment from the Asian NICs, in particular from Taiwan, the RoK and Singapore. The geography of investment has thus altered for the Asia-Pacific region and, indeed, for the world. The implications of shifting international FDI for the four ASEAN countries have been even greater than those flowing from the technological developments already mentioned (Phongpaichit, 1990a).

In part, Japan responded to the yen's appreciation, and to import restrictions imposed by the West, by transferring production facilities to countries with import quotas and those with currencies aligned to the US dollar (see Chapter 2). These moves aimed to reduce production costs and gain access to, or enlarge, export markets. The ability of Japanese industry to restructure rapidly and avoid the recessionary impact of protectionism and of the yen's appreciation is illustrated by events in the textiles, motor vehicle, steel, electronics and precision equipment industries (Onoki, 1990: 19–25).

In the case of textiles, efforts were made within Japan to diversify into other fields (such as machinery, dyes and genetically engineered drugs) and high-value segments like fashion materials. The Asahi Chemical Industry Co. Ltd, for example, reduced its dependence on textiles from 75 per cent of revenue in 1965 to 20 per cent in 1988 (United Nations Industrial Development Organization, 1989: 38). Lower-value segments were shifted offshore through Joint Ventures (JVs), and Japanese investment in Asia and elsewhere thus became an important element in the survival of its textile producers.

The Japanese motor vehicle industry took a similar route, locating abroad and closer to the consumer market (see Chapter 2). Exports of cars, trucks and buses declined from 6.7 million units in 1985 to 5.8 million in 1989, but this 13 per cent fall was compensated for by a 14 per cent increase in domestic sales (Japan Automobile Manufacturers Association, 1990: 14, 21). Existing alliances forged with US producers were redeveloped in the context of industrial restructuring which fostered new modes of cooperation aimed at cutting production costs. The 'global grid plan' of car making was reinstituted and the production of vehicle parts was transferred to developing countries and the NICs.

Japan's electronics industry boasted the fastest restructuring pace after 1985 with imports replacing exports. In the case of radio-cassette players, for instance, imports — predominantly from Asian suppliers — rose from 15 per cent of total sales in 1986 to 48 per cent in 1987. At the other extreme, Japan's exports of consumer electronics fell by 25 per cent in 1987 (United Nations Industrial Development Organization, 1989: 39). These trends are likely to intensify as Japanese medium and small-scale companies relocate abroad. Japanese producers seek to decrease yen-dominated costs by restructuring:

thus 40 per cent of Matsushita Electric Industrial Co. Ltd's 1991 exports were made locally, with Toshiba Corp., Hitachi Ltd and Sanyo Electric Co. Ltd also increasing production abroad.

Japanese industrial restructuring involved the rapid expansion of FDI: total investments abroad from 1984 through 1990 amounted to US$249,500 million (Table 11.2), two-thirds occurring during the 1988-90 period. Manufacturing activities absorbed a quarter of the outlays during the seven years to the end of 1990 with the amount increasing substantially during the latter three years. Investments in the manufacturing sector amounted to 27 per cent of the total investments by 1990 and the amount invested soared from US$2,500 million in 1984 to US$3,800 million in 1986, US$7,800 million in 1988 and US$16,000 million in 1989. It dipped marginally to US$15,000 in 1990 (Table 11.3). Overseas investment in manufacturing was followed by the intensification of that in banking, finance, insurance, commerce, services and transport. Such investments support those in the manufacturing sector and compensate for the reduced earnings from industrial products by the increased return from invisible trade.

A large proportion of the Japanese investments went to North America and Europe, especially in the electrical and transport industries, as these were seen as a buttress against protectionist moves. Asia was the third largest recipient, with great interest being shown in facilities making metal goods, chemicals and electrical machinery mainly to supply Japanese enterprises elsewhere.

The experience of Japan has inspired other developing countries (especially the NICs) to follow a similar path to remain competitive. A 40 per cent appreciation of the Taiwanese dollar in 1986 and 1987 and the relaxation in 1987 of the tight restrictions on moving foreign currency out of the country paved the way to free Taiwanese investment abroad. A slightly lower appreciation of the RoK *won* and recent current account surpluses exerted similar pressures towards offshore production (Yuan, 1990: 115).

Many of the investments by Taiwanese and RoK firms focused on Thailand, Malaysia and the Philippines. The withdrawal of the Generalised Systems of Preference from the four Asian NICs in February 1988 induced a further shift of investments to the four ASEAN countries.

Table 11.2: Japan's foreign direct investment by country and region, fiscal years 1984 to 1990 (US$ m.)

| **Region/country** | **1984** | **1985** | **1986** | **1987** | **1988** | **1989** | **1990** | **1984-90** |
|---|---|---|---|---|---|---|---|---|
| United States | 3,360 | 5,395 | 10,165 | 14,704 | 21,701 | 32,540 | 26,128 | 113,993 |
| Canada | 184 | 100 | 276 | 853 | 626 | 1,362 | 1,064 | 4,265 |
| *North America* | *3,544* | *5,495* | *10,441* | *15,357* | *22,328* | *33,902* | *27,192* | *118,258* |
| Indonesia | 374 | 408 | 250 | 545 | 586 | 631 | 1,105 | 3,899 |
| Hong Kong | 412 | 131 | 502 | 1,072 | 1,662 | 1,898 | 1,785 | 7,462 |
| Singapore | 225 | 339 | 302 | 494 | 747 | 1,902 | 840 | 4,849 |
| Republic of Korea | 107 | 134 | 436 | 647 | 483 | 606 | 284 | 2,697 |
| China | 114 | 100 | 226 | 1,226 | 296 | 438 | 349 | 2,749 |
| Thailand | 119 | 48 | 124 | 250 | 359 | 1,276 | 1,154 | 3,330 |
| Malaysia | 142 | 79 | 158 | 163 | 387 | 673 | 725 | 2,327 |
| Taiwan | 65 | 114 | 291 | 367 | 372 | 494 | 446 | 2,149 |
| Philippines | 46 | 61 | 21 | 72 | 134 | 202 | 258 | 794 |
| *East & Southeast Asia* | *1,628* | *1,435* | *2,327* | *4,868* | *5,569* | *8,230* | *7,054* | *31,119* |
| Panama | 1,671 | 1,533 | 2,401 | 2,305 | 1,712 | 2,044 | 1,342 | 13,008 |
| Brazil | 318 | 314 | 270 | 229 | 510 | 349 | 615 | 2,605 |
| Cayman Islands | 1 | 132 | 930 | 1,197 | 2,609 | 1,658 | 588 | 7,115 |
| Bahamas | 97 | 298 | 792 | 734 | 737 | 620 | 121 | 3,399 |
| Bermuda | 29 | 148 | 16 | 36 | 337 | 229 | 360 | 1,154 |
| *Central & S. America* | *2,290* | *2,616* | *4,737* | *4,816* | *6,428* | *5,238* | *3,628* | *29,753* |
| United Kingdom | 310 | 375 | 984 | 2,473 | 3,956 | 5,239 | 6,806 | 20,151 |
| Netherlands | 452 | 613 | 651 | 829 | 2,359 | 4,547 | 2,744 | 12,195 |
| Luxembourg | 315 | 300 | 1,092 | 1,764 | 657 | 654 | 224 | 5,006 |
| FRG | 245 | 172 | 210 | 403 | 409 | 1,083 | 1,242 | 3,764 |
| France | 117 | 67 | 152 | 330 | 463 | 1,136 | 1,257 | 3,522 |
| Switzerland | 229 | 60 | 91 | 224 | 454 | 397 | 666 | 2,121 |
| Spain | 140 | 91 | 86 | 283 | 161 | 501 | 320 | 1,582 |
| Belgium | 71 | 84 | 50 | 70 | 164 | 326 | 367 | 1,132 |
| *Europe* | *1,937* | *1,930* | *3,469* | *6,576* | *9,116* | *14,808* | *14,294* | *52,130* |
| Australia | 105 | 468 | 881 | 1,222 | 2,413 | 4,256 | 3,669 | 13,014 |
| *Oceania* | *157* | *525* | *992* | *1,413* | *2,669* | *4,618* | *4,166* | *14,540* |
| Liberia | 281 | 159 | 289 | 267 | 648 | 643 | 531 | 2,818 |
| *Africa* | *326* | *172* | *309* | *272* | *653* | *671* | *551* | *2,954* |
| Kuwait | 55 | 34 | 41 | 54 | 20 | 32 | 26 | 262 |
| *Middle East* | *273* | *45* | *44* | *62* | *259* | *66* | *27* | *776* |
| **Total** | **10,155** | **12,217** | **22,320** | **33,364** | **47,022** | **67,540** | **56,911** | **249,529** |

*Sources:* Japan, Ministry of Finance, 1991: 95; United Nations Industrial Development Organization, 1991: 51. Data refer to *notifications* of FDI rather than to actual flows.

Table 11.3: Japan's foreign direct investment by industry, fiscal years 1984 to 1990 (US$ m.)

| Sector | 1984 | 1985 | 1986 | 1987 | 1988 | 1989 | 1990 | Total 1951-90 |
|---|---|---|---|---|---|---|---|---|
| Food products | 118 | 90 | 127 | 328 | 418 | 1,300 | 821 | 4,085 |
| Textiles | 85 | 28 | 63 | 207 | 317 | 533 | 796 | 3,999 |
| Wood & paper products | 115 | 15 | 57 | 317 | 605 | 555 | 314 | 2,969 |
| Chemicals | 223 | 133 | 355 | 910 | 1,292 | 2,109 | 2,292 | 10,940 |
| Metals | 718 | 385 | 328 | 786 | 1,366 | 1,591 | 1,047 | 10,308 |
| Non-electrical machinery | 185 | 352 | 626 | 687 | 1,432 | 1,762 | 1,454 | 7,932 |
| Electrical machinery | 409 | 513 | 987 | 2,421 | 3,041 | 4,480 | 5,684 | 20,360 |
| Transport equipment | 437 | 627 | 828 | 1,474 | 592 | 2,053 | 1,872 | 10,880 |
| Other | 215 | 208 | 435 | 704 | 4,050 | 1,901 | 1,207 | 10,138 |
| *Manufacturing sub-total* | *2,505* | *2,352* | *3,806* | *7,832* | *13,805* | *16,284* | *15,486* | *81,613* |
| Agriculture and forestry | 26 | 12 | 15 | 98 | 161 | 151 | 153 | 1,358 |
| Fisheries | 24 | 42 | 52 | 44 | 93 | 47 | 61 | 739 |
| Mining | 484 | 598 | 669 | 512 | 1,013 | 1,262 | 1,328 | 16,539 |
| Construction | 112 | 94 | 250 | 87 | 309 | 646 | 300 | 2,389 |
| Trade and sales | 1,482 | 1,550 | 1,861 | 2,269 | 3,204 | 5,149 | 6,156 | 31,315 |
| Banking, finance, insurance | 2,085 | 3,805 | 7,240 | 10,673 | 13,105 | 15,395 | 8,047 | 65,319 |
| Services | 681 | 665 | 1,560 | 2,780 | 3,733 | 10,616 | 11,292 | 34,667 |
| Transport | 1,651 | 1,240 | 1,925 | 2,144 | 2,372 | 2,927 | 2,169 | 17,438 |
| Real estate | 430 | 1,207 | 3,997 | 5,427 | 8,641 | 14,143 | 11,107 | 45,849 |
| Other | 454 | 322 | 379 | 1,047 | 3 | 180 | 8 | 7,523 |
| *Non-manufacturing sub-total* | *7,429* | *9,536* | *17,949* | *25,080* | *26,546* | *50,517* | *40,620* | *223,136* |
| *Branch offices* | *221* | *329* | *566* | *452* | *583* | *739* | *806* | *5,464* |
| **Total** | **10,155** | **12,217** | **22,320** | **33,364** | **47,023** | **67,540** | **56,911** | **310,808** |

*Sources*: Japan, Ministry of Finance, 1991: 96; United Nations Industrial Development Organization, 1989: 51.

Uncertainties surrounding Hong Kong after 1997 have eroded investors' confidence and caused a massive outflow of capital, some to nearby ASEAN countries where it has been welcomed with appropriate deregulation on equity ownership of manufacturing firms and the liberalization of private foreign investment, particularly with respect to export-orientated products.

Singapore is characterized by a surplus of capital (having the highest saving rate — 40 per cent — in the world), a shortage of land and labour and related rising costs and, since April 1987, a policy of phasing out foreign workers and retaining only a handful with temporary work permits. As a result, many labour and land-intensive manufacturing firms have relocated across the causeway to Johor State in Malaysia which has greatly benefited from this economic twinning and has rapidly become that country's southern growth pole (Salem, 1988). These transfers may also reduce recruitment problems for Singapore's labour-intensive industries (Chang, 1989).

In general, surplus capital moves globally in search of the most attractive locations for production. The ASEAN four have gained popularity with Japan, Taiwan, Singapore, the RoK and Hong Kong as offering offshore production sites, a factor which has substantially altered the range of technological possibilities open to them, and will probably aid their success in the 1990s. Their geographical proximity to Japan and the Asian NICs, and their location in a region with a reputation for political stability and commitment to economic growth will further strengthen their prospects.

**Source and Characteristics of FDI in the 'ASEAN Four'**

FDI flows to the four ASEAN countries have increased in absolute terms since the early 1970s. During the 1977-85 period, FDI in Indonesia, Thailand, Malaysia and the Philippines accounted for 19, 12, 10 and 7 per cent, respectively, of total resource inflows. Whereas FDI accounts for 73, 62 and 62 per cent of the flows to Singapore, Taiwan and Hong Kong, in the ASEAN four it represents only a fraction of gross domestic capital formation. Private financial flows now overshadow official flows from developed countries.

As shown in Table 11.4, the major sources of FDI for the ASEAN countries have been Japan, the US, and the Asian NICs. In 1988, US direct investment, globally, reached a new high of US$326,900 million, of which US$18,900 million (5.8 per cent) went to the Asia-Pacific region (United Nations Industrial Development Organization, 1991: 46). In that year, US direct investment in the ASEAN four totalled US$1,653 million, or 8.7 per cent of its total investment in the Asia-Pacific region, whereas in 1989 it slowed to US$786 million, most of which went to Thailand.

A distinctive feature of FDI in the ASEAN group is the emergence of Japan and the Asian NICs as major suppliers of equity capital (Table 11.4). According to the Japanese Ministry of Finance, FDI to the ASEAN countries increased by over 667 per cent between 1986 and 1989. From the Japanese perspective, these countries are not major recipients of FDI (Table 11.2) as they receive only 4 per cent of its global total; from an Asian perspective, however, Japanese investment, which amounted to 40 per cent of FDI flows to all developing countries in the Asia-Pacific region in 1988, is significant to ASEAN. The share in ASEAN increased rapidly in 1989 and 1990, and in this latter year accounted for 58 per cent of Japanese FDI to all developing countries in the Asia-Pacific region. In each of the four ASEAN countries Japan is the largest or second-largest source of foreign investment.

East Asian sources have similarly gained significance. The Asian NICs invested US$283 million in the ASEAN four in 1986, and in 1988 they became the leading source with flows totalling US$3,648 million as against US$3,627 million from Japan. Japan overtook the Asian NICs again in 1989 with investments worth US$4,439 million or about a third of all investments in the ASEAN four, and together, they contributed 61 per cent of the FDI in 1989 (Table 11.4).

Among the four countries, Thailand was the main recipient of FDI from 1988 to 1990; nearly half the US$7,986 million it received in 1989 came from Japan and a quarter from the Asian NICs. Indonesia was the second largest recipient with the Asian NICs as its main source. In Malaysia, more than two-thirds of FDI was provided by Japan and the Asian NICs, especially Taiwan which in 1990 overtook Japan as the country's leading investor with US$2,300 million.

## Increasing Trade Interdependence in the Asia-Pacific Region

The impact of Japanese FDI on the process of industrialization in the ASEAN countries is even more substantial than data from Japan suggest. In 1984 Japanese companies overseas produced goods worth US$52,000 million which is equal to 4.2 per cent of that nation's GDP. The Ministry of International Trade and Industry in Tokyo has forecast that this will rise to US$228,000 million, 8.3 per cent of GDP, by 1992 and that 25 to 35 per cent of this will be

Table 11.4: Sources of foreign direct investment flows to ASEAN countries, 1986 to 1989 (US$ m.)

| Source | Year | Malaysia | Thailand | Indonesia | Philippines |
|---|---|---|---|---|---|
| **Taiwan** | 1986 | 34.6 | 35.7 | 17.3 | 0.4 |
| | 1987 | 98.5 | 299.2 | 7.9 | 9.0 |
| | 1988 | 146.7 | 849.9 | 913.0 | 109.3 |
| | 1989 | 367.6 | 867.9 | 47.0 | 148.7 |
| **Republic of Korea** | 1986 | 2.1 | 0.9 | 21.5 | – |
| | 1987 | 9.0 | 12.9 | 15.5 | 0.7 |
| | 1988 | 8.9 | –109,0 | 207.0 | 0.5 |
| | 1989 | 29.1 | 170.7 | 224.0 | 17.5 |
| **Hong Kong** | 1986 | 22.5 | 44.8 | 59.8 | 7.3 |
| | 1987 | 11.8 | 125.0 | 122.1 | 22.8 |
| | 1988 | 49.5 | 474.7 | 259.0 | 26.7 |
| | 1989 | 41.5 | 561.5 | 170.0 | 132.8 |
| **Singapore** | 1986 | 42.0 | 9.5 | 105.3 | 0.3 |
| | 1987 | 135.0 | 64.0 | 12.9 | 0.9 |
| | 1988 | 65.7 | 275.6 | 151.0 | 2.0 |
| | 1989 | 98.7 | 407.0 | 47.0 | 23.7 |
| ***Sub-total of NICs*** | *1986* | *101.2* | *90.9* | *84.3* | *8.0* |
| | *1987* | *254.3* | *501.1* | *158.4* | *33.5* |
| | *1988* | *270.8* | *1,709.2* | *1,530.0* | *138.5* |
| | *1989* | *536.9* | *2,007.1* | *488.0* | *322.7* |
| **Japan** | 1986 | 67.6 | 250.7 | 324.6 | 22.3 |
| | 1987 | 185.0 | 965.2 | 512.1 | 28.8 |
| | 1988 | 214.3 | 3,062.7 | 256.0 | 94.6 |
| | 1989 | 391.8 | 3,524.2 | 366.0 | 157.7 |
| **United States** | 1986 | 12.5 | 40.6 | 128.4 | 22.4 |
| | 1987 | 71.1 | 172.2 | 62.0 | 36.0 |
| | 1988 | 96.5 | 673.2 | 731.0 | 152.5 |
| | 1989 | 46.5 | 549.6 | 58.0 | 131.2 |
| **World** | 1986 | 427.9 | 579.1 | 800.4 | 78.2 |
| | 1987 | 745.5 | 1,949.2 | 1,239.7 | 166.6 |
| | 1988 | 767.7 | 6,249.1 | 4,409.0 | 451.4 |
| | 1989 | 1,245.1 | 7,985.8 | 2,651.0 | 804.2 |

*Source:* Adachi, 1990: 27.

located in ASEAN and other Asian countries. Japanese firms will thus add from US$55,000 million to US$65,000 million to Asia's industrial output by 1992, an amount equivalent to the current industrial output of the ASEAN group (Adachi, 1990: 6).

ASEAN's total exports grew 8.9 per cent annually from 1979 to 1989 and its imports by 9.6 per cent. In the latter year its total exports were valued at US$119,500 million and its imports at US$116,000 million (Than, 1991: 180). FDI has not only encouraged rapid industrialization in the four ASEAN countries but has also inspired greater intra-Asian trade which in 1989 amounted to US$310,000 million or 10 per cent of the world total. Japan is the largest trading partner of the ASEAN four, taking US$15,500 million, or 25 per cent of their total exports. The Asian NICs buy 21 per cent (US$13,500 million), and the US 20 per cent (US$12,400 million) (Adachi, 1990: 16) but Japan's contribution to the export growth of the ASEAN four and the Asian NICs is lessening. The major impetus now comes from intra-regional trade between the Asian NICs and the ASEAN four. Trade between the ASEAN countries is growing but only slowly because of the lack of complementarity among these economies.

ASEAN countries have been recording rapid gains in trade and investments which have served to cement the mutual dependence among Asia-Pacific economies, and led to the formation in 1987 of the Asia-Pacific Economic Cooperation (APEC) group of 15 member countries that aims to coordinate macro-economic policies such as exchange rates. Liberalizing trade links with the isolated economies of the People's Republic of China, Vietnam, Laos, Democratic People's Republic of Korea and Burma (Myanmar) has further strengthened this trend towards trade interdependence. Exports from Burma, Laos and Vietnam to ASEAN increased fivefold from US$21 million in 1979 to US$106 million in 1989, while ASEAN exports to these countries during the same period grew from US$132 million to US$186 million in 1989 (Than, 1991: 183–6). The ASEAN group is encouraging local investments into these mainland Southeast Asian countries.

A simulation model developed by the Japanese Economic Planning Agency suggests that that country could help to cushion the impact of a decline in trade with the US and 'fortress Europe' by liberalizing its imports from the ASEAN countries and the Asian NICs as a flow-on from its FDI in the four ASEAN states (Adachi, 1990). However, Phongpaichit (1988) found that only 29 per cent of Japanese firms investing in East and Southeast Asia did so with the aim of selling products in Japan; the rest sold either in the host country or in the US and Western Europe. As export-orientated industrialization in Asian countries is led by corporate hierarchies and networks and their investment strategies, there is a need for caution in claiming that Japan is completely open to manufactured exports from Asia.

## Comparative investment incentives in the four ASEAN countries

Various generous incentives are provided by the four ASEAN countries to attract FDI. In general, foreigners are entitled to the same rights and privileges as those enjoyed by local investors, although the former must adhere to certain restrictions. Performance requirements are stipulated and serve to maintain the government's bargaining power as well as supporting the economic manoeuvres of local technocrats. By and large, however, foreign enterprises can establish and run their businesses in any ASEAN country with little interference. The terms set on foreign exchange remittance are also liberal compared with those in other developing countries.

Although differing in detail, all four countries offer similar incentives. This is hardly surprising since they compete for FDI among themselves as well as with countries outside the region. The packages generally comprise a specific income tax holiday; duty-free imports or reduced taxes and import duties on capital equipment and intermediate inputs; accelerated depreciation allowances; and low-cost credit facilities. Export-orientated FDI projects are also eligible for special incentives, including a longer period of income tax exemption and a reduction of the tax payable on export earnings. Foreign companies located in less developed areas of the countries likewise qualify for extra incentives. There are also free trade and export-processing zones wherein firms are exempted from taxes and duties on imported capital equipment, raw materials and other intermediate products, and on their exports. In addition, ASEAN countries, fully aware that natural resources and comparative labour costs are not the most powerful magnets, are now also placing greater emphasis on socially cultivated differentials and the political and financial stability of the region as a whole. Foreign companies must adhere to various performance requirements. In exchange for the privileges offered, policy guidelines have been set to channel foreign (as well as local) investment into preferred manufacturing sub-sectors. Investors are also required to incorporate, and participate in, investment by local businesses, and to employ local workers.

The blandishments offered to foreign investors differ between the four countries and alter over time (Natarajan and Tan, 1992: 2–12). In Indonesia, for example, there have been moves towards deregulation and liberalization, and in 1985 the sectors in which FDI was permitted were expanded. Similarly, restrictions were relaxed on foreign investment in chemicals, industrial machinery, basic metal, and agricultural industries. In Malaysia, incentives were restructured. In October 1986, new manufacturing investment projects were granted pioneer status and provided with various inducements regardless of their level of capital investment. Greater emphasis has also been placed on export-orientated industries in which a 100 per cent foreign equity ownership is permitted; tax concessions are awarded for R & D and training; and emphasis is being placed on the greater use of local resources. In the Philippines, procedures for granting incentives were simplified in 1983, and in 1987 the Omnibus Investment Code of 1981 was revised to try to attract more FDI by offering various inducements, simplifying customs procedures and liberalizing terms of employment for expatriates. In Thailand, the incentives policy set by the Board of Investment gives priority to companies investing mainly for the domestic market, and locating in Bangkok and adjacent provinces. In all the four ASEAN countries the packaging of incentives and guarantees is constantly being redesigned to align them with exogenous stimuli and internal social and political interests (Salih and Young, 1987: 199). It is an explicit policy that these countries be integrated into the emerging Pacific Rim economy through FDI from Japan, the Asian NICs and the US.

## Intra-ASEAN investment

Comprehensive studies on intra-ASEAN investment are lacking although it is known to be significant. Singapore is the most important source of such funds whereas investment from the other ASEAN countries is still comparatively small (Table 11.4). In Singapore in 1988, 77 per cent of all investments in manufacturing were in the hands of wholly or majority foreign-owned enterprises: these accounted for 82 per cent of direct exports, 70 per cent of gross output, 65 per cent of value added and 53 per cent of employment. In turn,

Singapore invested in the ASEAN four US$1,440 million from 1986 through 1989 using JVs with other transnational corporations. It is now the eighth-largest investor in Indonesia with an investment in 34 projects worth US$315 million, 85 per cent of which was initiated during the 1986-88 period. About 22 per cent of Singapore's FDI in the ASEAN four went to that country.

Singapore has featured as the second-largest investor in Malaysia after Japan, with investments of US$242 million in 1986 through 1988 but the following year it dropped to third position behind Japan and Taiwan. In 1988, Singaporean companies accounted for 47 of the 101 applicants for manufacturing projects in Johor State, representing investments of US$99 million and an employment potential of 14,700. The Singapore Manufacturers' Association reported that 110 Singaporean companies set up factories in Johor State during the last nine months of 1988, compared with 58 in 1987. From 1986 through 1989 investments from Singapore to Malaysia amounted to US$341 million, about 10 per cent of total FDI received there during this four-year period.

Singapore has again entrenched its economic position in ASEAN by integrating its economy with its neighbours. It has diversified its investments and risks by each year concentrating the major portion of its FDI in a different country. In 1986 much of the investment was directed to Indonesia, followed by Malaysia in 1987 and by Thailand in 1988 and 1989. During these four years, only 2 per cent of its investments went to the Philippines (Table 11.4). Singapore, the fifth largest investor in Thailand after Japan, Taiwan, US and Hong Kong, committed US$756 million there from 1986 through 1989, or about 53 per cent of its total FDI in the ASEAN four.

As overseas capital began to invest in ASEAN countries, interest grew in the idea of this becoming a common market. Much of the initial effort went into trying to agree about reducing tariffs on goods moving between member countries and embarking on industrial cooperation schemes. Two arrangements in the early 1970s were the ASEAN Industrial Projects (AIP) and the ASEAN Industrial Complementation schemes. The former aimed to establish large-scale government-initiated projects 'which could utilize raw materials of member countries, create employment and contribute to economic growth' (Phongpaichit, 1990b: 55). In 1980 these initiatives were superseded by the ASEAN Industrial Joint Ventures (AIJV) scheme which has been described as 'the private sector equivalents of AIPs enjoying exclusivity and other privileges . . . but with various added elements of flexibility' (Chng, 1985: 43). A major benefit was the halving of tariffs on intra-regional trade on components between units of the same manufacturer (Phongpaichit, 1990b: 56). Originally to qualify as an AIJV a venture had to have at least 51 per cent ASEAN ownership but in October 1988 this was reduced to 40 per cent.

There are several justifications for the closer economic cooperation imposed on ASEAN countries by the organizational restructuring of large corporations. FDI has played an important role in the process of industrialization in all these nations, and can be effectively utilized to deliver greater benefits to the host economies. This is an important issue. Evidently FDI is beginning to inspire a degree of economic interaction within the ASEAN group that has not yet been attained cooperatively. Arguably, as these countries are in competition for investment inflows, effective cooperation on FDI issues could be difficult. Although competition prevails, foreign and local investors are none the less leaning towards organizational restructuring and industrial transformation and integration, with the aim of taking advantage of the dynamism in labour processes and the regional spatial division of labour to render industry globally competitive.

## Conclusion

Comparative advantages are not solely a matter of factor endowments and intensities. The learning process is additive, and experiences can be adopted and adapted to changing needs. The accessibility and affordability of, for instance, micro-electronic based innovations to the ASEAN countries means that the lag in the adaptation of new technologies between the developed countries, the NICs and some of the more advanced developing countries is decreasing. As neither the cheap labour advantage of the latter countries nor the automation options of the developed ones are absolutely attractive options, the balance is favouring the NICs and some developing countries where the abundance of skilled and semi-skilled labour and deepening technical levels are gaining importance. Reliability and speed reduce costs and make proximity significant so that by operating within the ASEAN group firms can manage inventories and material procurement more efficiently.

Some OECD countries (particularly the US) have tried to reduce the competitiveness of Japan and some of the Asian NICs through currency alignments (see Chapter 2). The ASEAN region thus represents a base from which export-orientated production can operate and so, as Japan's markets have become more open and domestic manufacturing costs continue to rise, many Japanese companies have relocated there. The surge in Taiwanese FDI reflects a similar tactic. FDI introduces technology to the host country since exploring firm-specific technological advantage is often the primary reason for relocation. This must surely raise concern over the foundation, and thus the durability, of local technology, and the vulnerability of industrial development occurring in the ASEAN region.

Japan and the Asian NICs have become both a supplier of capital and a market for ASEAN industry. There is the possibility that the US could push Asia down in its list of priorities because of other geopolitical concerns and involvements (Garten, 1991: 54). With the Japanese economy slumping in the last quarter of 1991 and in 1992 (Powell, 1992: 10) to negative growth and recording a sharp decline in the stock market, it is likely that the ASEAN group will have to contend with a downturn in its FDI programme. Such a downturn, however, will encourage the infrastructural and social support services to realign themselves to demand, thus creating a more conducive socially engineered environment when Japanese companies resume investing in the region and small suppliers in the *keiretsu* (subcontracting) system follow the larger corporations by also moving offshore. FDI is likely to take advantage of the growing intra-ASEAN consumer markets created by a period of prosperity and rapid economic growth since 1987.

# References

Adachi, F., 1990, 'The position of the Malaysian economy in the wider perspective of the western Pacific region' (paper presented to Roving Seminar on Industrial Transformation and Regional Development: Managing Regional Economies in a Borderless Age, Trengganu, Malaysia, 14-17 July).

Adelman, I., 1984, 'Beyond export led growth', *World Development,* 12, 937–49.

Adler, H.S. and Sneath, C.G., 1987, 'Acquiring companies in the U.S.A.', *Long Range Planning*, 20(2), 42–50.

Aglietta, M., 1979, *A Theory of Capital Regulation: The US Experience* (London: New Left Books).

Akat, A.S., 1984, *Alternatif Büyüme Stratejisi* [*Alternative Growth Strategies*] (İstanbul: İletişim).

Akder, H., 1987, 'Constant market share analysis of changes in Turkey's exports to EC (1981-1985)', *Yapı Kredi Economic Review*, 1(2), 33–42.

Akder, H., 1988, 'Turkey's export expansion in the Middle East 1980-1985', *The Middle East Journal*, 41, 553–67.

Aktan, O., 1985, 'The second enlargement of European Communities, probable effects on the members and the new entrants', *European Economic Review*, 28, 279–308.

Aktan, O. and Baysan, T., 1985, 'Türk ekonomisinin dünya ekonomisine enteğrasyonu: liberasyon, karşılaştırmalı üstünlük ve optimum politikalar [The integration of Turkish economy to the world economy: liberation, comparative advantage and optimum policies]', *Middle East Technical University Studies in Development*, 12, 409–507.

Albach, H., 1984, 'Kapitalausstattung und Entwicklung der Wirtschaft [Capital endowment and development of the economy]', in M. Bierich and R. Schmidt (eds), *Finanzierung Deutscher Unternehmen Heute* [*Financing German Enterprises Today*] (Stuttgart: Poeschel), 1–28.

Alesina, A. and Tabellini, G., 1988, *External Debt, Capital Flight and Political Risk* (London: Centre for Economic Policy Research, Working Paper 253).

Alkaçar, B., 1988, *Türkiye'nin Avrupa Topluluğuna Üyeliğinin Dış Ticaretimize Etkileri* [*The Effects of Turkey's Membership of EC on Turkish Foreign Trade*] (Ankara: Türktrade).

Alpar, C., 1982, *Az Gelişmiş Ülkelerin Dış Ticaret Sorunları ve Sanayileşme* [*The Problems of Foreign Trade and Industrialization in Underdeveloped Countries*] (Ankara: Turhan).

Alpar, C., 1989, 'GSD bir model olabilir mi? [Can GSD (Union of Ready Made Clothing Industrialists) be a Model?]', *Dünya*, 31 May, 2.

Alptekin, Y., 1988, 'Tekstil sektörü yol ayırımında [The textile sector is at the crossroads]', *Dış Ticarette Durum*, May-June, 4–10.

Amadeo, E.J. and Banuri, T., 1988a, 'Policy, governance, and the management of conflict', unpublished paper (Helsinki: World Institute for Development Economics Research).

Amadeo, E.J. and Banuri, T., 1988b, 'Worlds within the Third World labour market institutions in Asia and Latin America', unpublished paper (Helsinki: World Institute for Development Economics Research).

Andreff, W., 1984, 'International centralisation of capital', *Capital and Class*, 22, 59–80.

Aras, M., 1987, 'Görüşler [Personal views]', in *Türkiye'nin Dış Ticaretinde Banka Sistemi* [*The Turkish Banking System in Foreign Trade*] (Ankara: Türktrade).

Ash, N., 1991, 'Fulfilling the new state plan', *Euromoney (Special supplement: Czechoslovakia, Progress under Pressure)*, June, 11–14.

Ayata, S., 1989, 'Buldan ve çevresinde değişen üretim ve sosyal yapı [Changing production and social structure at Buldan and its environment]' (paper presented to the Social Science Congress of Turkey, 10-15 May).

Ayto, J. and Bollard, A., 1987, *New Zealand Distributive Trade* (Wellington: New Zealand Institute of Economic Research, Research Paper No. 34).

Baban, A.S., 1987, 'Türkiye'de yabancı sermaye [Foreign investment in Turkey]', *1987 Sanayi Kongresi Bildirileri* (Ankara: Türkiye Mimar ve Mühendis Odaları Birliği [Union of Chambers of Architects and Engineers]), 23–41.

Bakis, H., 1987, 'Telecommunications and the global firm', in F.E.I. Hamilton (ed.), *Industrial Change in Advanced Economies* (London: Croom Helm), 130–60.

Balassa, B., 1977, *Policy Reform in Developing Countries* (New York: Pergamon).

Balassa, B., 1978, 'Exports and economic growth: further evidence', *Journal of Development Economics*, 5, 131–89.

Balkır, C., 1987, 'Görüşler [Personal views]', in *1987 Yılında Dış Ticarette Beklentiler Semineri* (Ankara: Türktrade), 59–82.

Bank for International Settlements, 1992, *62nd Annual Report 1st April 1991 — 31st March 1992* (Basle: BIS).

Barclays Bank Ltd, 1979, 'Barclays briefing: Eurobonds', *The Economist*, 20 October.

Begg, I, 1992, 'Spatial impact of completion of the EC internal market for financial services, *Regional Studies*, 26 (4), 333–47.

Benzes, O., 1988, 'GSD: dernekten şirkete [From association to firm]', *Dış Ticarette Durum*, May-June, 36–8.

Berg, A. and Sachs, J., 1988, 'The debt crisis: structural explanations of country performance', *Journal of Development Economics*, 29, 271–306.

Bhagwati, J., 1964, 'The pure theory of international trade: a survey', *Economic Journal*, 74, 1–84.

Bhaskar, R., 1979, *The Possibility of Naturalism* (New Jersey: Humanities Press).

Bluestone, B. and Harrison, B., 1982, *The Deindustrialization of America: Plant Closings, Community Abandonment, and the Dismantling of Basic Industry* (New York: Basic Books).

Boddy, M., 1981, 'The property sector in late capitalism: the case of Britain', in M. Dear and A. Scott (eds), *Urbanisation and Urban Planning in Capitalist Society* (London: Methuen), 267–87.

Böhme, H., 1978, *An Introduction to the Social and Economic History of Germany: Politics and Economic Change in the Nineteenth and Twentieth Centuries* (New York: St Martin's Press) [originally published, 1972, as *Prolegomena zu einer Sozial- und Wirtschaftsgeschichte Deutschlands im 19. und 20. Jahrhundert* (Suhrkamp Verlag)].

Bollard, A. and Easton, B. (eds), 1985, *Markets, Regulation and Pricing: Six Case Studies* (Wellington: New Zealand Institute of Economic Research, Research Paper No. 31).

Bonus, H. and Schmidt, G., 1990, 'The cooperative banking group in the Federal Republic of Germany: aspects of institutional change', *Journal of Institutional and Theoretical Economics*, 146, 180–207.

Boratav, K., 1988, *Türkiye İktisat Tarihi* [*Economic History of Turkey*] (İstanbul: Gerçek).

Boyer, R., 1986, *La Théorie de la Régulation: une Analyse Critique* [*The Theory of Régulation: A Critical Analysis*] (Paris: La Découverte) [English translation, Columbia University Press, 1988].

Boyer, R., 1988, 'Technical change and the theory of "Régulation"', in G. Dosi, C. Freeman, R. Nelson, G. Silverberg and L. Soete (eds), *Technical Change and Economic Theory* (London: Pinter), 67–94.

Boyer, R., 1990, *The Regulation School: A Critical Introduction* (New York: Columbia University Press).

Brierley Investments Ltd, 1980-1988, *Annual Report* (Wellington: BIL).

Brierley Investments Ltd, 1985a, *Director's Report* (Wellington: BIL).

Brierley Investments Ltd, 1985b, *Directory of Principal Investments* (Wellington: BIL).

Britton, S. and Le Heron, R., 1987, 'Regions and restructuring in New Zealand: issues and questions in the 1980s', *New Zealand Geographer*, 43, 129–39.

Britton, S. and Perry, M., 1987, *Enterprises and Economic Restructuring in the Auckland Region* (Auckland: University of Auckland).

Bromley, D.W., 1989, *Economic Interests and Institutions. The Conceptual Foundations of Public Policy* (New York: Basil Blackwell).

Browett, J. and Leaver, R., 1989, 'Shifts in the global capitalist economy and the national economic domain', *Australian Geographical Studies*, 27, 31–46.

Bruck, C., 1989, *The Predators' Ball: The Inside Story of Drexel Burnham and the Rise of the Junk Bond Raiders* (New York: Penguin).

Bryan, R., 1987, 'The state and internationalisation of capital: an approach to analysis', *Journal of Contemporary Asia*, 17, 253–75.

Buchanan, J., 1986, *Liberty, Market and State: Political Economy in the 1980s* (Brighton: Wheatsheaf Books).

Buhl, I. and Schulz, E., 1991, 'Ausländische Investitionen. Joint ventures, Privatisierung, Wirtschaftssonderzonen [Foreign investments, Joint Ventures, privatization, special economic zones]', in Deutsche Bank, *Osteuropa im Aufbruch [Eastern Europe at the Break-up]* (Frankfurt am Main: Deutsche Bank), 78–85.

Burstein, D., 1990, *Yen! Japan's New Financial Empire and Its Threat to America* (New York: Fawcett Columbine).

Büschgen, H. E., 1986, *Internationales Finanzmanagement [International Financial Management]* (Frankfurt am Main: Knapp).

Büschgen, H.E., 1990a, 'Leasing und EC-Binnenmarkt [Leasing and the EC Single Market]', *Finanzierung, Leasing, Factoring*, 1, 3–9.

Büschgen, H.E., 1990b, 'Neben Auflockerungserscheinungen wächst auch Tendenz zur Kooperation [Despite dispersal tendencies cooperation processes are increasing]', *Handelsblatt* no. 93, B24.

Calverly, J., 1985, *Country Risk Analysis* (London: Butterworths).

Cameron, R. (ed.), 1976, *Banking in the Early Stages of Industrialization: A Study in Comparative Economic History* (New York: Oxford University Press).

Carew, E., 1986, *New Zealand's Money Revolution* (Wellington: Allen & Unwin/Port Nicholson Press).

Chandler, A.D., 1962, *Strategy and Structure* (Cambridge, Mass.: M.I.T. Press).

Chang, M.K., 1989, *Industrial Transformation and Regional Development in Asean: The Impact of Singapore* (Nagoya: United Nations Centre for Regional Development).

Channon, D.F., 1973, *The Strategy and Structure of British Enterprise* (Boston: Harvard University Press).

Charap, J. and Dyba, K., 1991, 'Transition to a market economy. The case of Czechoslovakia', *European Economic Review* 35(2/3), 581–90.

Chick, V. and Dow, S.C., 1988, 'A post-Keynesian perspective on the relation between banking and regional development', in P. Arestis (ed.), *Post-Keynesian Monetary Economics: New Approaches to Financial Modelling* (Aldershot: Elgar), 219–50.

Chng, M.K., 1985, 'ASEAN economic co-operation: the current status', *Southeast Asian Affairs*, 4, 40–53.

Cho, D.S., 1987, *The General Trading Company: Concept and Strategy* (New York: Lexington).

Clapham, C., 1987, 'The Third World state', in T. Miljan (ed.), *The Political Economy of North-South Relations* (Peterborough: Broadview Press), 76–8.

Clark, G., Gertler, M.S. and Whiteman, J., 1986, *Regional Dynamics: Studies in Adjustment Theory* (Boston: Allen & Unwin).

Coşkun, A., 1988, 'İhraatçı birlikler hakkında iki görüş [Two views on export corporations]', *Dış Ticarette Durum*, May-June, 12–13.

Coffee, J.C., Lowenstein, L. and Rose-Ackerman, S. (eds), 1988, *Knights Raiders and Targets: The Impact of the Hostile Takeover* (New York: Oxford University Press).

Cohen, R.B., 1981, 'The new international division of labor, multinational corporations and urban hierarchy', in M. Dear and A.J. Scott (eds), *Urbanization and Urban Planning in Capitalist Society* (London: Methuen), 287–315.

Cohen, St S. and Zysman, J, 1987, *Manufacturing Matters, The Myth of the Post-industrial Economy* (New York: Basic Books).

Cooke, P., 1983, *Theories of Planning and Spatial Development* (London: Hutchinson).

Cooke, T., 1986, *International Mergers and Acquisitions* (Oxford: Basil Blackwell).

Corbridge, S., 1988, 'The debt crisis and the crisis of global regulation', *Geoforum*, 19, 109–30.

Corbridge, S., 1989, 'Debt, the nation-state and theories of the world economy' in D. Gregory and R. Walford (eds), *Horizons in Human Geography* (London: Macmillan), 341–60.

Coyne, J. and Wright, M. (eds), 1986, *Divestment and Strategic Change* (Oxford: Philip Allan).

Crockett, A.D. and Nsouli, S.M., 1977, 'Exchange rate policies for developing countries', *Journal of Development Studies*, 13, 125–43.

Cruszecki, P., 1991, 'Privatisation in Poland 1990', *Communist Economies and Economic Transformation*, 3(2), 141–54.

Curham, J.P., Davidson, W. and Suri, R., 1977, *Tracing the Multinationals* (Cambridge, Mass.: Ballinger).

Cusumano, M.A., 1985, *The Japanese Automobile Industry: Technology and Management at Nissan and Toyota* (Cambridge, Mass.: The Council on East Asian Studies, Harvard University).

Daly, M., 1984, 'The revolution in international capital markets: urban growth and Australian cities', *Environment and Planning A*, 16, 1003–20.

Daly, M.T. and Logan, M.I., 1986, 'The international financial system and national economic development patterns', in D. Drakakis-Smith (ed.), *Urbanisation in the Developing World* (London: Croom Helm), 37–62.

Daly, M.T. and Logan, M.I., 1989, *The Brittle Rim: Finance, Business and the Pacific Region* (Melbourne: Penguin).

Dear, M., 1988, 'La reconstruction de la géographie humaine [The reconstruction of human geography]', in G.B. Benko (ed.), *Les Nouveaux Aspects de la Théorie de la Géographie à la Sociologie* [*The New Aspects of Social Theory. From Geography to Sociology*] (Caen: Paradigme), 55–75.

Debenham, Tewson and Chinnocks, 1982, *Money into Property* (London: DTC).

Debenham, Tewson and Chinnocks, 1989, *Money into Property* (London: DTC).

Deutsche Bank, 1990, *Annual Report* (Frankfurt am Main: Deutsche Bank).

Deutsche Bundesbank, 1989, 'Längerfristige Entwicklung des Bankensektors und Marktstellung der Kreditinstitutsgruppen [Long-term development in the banking sector and the marketing position of groups of credit institutions]', *Monatsberichte*, 41(4), 13–22, 53–72.

Deutsche Bundesbank, 1993, 'Die Entwicklung des deutschen Auslandsvermögens und der Kapitalerträge [The development of German foreign assets and capital returns]', *Monatsberichte der Deutschen Bundesbank*, 45(1), 43–57.

Devecioğlu, T., 1988, 'Yerli şirketlere yabancı damat [Foreign sons-in-law for domestic firms]', *Ekonomik Panorama*, 25 December, 22–3.

Devlet Planlama Teşkilatı [State Planning Organization], 1988, *1989 Yılı Programı* [*1989 Annual Programme*] (Ankara: DPT).

de Vroey M., 1984, 'A regulation approach interpretation of the contemporary crisis', *Capital and Class*, 23, 454–56.

Dicken, P., 1992, *Global Shift: The Internationalization of Economic Activity* (London: Paul Chapman Publishing).

Ding, Shi-cheng, 1990, 'The Golden Delta of Northeast Asia in the future — the delta of Tumen River' (paper presented to International Conference on Co-operation in Economic Development in the Coastal Area of Northeast Asia, Changchun, PRC, 16-18 July).

Done, K. and Garnett, N., 1989, 'Being special is not enough', *Financial Times*, 23 September, 6.

Douglass, M., 1990, 'The globalization of industrialization in Southeast Asia: rethinking regional development theory and policy' (paper presented to Roving Seminar on Industrial Transformation and Regional Development: Managing Regional Economies in a Borderless Age, Trengganu, Malaysia, 14-17 July).

Drucker, P., 1986, 'The changed world economy', *Foreign Affairs*, 3, 768–91.

Dugan, A., 1990, 'Banks on the firing line', *Euromoney*, September, 119–25.

Dunford, M., 1990, 'Theories of regulation', *Environment and Planning D: Society and Space*, 8, 297–322.

Dunnett, A., 1989, 'The role of the exchange rate in the decline of UK manufacturing', *The Royal Bank of Scotland Review*, 161, 13–25.

Easterwood, J.C., Seth, A. and Singer, R.F., 1989, 'The impact of leveraged buyouts on strategic direction', *California Management Review*, 32(1), 30–43.

Eckstein, W., 1988, 'Wirtschaftsorganisationen des Leasing [Industrial organizations of leasing]', in K.F. Hagenmüller and G. Stoppek (eds), *Leasing-Handbuch für die Betriebliche Praxis* [*Handbook of Leasing for Managerial Practice*] (Frankfurt am Main: Knapp), 159–82.

Economic and Social Council Economic Comission for Europe, Committee on the Development of Trade, 1988, *East-West Joint Ventures: Economic, Business, Financial and Legal Aspects* (New York: United Nations, Sales no. E.88.II.E.18).

Economou, P., 1990, 'Enterprises from Eastern Europe and the USSR', *The CTC Reporter*, 30, 46–7.

Edwards, C., 1985, *The Fragmented World: Competing Perspectives in Trade, Money and Crises* (London: Methuen).

Edwards, C., 1988, 'The debt crises and development: a comparison of major economic theories', *Geoforum*, 19, 3–28.

Edwards, J. and Fischer, K., 1991, *An Overview of the German Financial System* (Cambridge: Cambridge University: CEPR).

Ellis, J.A., 1976, *Industrial Concentration* (Wellington: New Zealand Institute of Economic Research, Research Paper No. 20).

El-Rifai, G., 1990, 'Opening statement' (paper presented to Hungary Investment Promotion Conference, Budapest, 10-12 September).

Eraydin, A. and Eraydin, H., 1989 'Turizm sermayesinin oluşumu ve mekansal arayışları [The formation and spatial tendencies of tourism capital]', *Turizm Yapıları Uygulamalı Sempozyumu* (İstanbul: Yıldız Üniversitesi), 156–65.

Erdal, B., 1986, *Türk Ticaretinde Yapısal Değişme (1980-1986)* [*Structural Change in Turkish Foreign Trade (1980-1986)*] (Ankara: İhracaatı Geliştirme ve Destekleme Merkezi).

Evans, P., 1979, *Dependent Development* (Princeton: Princeton University Press).

Evans, P. and Plumb, C., 1984, 'The property requirements of knowledge based industries', *Land Development Studies*, 1, 131–44.

Ewers, H.J. and Wettmann, R., 1980, *Innovationsorientierte Regionalpolitik* [*Innovation Oriented Regional Policy*] (Bonn: Schriftenreihe 'Raumordnung' des Bundesministers für Raumordnung, Bauwesen und Städtebau 06.042 ['Regional Policy' Series of the Federal Minister for Regional Policy, Building and Urban Development 06.042]).

Faegin, J., 1982, 'Urban real estate speculation in the US: implications for social science and urban planning', *International Journal of Urban and Regional Research*, 6, 35–60.

Faegin, J., 1987, 'The secondary circuit of capital: office construction in Houston, Texas', *International Journal of Urban and Regional Research*, 11, 172–92.

Fagan, R.H., 1988, 'Australia in the global economy' (paper presented to the Conference of the IGU Commission on Industrial Change, Rutherglen, Tasmania, 22-26 August).

Fagan, R.H., 1990, 'Elders IXL Ltd: finance capital and the geography of corporate restructuring', *Environment and Planning A*, 22, 647–66.

Fagan, R.H. and Le Heron, R.B., 1990, 'Reinterpreting the geography of production', unpublished paper (North Ryde: Macquarie University).

Fallows, J., 1989, 'Containing Japan', *The Atlantic Monthly*, 263(5), 40–54.

Fletcher, H.A., 1982, 'The role of the private sector in resource development', in *Proceedings, Eleventh New Zealand Geographic Conference* (Christchurch: New Zealand Geographical Society), 5–7.

Flight, H. and Lee-Swan, B., 1988, *All You Need Know About Exchange Rates* (London: Sidgwick and Jackson).

Florida, R.L. and Kenney, M., 1988, 'Venture capital, high technology and regional development', *Regional Studies*, 22, 33–48.

Fothergill, S., Monk, S. and Perry, M., 1987, *Property and Industrial Development* (London: Hutchinson).

Franklin, S.H., 1978, *Trade Growth and Anxiety* (Wellington: Methuen).

Frey, B.S., 1984, *International Political Economics* (Oxford: Basil Blackwell).

Friedmann, J., 1986, 'The world city hypothesis', *Development and Change*, 17, 69–83.

Fryer, D., 1988, 'The political geography of international lending by private banks', *Transactions, Institute of British Geographers*, n.s., 12, 412–32.

Gallagher, M., 1990, 'Poles on top in Eastern Europe', *Euromoney*, September, 130–3.

Garten, J.E., 1991, 'Asia and the new economic order', *Far Eastern Economic Review*, 11 April, 54.

George, S., 1988, *A Fate Worse Than Debt* (London: Penguin).

Gerke, W., 1984, 'Finanzstrategien der Banken im Wandel [Changing financial strategies of banks]', in E. Gaugler, O.H. Jacobs and A. Kieser (eds), *Strategische Unternehmensführung und Rechnungslegung* [*Strategic Management and Rendering of Accounts*] (Stuttgart: Poeschel), 117–31.

Gertler, M.S., 1988, 'The limits to flexibility: comments on the Post-Fordist vision of production and its geography', *Transactions of the Institute of the British Geographers*, 13, 419–32.

Gibbs, D., 1991, 'Venture capital and regional development: the operation of the venture capital industry in Manchester', *Tijdschrift voor Economische en Sociale Geografie*, 82 (4), 241–53.

Gibbs, D.C. and Gentle, C.J.S., 1990, 'Global financial dynamics, recent growth of financial services and Manchester's space economy: some preliminary evidence', *Tijdschrift voor Economische en Sociale Geografie*, 81, 110–22.

Gibson, K. and Horvath, R., 1983, 'Global capital and the restructuring crisis in Australian manufacturing', *Economic Geography*, 59, 178–94.

Giddens, A., 1984, *The Constitution of Society* (Cambridge: Polity Press).

Goldsmith, R.W., 1983, *The Financial Development of Japan, 1868-1977* (New Haven, Ct: Yale University Press).

Greater London Council, 1986, *London Financial Strategy* (London: GLC).

Green, G.P., 1987, *Finance Capital and Uneven Development* (Boulder: Westview Press).

Guild, I. and Harris, R., 1985, *Forfaiting: An Alternative Approach to Export Trade Finance* (Cambridge: Woodhead-Faulkner & Euromoney Publications).

Gwynne, R.N., 1979. 'Oligopolistic reaction', *Area*, 11, 316–19.

Hall, M., 1987, *Financial Deregulation. A Comparative Study of Australia and the United Kingdom* (London: Macmillan).

Hamer, E., 1988, 'Die Bedeutung der Spezialfinanzierungsinstitute für mittelständische Unternehmen [The significance of special financing institutions for medium-size enterprises]', unpublished paper (Hannover: Mittelstandsinstitut Niedersachsen e.V.).

Hamilton, F.E.I., 1990, 'A global region in the melting-pot?', *Geoforum*, 21, 145–61.

Hamilton, R.T., 1986, 'The extent and nature of diversification in New Zealand manufacturing industries', *New Zealand Economic Papers*, 20, 77–91.

Händel, W. and Patterson, A., 1990, 'Strukturwandel im Markt für Finanzdienstleistungen [Structural change in the market for financial services]', *DBW Die Betriebswirtschaft*, 50, 157–69.

Hänkel, W., 1989, 'Kapitalmärkte und Finanzinstitutionen im Entwicklungsprozess [Capital markets and financial institutions in development]', in H. Körner (ed.), *Zur Analyse von Institutionen im Entwicklungsprozess und in der Internationalen Zusammenarbeit [Towards an Analysis of Institutions in the Development Process and in International Cooperation]* (Berlin: Schriften des Vereins für Sozialpolitik, No. 186), 169–202.

Harper, D.A., 1986, *The Financial Services Industry: Effects of Regulatory Reform* (Wellington: New Zealand Institute of Economic Research, Research Paper no. 35).

Harris, N., 1987, *The End of the Third World* (London: Penguin).

Harvey, D., 1982, *The Limits to Capital* (Oxford: Basil Blackwell).

Harvey, D., 1989, *The Urban Experience* (Oxford: Basil Blackwell).

Hauser, J., 1987, 'Zagraniczne przedsiebiorstwa drobnej wytwórczości w Wielkoposce [Small foreign manufacturing enterprises in Wielkopolska]', *Kronika Wielkopolska*, 1(44), 148–79.

Hay, D.A. and Morris, D.J., 1979, *Industrial Economics* (Oxford: Oxford University Press).

Healey and Baker, 1990, *Quarterly Investment Report* (March) (London: Healey and Baker Research Services).

Heffernan, S.A., 1986, *Sovereign Risk Analysis* (Worcester: Allen & Unwin).

Heiduk, G., Ladyka, S., Misala, J. and Wingender, P. (eds), 1991, *Deutsch-Polnische Joint Ventures. Ergebnisse einer Befragung* [*German-Polish Joint Ventures. Results of a Survey*] (Hamburg: Duisburger Volkswirtschaftliche Schriften 10, Steuer-und Wirtschaftsverlag).

Henneberry, J., 1988, 'Conflict in the industrial property market', *Town Planning Review*, 59, 241–62.

Hepworth, M. E., 1989, 'The electronic comeback of information space', *Tijdschrift voor Economische en Sociale Geografie*, 80, 3–42.

Hepworth, M., 1990, *Geography of the Information Economy* (London: The Guildford Press).

Herr, H., 1987, *Der Euro-DM-Markt: Theoretische Erfassung, empirische Entwicklung und Einfluss auf die nationale Geldpolitik* [*The Euromoney Market: Theoretical Recording, Empirical Growth and Impact on National Monetary Policy*], Discussion Paper IIM/LMP 87-7 (Berlin: Wissenschaftzentrum).

Hillier Parker Research, 1987, *Industrial Contour Map: Rents and Yields* (London: Hillier Parker May and Rowden).

Hirn, W., 1990, 'Hohe Temperatur. Zwei Studien drängen die EC zum Abbau von Takeover-Barrieren. Auch die Deutschen haben hohe Hürden [High temperature. Two studies push the EC to reduce takeover barriers. The Germans, too, have high hurdles]', *Wirtschaftswoche*, 44 (1/2), 104–6.

Holly, B.P., 1987, 'Regulation, competition and technology: the restructuring of the US commercial banking system', *Environment and Planning A*, 19, 633–52.

Honda, K., 1992, 'Micro issues distort U.S.-Japan trade ties', *Nikkei Weekly*, 11 April, 6.

Hungary, Ministry of Foreign Affairs, 1991, *Investment by Foreigners in Hungary* (Budapest: Fact Sheets on Hungary 7).

Huxley, M. and Berry, M., 1988, 'Big build: property capital, the state and urban change in Australia' (paper presented to 26th International Geographical Union Congress, Sydney, Australia).

İhracaatı Geliştirme ve Destekleme Merkezi [Centre for Development and Support of Export Activities], 1988a, *Türk Dış Ticaretinde Yapısal Değişme (1980-1986)* [*Structural Change in Turkish Foreign Trade (1980-1986)*] (Ankara: IGEME).

İhracaatı Geliştirme ve Destekleme Merkezi [Centre for Development and Support of Export Activities], 1988b, *Foreign Trade and Investment Measures* (Ankara: IGEME).

International Monetary Fund, 1986, *World Economic Outlook April 1986* (Washington D.C.: IMF).

International Stock Exchange, 1990, *Information on Personal Shareholding* (London: Retail Marketing Unit, ISE).

International Trade Centre, 1987, *Export Agencies: The Role in Promoting Exports of Small and Medium Sized Enterprises in Developing Countries* (Geneva: ITC).

İstanbul Sanayi Odası [Istanbul Chamber of Industry], 1984, *Sanayide Fon Akımı ve Finans Yollarındaki Değişim* [*The Flow of Funds in Industry and the Changes in Financial Mechanisms*] (İstanbul: Can Matbaası).

İstanbul Sanayi Odası [Istanbul Chamber of Industry], 1988, *Yılı İhracaat Durumu ve Anket Sonuçları* [*Conditions in Export Activities and the Results of the Interviews*] (İstanbul: ISO).

James, C., 1984, 'Occupational pensions: the failure of private welfare', *Fabian Pamphlet No 497* (London: Fabian Society).

Japan Automobile Manufacturers Association, 1990, *Motor Vehicle Statistics of Japan 1990* (Tokyo: JAMA).

Japan, Ministry of Finance, 1991, *Financial Statistics of Japan, 1991* (Tokyo: Ministry of Finance, Institute of Fiscal and Monetary Policy).

Jenkins, R., 1984, 'Divisions over the international division of labour', *Capital and Class*, 22, 28–57.

Jennings, R. and Mazzeo, M., 1986, 'Resisting takeovers isn't always bad', *Business Horizons*, 29(2), 56–60.

Jesson, B., 1987, *Behind the Mirror Glass* (Auckland: Penguin).

Jessop, B., 1988, 'Regulation theory, post-fordism and the state', *Capital and Class*, 34, 147–68.

Jessop, B., 1989, 'Regulation theories in retrospect and prospect' (revised paper first presented at the International Conference on Regulation Theory, Barcelona, 16-18 June 1988).

Johnson, P. and Ash, T.G., 1990, 'Entering the "age of deals": two views on how to reconstruct the continent', *World Press Review*, March, 24–6.

Kafka, A., 1978, 'The new exchange rate regime and the developing countries', *Journal of Finance*, 33, 795–802.

Kammer, J.F., 1986, 'Financial management and international banks: the policy of BASF', in D.B. Zenoff (ed.), *Corporate Finance in Multinational Companies* (London: Euromoney Publications), 107–13.

Kazgan, G., 1985, *Ekonomide Dışa Açık Büyüme* [*Extroverted Economic Development*] (İstanbul: Altın Kitaplar).

Kazgan, G., 1987, *Prospects for Turkey's Accession to the Community with Special Reference to Competitiveness* (Istanbul: Association of Turkish Industrial and Business Entrepreneurs).

Kazgan, G., 1989, 'Türk imalat sanayinin AT ile ilgili beklentileri ve rekabet koşulları [The expectations of Turkish manufacturing industry from EC and the conditions of competition]', *Dış Ticarette Durum*, 14(1-2), 33–5.

Killick, T., 1983, 'The possibilities of development planning', in M.P. Todaro (ed.), *The Struggle for Economic Development* (New York: Longman), 351–69.

Kindleberger, C.P., 1983, 'International banks as lenders or followers of international business: a historical perspective', *Journal of Banking and Finance*, 7, 583–95.

Kırım, A., 1989, 'Şirketler nasıl kabuk değiştirdi [How the firms have changed their skins]', *Ekonomik Panorama*, 26 February, 22–3.

Kornai, J., 1980, *The Economics of Shortage* (Amsterdam: North Holland).

Kornai, J., 1989, *Régi és új Ellentmondások* [*Old and New Contradictions*] (Budapest: Magvetö, Gyorsuló Ido Sorozat).

Korum, U., 1987, 'Görüşler [Personal views]', in *1987 Yılında Dış Ticarette Beklentiler Semineri*, (Ankara: Türktrade), 85–9.

Központi Statisztikai Hivatal, 1991, *Gazdaságstatisztikai Evköyv* [*Yearbook on Economic Statistics*] (Budapest: KSH).

Központi Statisztikai Hivatal, 1992, *Gazdaságstatisztikai Evkönyv* [*Yearbook on Economic Statistics*] (Budapest: KSH).

Krugman, P., 1988, *Financing vs. Forgiving: A Debt Overhang* (Cambridge, Mass.: National Bureau of Economic Research, Working Paper No. 2486).

Kurm, M., 1989, 'Der Exportweltmeister bei Finanzen in der zweiten Liga [The world champion in exports second division in financial services]', *Handelsblatt* no. 59, 12.

Kuznets, P., 1988, 'An East Asian model of economic development: Japan, Taiwan and South Korea', *Economic Development and Cultural Change (Supplement: Why Does Overcrowded, Resource Poor East Asia Succeed — Lessons for the LDCs)*, 36(3), 11–43.

Langdale, J.V., 1985, 'Electronic funds transfer and the internationalization of the banking and finance industry', *Geoforum*, 16, 1–13.

Langdale, J.V., 1987, 'Telecommunications and electronic information services in Australia', in J.F. Brotchie, P. Hall and P.W. Newton (eds), *The Spatial Impact of Technological Change* (Totowa, NJ: Barnes & Noble), 89–103.

Langdale, J.V., 1989, 'The geography of international business telecommunications: the role of leased networks', *Annals of the Association of American Geographers*, 79, 501–22.

Läpple, D., 1986, '"Süd-Nord-Gefälle": Metapher für die räumlichen Folgen einer Transformationsphase: Auf dem Weg zu einem post-tayloristischen Entwicklungsmodell? ["South-North Divide": A metaphor for spatial consequences of a transformation phase: towards a post-tayloristic model of development?]', in J. Friedrichs, H. Häussermann and W. Siebel (eds), *Süd-Nord-Gefälle in der Bundesrepublik? Sozialwissenschaftliche Analysen* [*South-North-Divide in the Federal Republic? Analyses in Social Science*] (Opladen: Westdeutscher Verlag), 97–116.

Laulajainen, R., 1981, 'Three tests on locational matching', *Geografiska Annaler*, 63 B(1), 35–45.

Lebkowski, M. and Monkiewicz, J., 1987, 'CMEA direct investments in the Western countries: the case of Poland', *Journal of World Trade Law*, 21(3), 27–38.

Leborgne, D. and Lipietz, A., 1989, 'Deux stratégies sociales dans la production des nouveaux espaces économiques [Two social strategies of producing new economic spaces]', Intervention au colloque international Les Nouveaux Espaces Industriels, Un Survol International [paper to international colloquium on The New Industrial Spaces, An International Overview], Paris, 21-22 March (Paris: CEPREMAP).

Le Heron, R.B., 1977, 'Patterns of company control and regional development in New Zealand', *Pacific Viewpoint*, 18, 58–78.

Le Heron, R.B., 1980, 'The diversified corporation and development policy — New Zealand's experience', *Regional Studies*, 14, 201–17.

Le Heron, R.B., 1990a, 'Goodman Fielder Wattie: good food worldwide?: internationalisation and performance', in M. de Smidt and E. Wever (eds), *The Corporate Firm in a Changing World Economy* (London: Routledge), 100–19.

Le Heron, R.B., 1990b, 'New Zealand agriculture and changes in the agriculture-finance relation during the 1980s', unpublished paper (Palmerston North: Massey University).

Le Heron, R., Roche, M. and Anderson, G., 1989, 'Reglobalisation of New Zealand's food and fibre system: organisational dimensions', *Journal of Rural Studies*, 5, 395–404.

Leinbach, T.R. and Amrhein, C., 1987, 'A geography of the venture capital industry in the US', *Professional Geographer*, 39, 146–58.

Leland, H.E., 1989, 'LBOs and taxes: no one to blame but ourselves?', *California Management Review*, 32(1), 19–29.

Leyshon, A. and Thrift, N.J., 1992, 'Liberalisation and consolidation: the Single European Market and the remaking of European financial capital', *Environment and Planning A*, 24, 49–81.

Linge, G.J.R., 1991, 'Just-in-time: more or less flexible?', *Economic Geography*, 67, 316–32.

Linge, G.J.R., 1992, 'Developments in Russia's Far East and their implications for the Pacific Basin', *Australian Geographical Studies*, 30(2), 125–41.

Linge, G.J.R. and Forbes, D.K. (eds), 1990, *China's Spatial Economy: Recent Developments and Reforms* (Hong Kong: Oxford University Press).

Linge, G.J.R. and Hamilton, F.E.I., 1981, 'International industrial systems', in F.E.I. Hamilton and G.J.R. Linge (eds), *Spatial Analysis, Industry and the Industrial Environment, Volume 2 International Industrial Systems* (Chichester: John Wiley), 1–117.

Lipietz, A., 1985, 'The world crises: the globalization of the general crises of Fordism', *IDS Bulletin*, 16, 6–11.

Lipietz, A., 1986, 'New tendencies in the international division of labor: regimes of accumulation and modes of regulation', in A.J. Scott and M. Storper (eds), *Production, Work, Territory: The Geographical Anatomy of Industrial Capitalism* (Boston: Allen & Unwin), 16–40.

Lipietz, A., 1989, 'The debt problem: European integration and the new phase of world crises', *New Left Review*, 178, 37–50.

Liviatan, O., 1984, 'A macro-absorption approach for estimating the foreign debt burden', *Economic Development and Cultural Change*, 32, 803–18.

McConnell, J.E., 1983, 'The international location of manufacturing investments: recent behaviour of foreign-owned corporations in the United States', in F.E.I. Hamilton and G.J.R. Linge (eds), *Spatial Analysis, Industry and the Industrial Environment, Volume 3 Regional Economics and Industrial Systems* (Chichester: John Wiley), 337–58.

McGee, T.G., 1986, 'Circuits and networks of capital: the internationalisation of the world economy and national urbanisation', in D. Drakakis-Smith (ed.), *Urbanisation in the Developing World* (London: Croom Helm), 23–36.

McKillop, D.G. and Hutchinson, R.W., 1990, *Regional Financial Sectors in the British Isles* (Aldershot: Avebury).

McMillan, C., 1987, *Multinationals from the Second World: Growth of Foreign Investment by Soviet and East European Enterprises* (London: MacMillan Press for the Trade Policy Research Centre).

McMillan, C. (ed.), 1989, *The East-West Business Directory* (Ottawa: Carlton University, Duncan Publishing).

McNaughton, R.B. and Green, M.B., 1989, 'Spatial patterns of Canadian venture capital investments', *Regional Studies*, 23, 9–18.

Magowan, P.A., 1989, 'The case for LBOs: the Safeway experience', *California Management Review*, 32(1), 9–18.

Maitland, A., 1989, 'The little dragons: candidates for the US blacklist', *Financial Times*, 25 May (Survey), vi.

Mandel, E., 1975, *Late Capitalism* (London: Verso).

Manikowska, B., Matykowski, R. and Stryjakiewicz, T., 1985, 'Tendencje lokalizacyjne i struktura przestrzenna przedsiebiorstw polonijno-zagranicznych w Polsce [The locational tendencies and spatial structure of foreign enterprises in Poland]', *Czasopismo Geograficzne*, 56(3–4), 356–77.

Markusen, A., 1985, *Profit Cycles, Oligopoly and Regional Development* (Cambridge, Mass.: MIT Press).

Marshall, M., 1987, *Long Waves of Regional Development* (London: Methuen).

Martin, R., 1989, 'The growth and geographical anatomy of venture capitalism in the United Kingdom', *Regional Studies*, 23, 389–403.

Massey, D., 1984, *Spatial Divisions of Labour: Social Structures and the Geography of Production* (London: Macmillan).

Maycock, J., 1986, *Financial Conglomerates: The New Phenomenon* (Aldershot: Gower).

Medlock, A., 1989, 'Storm under the French umbrella: devaluation is threatening the Franc Zone', *Financial Times*, 24 May, 24.

Mistry, P.S., 1987, 'Globalization of financial markets: implications for Asian developing countries', *International Journal of Development Banking*, 5, 3–20.

Moffitt, M., 1983, *The World's Money: International Banking from Bretton Woods to the Brink of Insolvency* (New York: Simon & Schuster).

Molyneux, P., 1989, '1991 and its impact on local and regional banking markets', *Regional Studies*, 23, 523–33.

Moran, M., 1981, 'Finance capital and pressure-group politics in Britain', *British Journal of Political Finance*, 11, 381–404.

Muth, M., 1989, 'Im Wettbewerb am Finanzdienstleistungsmarkt wird es entscheidend auf das Vertriebskonzept ankommen [Market competition for financial services depends on marketing concept]', *Handelsblatt* no. 84, B17.

Narver, J.C., 1964, *Conglomerate Mergers and Market Competition* (Berkeley: University of California Press).

Natarajan, S. and Tan, J.M., 1992, *The Impact of Investments in Malaysia, Singapore & Thailand* (Singapore: Institute of Southeast Asian Studies).

National Bank of Hungary, 1988, *New Banking System in Hungary 1987* (Budapest: NBH, International Monetary Department).

National Bank of Hungary, 1989, *Banking System in Hungary 1989* (Budapest: NBH).

Newberry, D.M., 1991, 'Reform in Hungary: sequencing and privatisation', *European Economic Review*, 35(2/3), 571–80.

New Zealand Planning Council, 1988, *The Regulated Economy* (Wellington: NZPC).

Nilsson, J-E., 1991, 'Managing the spatial aspects of industrial change in Sweden', in D.C. Rich and G.J.R. Linge (eds), *The State and the Spatial Management of Industrial Change*, Routledge: London, 146–57.

North, D.C., 1986, 'The new institutional economics', *Journal of Institutional and Theoretical Economics*, 142, 230–7.

Nove, A., 1983, *The Economics of Feasible Socialism* (London: Allen & Unwin).

O'Brien, R., 1992, *Global Financial Integration: The End of Geography* (London: Pinter).

O'Connor, D., 1989, *Microelectronics-Based Innovations: Strategic Implications for Selected Industries in the Second-tier Newly Industrializing Economies (NIEs) of Southeast Asia* (Paris: OECD Development Centre Research Project)

O'Connor, J., 1984, *Accumulation Crisis* (New York: Basil Blackwell).

Olgun, H. and Togan, S., 1984, *Türk Ekonomisinin Dünya Ekonomisine Enteğrasyonu* [*Integration of the Turkish Economy into the World Economy*] (İstanbul: Enka).

Onoki, S., 1990, 'Restructuring and innovation in the regional industries of Aichi Prefecture in the context of the global economy' (paper presented to Roving Seminar on Industrial Transformation and Regional Development: Managing Regional Economies in a Borderless Age, Trengganu, Malaysia, 14-17 July).

Organisation for Economic Co-operation and Development, 1986, *Venture Capital: Context, Development and Policies* (Paris: OECD).

Orta Doğu Teknik Üniversitesi [Middle East Technical University], İşletmecilik ve Yönetim Sistemleri Merkezi [Center for Management and Administration Systems], 1989a, *Bursa Tekstil ve Hazır Giyim Envanteri, Eğilimler: Teknoloji [Inventory of Textile and Ready Made Clothing Industry in Bursa, Trends: Technology]* (Ankara: IGEME).

Orta Doğu Teknik Üniversitesi [Middle East Technical University], İşletmecilik ve Yönetim Sistemleri Merkezi [Center for Management and Administration Systems], 1989b, *Bursa Tekstil ve Hazır Giyim Envanteri, Eğilimler: İhraacat [Inventory of Textile and Ready Made Clothing Industry in Bursa, Trends: Exports]* (Ankara: IGEME).

Oshima, H.T., 1988, 'Human resources in East Asia's secular growth', *Economic Development and Cultural Change (Supplement: Why Does Overcrowded, Resource Poor East Asia Succeed — Lessons for the LDCs)*, 36(3), 117–18.

Özel, M., 1988a, *Dış Ticaret Sermaye Şirketler [Foreign Trade Firms]* (Ankara: Türktrade-Grafik).

Özel, M., 1988b, 'Trading companies go international', *Türktrade Trade and Business Review*, 1, 12–19.

Patton, M., 1988, *İhracaata Yönelik Sanayileşme [Export Led Industrialization]* (Ankara: Türktrade Research Centre Series No.1).

Paul, W., 1989, 'Financial strategies of BASF in view of its multinational activities' (paper presented to the Conference of the IGU Commission on Industrial Change, Eppenhain, September 1989).

Pfeiffer, H., 1989, 'BASF und die Deutsche Bank. Eine Fallstudie zum Bankeneinfluß in der Wirtschaft [BASF and the Deutsche Bank. A case study of the economic influence of banks]', *Wirtschafts- und Sozialwissenschaftliches Institut Mitteilungen*, 42(1), 9–16.

Philipp, A. (ed.), 1985, *Pension Funds and their Advisers* (London: AP Information Services).

Phongpaichit, P., 1988, 'Decision-making on overseas direct investment by Japanese small and medium industries in ASEAN and the Asian NICs', *ASEAN Economic Bulletin*, 4(8), 302–15.

Phongpaichit, P., 1990a, 'Japanese investments in the Asean after the yen appreciation, in S.L. Ying (ed.), *Foreign Direct Investment in Asean* (Kuala Lumpur: University of Malaya), 92–111.

Phongpaichit, P., 1990b, *The New Wave of Japanese Investment in ASEAN* (Singapore: Institute of Southeast Asian Studies).

Piore, M.J. and Sabel, C.F., 1984, *The Second Industrial Divide: Possibilities for Prosperity* (New York: Basic Books).

Pogodda, F., 1989, 'Leasing: Europa 1993', *Finanzierung, Leasing, Factoring*, 3, 90–3.

Pohl, H., 1982, 'Das deutsche Bankwesen 1806-1841 [German Banking 1806-1841]', in *Deutsche Bankgeschichte 2 [History of German Banking 2]* (Frankfurt am Main: Knapp), 96–115.

Pohle, K., 1986, 'Treasury management in a global company: Schering AG', in D.B. Zenoff (ed.), *Corporate Finance in Multinational Companies* (London: Euromoney Publications), 59–63.

Poland, Information and Negotiation Centre of the Ministry of Privatization, 1991, *Information Guide to the Ministry* (Warsaw: the Ministry.

Powell, B., 1992, 'Japan: The big slump', *Newsweek*, 23 March, 10–15.

Pratt, A.C., 1989, 'Towards an explanation of the location and form of industrial estates in Cornwall in 1984: a critical realist approach', unpublished PhD dissertation (Exeter: University of Exeter).

Property Advisory Group, 1975, *Commercial Property Development: First Report* (London: Department of the Environment, HMSO).

Rapkin, D.P. and Avery, W.P., 1986, 'World markets and political instability within less developed countries', *Cooperation and Conflict*, 21, 99–117.

Rawls, J., 1971, *A Theory of Justice* (Cambridge, Mass.: Harvard University Press).

Rees, J., 1978, 'On the spatial spread and oligopolistic behavior of large rubber companies', *Geoforum*, 9, 319–30.

Reid, S.R., 1976, *The New Industrial Order* (New York: McGraw-Hill).

Reinmann, B.C., 1989, 'Creating value to keep the raiders at bay', *Long Range Planning*, 22(3), 18–27.

Riddell, P., 1989, 'US worries and foreign investment: the task of matching sense and sensibilities', *Financial Times*, 15 September, 22.

Rimmer, P., 1988, 'Japanese construction contracting enterprises and global restructuring: Tokyo's Kumagai Gumi in Hong Kong, Curaçao, Dallas and Sydney' (paper presented to Workshop on Enterprises and Restructuring, Australian Defence Force Academy, Canberra).

Roberts, J., 1987, *Politicians, Public Servants and Public Enterprises* (Wellington: Victoria University).

Roche, D., 1990, 'Deflationärer Schock [Deflationary shock]', *Wirtschaftswoche*, 44(28), 90–1.

Rothwell, R. and Zegveld, W., 1985, *Reindustrialization and Technology* (Harlow: Longman).

Rowley, A., 1988, 'Waning of the NICs?', *Far Eastern Economic Review*, 18 August, 79.

Ryniewicz, I., 1991, 'Foreign investments in 1990: still with the foot on the brake', *Polish Business Review*, 5/6, 12–18.

Sabel, C., Herrigel, G.B., Deeg, R. and Kazis, R., 1987, *Regional Prosperities Compared: Massachusetts and Baden-Württemberg in the 1980's* (Berlin: Wissenschaftszentrum Berlin, discussion papers IIM/LMP 87–10b).

Sachs, J., 1984, *Theoretical Issues in International Borrowing* (Princeton: Princeton University Studies in International Finance No. 54).

Sadzikowski, W., 1989, 'Kiedy socjalistyczne joint ventures? [When socialist joint ventures?]', *Wektory Gospodarki*, 1, 21–3.

Salem, E., 1988, 'Twinned hinterlands: Johor and Singapore develop closer economic and industrial ties', *Far Eastern Economic Review*, 18 August, 76–7.

Salih, K. and Young, M.L., 1987, 'Social forces, the state and the international division of labour: the case of Malaysia', in J. Henderson and M. Castells (eds), *Global Restructuring and Territorial Development* (London: Sage), 168–202.

Sasaki, J., 1990, 'SII talks: a dangerous effort to prove that Japan and the U.S. can get along', *Japan Economic Journal*, 4 August, 8.

Sassen, S., 1989, 'Finance and business services in New York City: international linkages and domestic effects', in L. Ridwin and H. Sazanami (eds), *Deindustrialization and Regional Economic Transformation: The Experience of the United States* (Boston: Unwin Hyman), 132–54.

Savage, J., 1986, *Economic Liberalisation and the Outlook for Manufacturing* (Wellington: New Zealand Institute of Economic Research).
Savage, J., 1988, *Financial Centre Prospects for New Zealand* (Wellington: New Zealand Institute of Economic Research, Monograph No. 41).
Sayer, A., 1984, *Method in Social Science: A Realist Approach* (London: Hutchinson).
Sayer, A., 1985, 'The difference that space makes', in D. Gregory and J. Urry (eds), *Social Relations and Spatial Structures* (London: Macmillan), 49–66.
Sayer, A., 1986, 'New developments in manufacturing: the just-in-time system', *Capital and Class*, 30, 43–72.
Schamp, E.W., 1988, 'International competition, industrial change and regional development in the Federal Republic of Germany: an introduction', *Zeitschrift für Wirtschaftsgeographie*, 32, 169–78.
Schoenberger, E., 1989, 'Thinking about flexibility: a response to Gertler', *Transactions of the Institute of British Geographers*, 14, 98–108.
Scott, A., 1988, *New Industrial Spaces* (London: Pion).
Scott, J., 1986, *Capitalist Property and Financial Power. Comparative Study of Britain, the United States and Japan* (Brighton: Wheatsheaf Books).
Şenses, F., 1988, *Türkiye'nin Avrupa Topluluğuna Üyeliğinin Dış Ticaretimize Etkileri* [*The Effects of Turkey's Membership of EC on Turkish Foreign Trade*] (Ankara: Türktrade).
Şenses, F., 1989, 'The nature and main characteristics of recent Turkish growth in export of manufactures', *Developing Economies*, 28 (1), 19–33.
Shachar, A., 1990, 'The global economy and world cities' in A. Shachar and S. Öberg (eds), *The World Economy and the Spatial Organization of Power* (Aldershot: Avebury), 149–60.
Shachar, A. and Öberg, S., 1990, 'The world economy and the spatial organization of power: research agenda', in A. Shachar and S. Öberg (eds), *The World Economy and the Spatial Organization of Power* (Aldershot: Avebury), 3–12.
Sim, P., 1983, 'Choosing areas of property investment', in A. Philipp (ed.), *Pension Funds and their Advisers* (London: AP Financial Registers), 105–11.
Simon, H., 1957, *Models of Man* (New York: Wiley & Sons).
Singh, M.S., 1989, 'Asean: regional co-operation and industrial development' (paper presented at Chubu University, Kasugai, 10 May).

Singh, M.S. and Chi, S.C., 1981, 'Spatial dynamics in the growth and development of multinational corporations in Malaysia', in F.E.I. Hamilton and G.J.R. Linge (eds), *Spatial Analysis, Industry and the Industrial Environment, Volume 2 International Industrial Systems* (Chichester: John Wiley), 481–507.

Städtler, A., 1988, 'Gegenwart und Zukunft des Leasingmarktes in der Bundesrepublik [Present and Future of the Leasing Market in the Federal Republic]', in K.F. Hagenmüller and G. Stoppek (eds), *Leasing-Handbuch für die Betriebliche Praxis* [*Handbook of Leasing for Managerial Practice*] (Frankfurt am Main: Knapp), 183–213.

Städtler, A., 1990, 'Hochkonjunktur in der Leasingbranche [Boom in the leasing section]', *Finanzierung, Leasing, Factoring*, 1, 10–12.

Steed, G.P.F., 1968, 'The changing milieu of a firm: a case study of a shipbuilding concern', *Annals of the Association of American Geographers*, 58, 506–25.

Steinriede, W., 1989, 'Firmenkunden fordern immer stärker maßgeschneiderte Komplett-Lösungen [Corporate customers increasingly expect tailor-made solutions]', *Handelsblatt* no. 84, B4.

Suarez-Villa, L., 1987, 'Entrepreneurship and the international diffusion of innovations in manufacturing: a general approach', *Scienze Economiche e Commerciali*, 34, 369–92.

Swedberg, R., 1987, 'Oil shocks, the private banks and the origins of the debt crisis', *International Social Science Journal*, 38, 323–35.

Swoboda, A.K., 1986, 'Credibility and viability in international monetary arrangements: the internal logic, requirements and implications of alternative exchange rate systems', *Finance and Development*, 23(3), 15–18.

Swyngedouw, E., 1992, 'The mammon quest. "Globalisation", interspatial competition and the monetary order: the construction of new scales', in M. Dunford and G. Kafkalas (eds), *Cities and Regions in the New Europe: the Global-Local Interplay and Spatial Development Strategies* (London Belhaven Press), 39–67.

Tarnowski, P., 1989, 'Mieszane spółki, mieszane uczucia [Joint ventures, mixed feelings]', *Polityka*, 7, 18.

Taylor, M. and Thrift, N., 1981, 'British capital overseas: direct investment and corporate development in Australia', *Regional Studies*, 15, 183–212.

Taylor, M. and Thrift, N., 1983, 'The role of finance in the evolution and functioning of industrial systems', in F.E.I. Hamilton and G.J.R. Linge (eds), *Spatial Analysis, Industry and the Industrial Environment, Volume 3 Regional Economies and Industrial Systems* (Chichester: John Wiley), 359–85.

Taylor, M. and Thrift, N. (eds), 1986, *Multinationals and the Restructuring of the World Economy* (London: Croom Helm).

Ter Hart, H.W. and Piersma, J., 1990, ' Direct representation in international financial markets: the case of foreign banks in Amsterdam', *Tijdschrift voor Economische en Sociale Geografie*, 81, 82–93.

Tew, B., 1977, *The Evolution of the International Monetary System 1945–1977* (London: Hutchinson).

Than, M., 1991, 'ASEAN, Indo-China and Myanmar: towards economic co-operation?', *ASEAN Economic Bulletin*, 8(2), 173–93.

Thiessen, F., 1988, *Standorttheorie für Internationale Finanzzentren* [*Location Theory for International Financial Centres*], (Cologne: Nomos, Untersuchungen zur Wirtschaftspolitik [Studies in Economic Policy] 74).

Thomas, W.A., 1978, *The Finance of British Industry, 1918-1976* (London: Methuen).

Thompson, C., 1989, 'The geography of venture capital', *Progress in Human Geography*, 13, 62–98.

Thompson, G., 1977, 'The relationship between the financial and industrial sector in the United Kingdom', *Economy and Society*, 6, 235–83.

Thrift, N., 1986a, 'The geography of international economic disorder', in R.J. Johnston and P.J. Taylor (eds), *A World in Crisis? Geographical Perspectives* (Oxford: Basil Blackwell), 12–67.

Thrift, N., 1986b, 'The internationalisation of producer services and the integration of the Pacific basin property market', in M. Taylor and N. Thrift (eds), *Multinationals and the Restructuring of the World Economy* (London: Croom Helm), 142–92.

Thrift, N., 1987, 'The fixers: the urban geography of international commercial capital', in J. Henderson and M. Castells (eds), *Global Restructuring and Territorial Development* (London: Sage), 203–33.

Thrift, N.J., 1990, 'The perils of the international financial system', *Environment and Planning A*, 22, 1135–7.

Thrift, N. and Leyshon, A., 1988, '"The gambling propensity": banks, developing country debt exposure and the New International Financial System', *Geoforum*, 19, 55–69.

Tickell, A. and Peck, J.A., 1992, 'Accumulation, regulation and the geographies of post-Fordism: missing links in regulationist research', *Progress in Human Geography*, 16 (2), 190–218.

Togan, S., Olgun, H. and Akder, H., 1988, *External Economic Relations of Turkey* (Ankara: Türktrade).

Tonak, A., 1989, 'Yabancı sermaye üzerine [On foreign capital]', *Ekonomik Panorama*, 12 March, 16–17.

Trescott, P.B., 1963, *Financing American Enterprise: The Story of Commercial Banking* (New York: Harper & Rowe).

Tugendhat, C., 1971, *The Multinationals* (London: Eyre and Spottiswoode).

Türel, Ö., 1987, 'Türkiye'de sanayinin gelişimine genel bakış [General overview of industrial development in Turkey]', *1987 Sanayi Kongresi Bildirileri* [Proceedings of 1987 Industrial Congress], (Ankara: Türkiye Mimar ve Mühendis Odaları Birliği [Union of Chambers of Architects and Engineers]), 1–22.

Turkey, State Planning Organization, 1985, *V.Beş Yıllık Kalkınma Planı Öncesinde Gelişmeler [Developments Prior to Fifth Five Year Plan]* (Ankara: DPT).

Turkey, State Planning Organization, 1985 to 1991, *Main Economic Indicators* (Ankara: Başbakanlık).

Turkey, State Planning Organization, 1987, 1989, *Yabancı Sermaye Raporu [Report on Foreign Investment]* (Ankara: DPT).

Türkiye İhracaat ve İthalatçılar Derneği [Importers and Exporters Association of Turkey], 1989, *A Bridge for Trade Between Turkey and the World* (Ankara: Grafik).

Türkiye Sanayici ve İş Adamları Derneği [Association of Turkish Industrial and Business Entrepreneurs], 1986, *Dış Ticaret Raporu, İthalat ve İhracaata Sorunlar ve Öneriler [The Problems and Proposals on Exports and Imports]* (İstanbul: TUSIAD).

Türkiye Ticaret, Sanayi, Deniz Ticaret Odaları ve Borsaları Birliği [Turkish Association of Chambers and Stock Exchange Markets of Trade, Industry and Marine Trade], 1987, *Dış Ticaret Mevzuatşı* [*Foreign Trade Legislation*] (Istanbul: TTSOBB).

Türktrade, 1988, *The Foreign Trade Association of Turkey and Turkish Economy in Brief* (Ankara: Grafik).

Tussie, D., 1987, *The Less Developed Countries and the World Trading System* (London: Frances Pinter).

Underhill, G.R.D., 1991, 'Markets beyond politics? The state and the internationalisation of financial markets', *European Journal of Political Research*, 19, 197–225.

United Kingdom, 1973, 'Memorandum of the Department of Trade and Industry minutes of evidence to the Select Committee on Regional Development Initiatives', *House of Commons Papers*, No. 85–1 (London: HMSO).

United Nations Centre on Transnational Corporations, 1988, *Joint Ventures as a Form of International Economic Co-operation*, (New York: United Nations, Sales no.E88.II.A.12).

United Nations Department of Economic and Social Affairs, 1973, *Multinational Corporations in World Development* (New York: United Nations, Sales no. E.73.II.A.11).

United Nations Economic and Social Council, 1978, *Transnational Corporations in World Development: A Re-examination* (New York: United Nations, Sales no. E.78.II.A.5).

United Nations Industrial Development Organization, annual, *Industry and Development: A Global Report* (Vienna: UNIDO).

United Nations Transnational Corporations and Management Division, Department of Economic and Social Development, 1992, *World Investment Report 1992, Transnational Corporations as Engines of Growth* (New York: United Nations, Sales no. E.92.II.A.19).

Urry, J., 1981, *The Anatomy of Capitalist Society* (London: Macmillan).

Utton, M.A., 1977, 'Large firm diversification in British manufacturing industry', *The Economic Journal*, 87, 96–113.

Utton, M.A., 1981, *The Political Economy of Big Companies* (London: Macmillan).

Vernon, R., 1992, 'Transnational corporations: where are they coming from, where are they headed?', *Transnational Corporations*, 1(2), 73–35.

Vos, G.T.B. and Zurawicki, L., 1984, 'International trading companies for developing countries — Latin America', *Middle East Technical University Studies in Development*, 11(3-4), 307–25.

Vukmir, B., 1989, 'Latest developments in the joint venture legislation in Eastern Europe', *The CTC Reporter*, 28, 34–9.

Wachtel, H., 1986, The Money Mandarins: *The Making of a Supranational Economic Order* (New York: Pantheon).

Walker, R., 1988, 'The geographical organization of production systems', *Environment and Planning D: Society and Space*, 6, 377–408.

Walker, R. and Storper, M., 1981 'Capital and industrial location', *Progress in Human Geography*, 5, 473–509.

Walter, J., 1985, 'Erklärungskonzepte zum Internationalisierungsprozeß der Banken [Explanatory concepts of the internationalization of banks]', in H.J. Krümmel (ed.), *Internationales Bankgeschäft* [*International Banking*] (Berlin: Beihefte zu Kredit und Kapital 8), 163–93.

Warf, B., 1989, 'Telecommunications and the globalization of financial services', *Professional Geographer*, 41, 257–71.

Wassermann, H., 1987, 'Leasing 1987', *Finanzierung, Leasing, Factoring*, 5, 186–201.

Wassermann, H., 1988, 'Leasing 1988', *Finanzierung, Leasing, Factoring*, 5, 194–206.

Wassermann, H., 1989, 'Leasing 1989', *Finanzierung, Leasing, Factoring*, 6, 217–30.

Wassermann, H., 1990, 'Leasing 1990', *Finanzierung, Leasing, Factoring*, 6, 226–38.

Weichert, R., 1987, *Probleme des Risikokapitalmarktes in der Bundesrepublik. Ursachen, Auswirkungen, Lösungsmöglichkeiten* [*Problems of the Risk Capital Market in the Federal Republic. Causes, Consequences and Possibilities for Solution*] (Tübingen: Mohr, Kieler Studien 213).

Wheeler, J.O., 1986, 'Corporate spatial links with financial institutions: the role of the metropolitan hierarchy', *Annals of the Association of American Geographers*, 76, 262–74.

Wiznitzer, L., 1990, 'French domination of African colonies in former "commonwealth" uncertain', *Japan Times*, 26 July, 7.

World Bank, 1985, *World Development Report, 1985: International Capital and Economic Development* (New York: Oxford University Press for the World Bank).

World Bank, 1988, *World Development Report 1988: Public Finance in Development* (New York: Oxford University Press for the World Bank).

World Bank, 1989, *World Development Report, 1989: Financial Systems* (New York: Oxford University Press for the World Bank).

World Bank, 1990, *World Development Report, 1990: Poverty* (New York: Oxford University Press for the World Bank).

World Bank, 1991, *World Development Report 1991: The Challenge of Development* (New York: Oxford University Press for the World Bank).

World Bank, 1992, *World Development Report 1992: Development and the Environment* (New York: Oxford University Press for the World Bank).

Yabancı Sermaye Derneği [Union of Foreign Investment], 1988, *Foreign Capital Legislation in Turkey* (İstanbul: YASED).

Yeşilada, B.A. and Füsunoğlu, M., 1988, 'Türkiye'nin Avrupa Topluluğuna Üyeliğinin Dış Ticaretimize Etkileri', *in Türkiye'nin Avrupa Topluluğuna Üyeliğinin Dış Ticaretimize Etkileri [The Effects of Turkey's Membership of EC on Turkish Foreign Trade]* (Ankara: Türktrade), 89–131.

Yonekawa, S., 1983, *General Trading Companies* (Tokyo: United Nations University).

Yuan, L.T., 1990, 'NIC investments in Asean: the pattern in the eighties', in S.L. Ying (ed.), *Foreign Direct Investment in Asean* (Kuala Lumpur: University of Malaya), 112–35.

Zenoff, D.B., 1986, 'Perspectives on financial management in international corporations', in D.B. Zenoff (ed.), *Corporate Finance in Multinational Companies* (London: Euromoney Publications), 3–10.

# Index

Bei Fragen zur Produktsicherheit wenden Sie sich bitte an:
If you have any questions regarding product safety,
please contact:

Walter de Gruyter GmbH
Genthiner Straße 13
10785 Berlin
productsafety@degruyterbrill.com